GARY LINEKER: A PORTRAIT OF A FOOTBALL ICON

CHRIS EVANS

GARY LINEKER: A PORTRAIT OF A FOOTBALL ICON

BLOOMSBURY SPORT
LONDON · OXFORD · NEW YORK · NEW DELHI · SYDNEY

For Isabelle

BLOOMSBURY SPORT
Bloomsbury Publishing Plc
50 Bedford Square, London, WC1B 3DP, UK
29 Earlsfort Terrace, Dublin 2, Ireland

BLOOMSBURY, BLOOMSBURY SPORT and the Diana logo are trademarks of Bloomsbury Publishing Plc

First published in Great Britain 2025

Copyright © Chris Evans, 2025

Chris Evans has asserted his right under the Copyright, Designs and Patents Act, 1988, to be identified as Author of this work

For legal purposes the Acknowledgements on p. 274 constitute an extension of this copyright page

All rights reserved. No part of this publication may be: i) reproduced or transmitted in any form, electronic or mechanical, including photocopying, recording or by means of any information storage or retrieval system without prior permission in writing from the publishers; or ii) used or reproduced in any way for the training, development or operation of artificial intelligence (AI) technologies, including generative AI technologies. The rights holders expressly reserve this publication from the text and data mining exception as per Article 4(3) of the Digital Single Market Directive (EU) 2019/790

Bloomsbury Publishing Plc does not have any control over, or responsibility for, any third-party websites referred to or in this book. All internet addresses given in this book were correct at the time of going to press. The author and publisher regret any inconvenience caused if addresses have changed or sites have ceased to exist, but can accept no responsibility for any such changes

Every reasonable effort has been made to trace copyright holders of material reproduced in this book, but if any have been inadvertently overlooked the publishers would be glad to hear from them.

A catalogue record for this book is available from the British Library

Library of Congress Cataloguing-in-Publication data has been applied for

ISBN: HB: 978-1-3994-1699-3; TPB: 978-1-3994-2639-8; eBook: 978-1-3994-1700-6; ePDF: 978-1-3994-1701-3

2 4 6 8 10 9 7 5 3 1

Typeset in Adobe Garamond Pro by Deanta Global Publishing Services, Chennai, India
Printed and bound in Great Britain by CPI Group (UK) Ltd., Croydon, CR0 4YY

To find out more about our authors and books visit www.bloomsbury.com and sign up for our newsletters

CONTENTS

Prologue   vii

1. On the market (1960–1968)   1
2. Early instincts (Aylestone Road, 1968–1976)   9
3. City boy (Leicester City, 1976–1981)   19
4. Big break (Leicester City, 1982–1984)   35
5. Call-up (England, 1984)   51
6. Moving on (Leicester City, 1984–1985)   63
7. Goodison goals (Everton, 1985–1986)   73
8. One game in Mexico (England, 1986)   91
9. A Nou adventure (Barcelona, 1986–1988)   107
10. Euro failure (England, 1988)   123
11. Catalonian cull (Barcelona, 1988–1989)   133
12. A return home (Tottenham, 1989–1990)   147
13. The Italian job (England, 1990)   161
14. White-hot Lane (Tottenham, 1990–1991)   179
15. So long, farewell... (Tottenham, 1991–1992)   195
16. Captaincy, records and fall-outs (England, 1990–1992)   205
17. A new adventure (Nagoya Grampus Eight, 1992–1994)   221
18. Star turn (1994–2000)   235
19. Standing up (2000–ongoing)   251

Epilogue   263
List of images   266
References and sources   270
Acknowledgements   274

PROLOGUE

6 June 1986, Mexico

*'Questions were coming and Lineker knew
some of them would be about him.'*

The browbeaten striker looked forlornly to the floor, the whistles of derision ringing in his ears. The stadium may only have been partially full of travelling England fans but the seething frustration was unmistakable as their emotion poured on to the pitch.

Lining the sparse terraces draped in Union Flags, the ragtag collection of supporters – many of them shirtless – got as close to the pitch as possible to spew their thoughts at their own players. England's raucous band of followers had proudly sung about backing their team 'over land and sea' only two hours earlier, but the tide had turned after what they'd witnessed.

The excesses of earlier in the day were now in plain sight. The vitriol normally saved for rival fans and players was raining down on their own countrymen instead, like volleys of friendly fire. Nobody was spared. Least of all the normally sharp-shooting marksman whose run without scoring for his country had stretched to yet another match.

He was pouring with sweat, white shirt and tight blue shorts drenched as a sign of his efforts, but Gary Lineker hadn't seen any fruits for his labours. Neither had his Three Lions teammates, much to the ire of the England contingent in the stands.

The next day's newspapers would describe the performance as a 'disaster', a 'disgrace', a 'day of shame'. England had been tepid. Toothless. Benign.

Two matches into the 1986 World Cup and England had failed to win a game or even score a single goal. If that run stretched into a third match, then a talented squad would be on the next plane home. There, they'd be greeted by the ferocity they'd lacked so far in Mexico; an unforgiving crowd of fans would make their dissatisfaction known.

If the several thousand angry supporters in Mexico were making their feelings heard, the millions more at home watching grainy images that proclaimed 'Inglaterra 0' for the second match running would be even louder.

The post-mortem had started even before Bobby Robson's men were dead and buried. If they got a win against Poland in England's final group game, they'd still progress to the last-16 of the competition, but listening to the pundits on TV, radio and in newspapers, you'd think that another underwhelming display was a foregone conclusion.

Questions were coming and Lineker knew some of them would be about him. The striker had been in irresistible form domestically all season, but his latest blank in an England shirt had meant he'd now gone six international matches without a goal. How could a forward who had plundered 40 goals for Everton in the past season look so impotent when playing for his country?

It wasn't an unusual phenomenon. In recent years, England had had a series of forwards whose careers had followed a similar trend, scoring freely in the First Division but never quite cutting it when they stepped up. It was starting to look as though Lineker might be the latest cab off the rank, another goalscorer who couldn't hit the levels needed to succeed internationally. Perhaps it was time to go in a different direction.

England's 0–0 draw with Morocco had been a low point. Lineker had tirelessly run the channels, fought for flick-ons from strike partner Mark Hateley, attempted to find pockets of space around the North Africans' goal. There was no questioning his industry,

PROLOGUE

but all he had to show for it was a first-half run into the box before being hustled to a tight angle away from goal and seeing his shot charged down by goalkeeper Badou Zaki.

It had been a similar story in the tournament's opening match a few days earlier. A 1–0 defeat to Portugal had offered little in the way of goalscoring opportunities for Lineker. He'd toiled and scrambled, bumped and barged, but had cut a frustrated figure as the Portuguese stifled England's attacking efforts. When an opportunity did fall to the number 10, he squeezed his shot beneath the goalkeeper only to see the ball cleared by the desperate covering run of defender António Oliveira. The images of Lineker's hands on his head and resting on his hips, blowing out his cheeks, were becoming all too common.

It's true that the Leicester-born striker had hardly been swimming in a conveyor belt of chances supplied from the players behind him, but his trend without scoring had stretched back longer than just England's disappointing start to the World Cup. He hadn't scored in the four games leading up to the tournament, meaning he hadn't netted since the previous year.

That hat-trick against Turkey, paired with a brace against the USA a few months earlier, papered over the cracks of Lineker's early international efforts. Six goals in his opening 15 England matches was a respectable return, if not hugely prolific, but he'd only scored in three of those matches – failing to find the net on 12 occasions. It was all well and good adding to his numbers against the weaker nations, but he needed to show he was more than simply a flat-track bully.

There were some pundits out there who thought Lineker should be one of a number of changes that Robson made to rescue his side's ailing Mexico '86 campaign. England's 1966 World Cup-winning manager Alf Ramsey was one of them, using his *Daily Mirror* column to call for a new-look frontline that 'would offer England a variation in their attacking ideas'. Being dropped at this stage of his career would be damaging for Lineker.

So when the team was revealed for the crucial final group game with Poland, it was a relief for Lineker to hear his name still in the starting XI. His strike partner for those opening two matches, Mark Hateley, had made way for Newcastle United's jinky creative Peter Beardsley, who – along with a handful of other changes, including Steve Hodge, Peter Reid and Trevor Steven – was expected to change the way England played. More speed and ingenuity should create a higher frequency of better chances for Lineker.

As he stepped on to the Estadio Universitario pitch in Monterrey, Lineker must have been aware of how important the ensuing 90 minutes would be for his England career. The sense of occasion must have been huge, even if the setting itself wasn't. Those same supporters who had been bubbling with resentment against Morocco were back again, gathered together to make the most noise they could muster in the vast, open-aired stands – creating a monophonic sound that echoed around the partially empty space.

England and Lineker couldn't afford for the unusual atmosphere to impact the performance on the pitch. If they failed to score again and the Three Lions crashed out of the World Cup without getting out of the groups, then the criticism would grow, and the striker's goal drought could be one of the reasons cited.

A match against Poland was no gimme, though. On paper, the Eagles posed much stronger competition than Portugal and Morocco had in the previous two games. They'd finished third at the 1982 World Cup four years earlier, only losing to eventual winners Italy, and had topped their qualifying group to be one of the top six seeds for the tournament. After a win and a draw in their opening two matches in 1986, they only needed to avoid defeat to progress at England's expense. The allowance for error couldn't be thinner.

A little over half an hour after that career-defining match with Poland kicked off, Lineker was surrounded by the whistles and cries of England fans once again. But this time, instead of staring down towards his feet, he was looking up to the heavens. Neck craning upwards, fists clenching in tight balls, face grimacing with joy.

The Three Lions striker had just bagged the third of a first-half hat-trick, secured in a 24-minute blitz that left opponents Poland at the mercy of a goalscorer extraordinaire. Each finish, all from

PROLOGUE

only a matter of yards out, was evidence of a poacher at the peak of his powers, capable of ghosting into the exact space the ball would drop, before ruthlessly dispatching it in a flash.

While the relief of kick-starting England's laboured 1986 World Cup campaign was fuelling Lineker's unabashed celebrations, the significance of his treble was far greater than anyone could have realised at the time. The doubts that had existed less than an hour before had dissipated. A crucial career crossroads had been passed and would soon be a distant memory.

The three goals he scored had great national significance in helping England to progress to the last-16 of the World Cup, but they'd prove to have even greater personal significance. This was the catalyst for Gary Lineker to become a global football icon.

England's number 10 had just announced himself to the world.

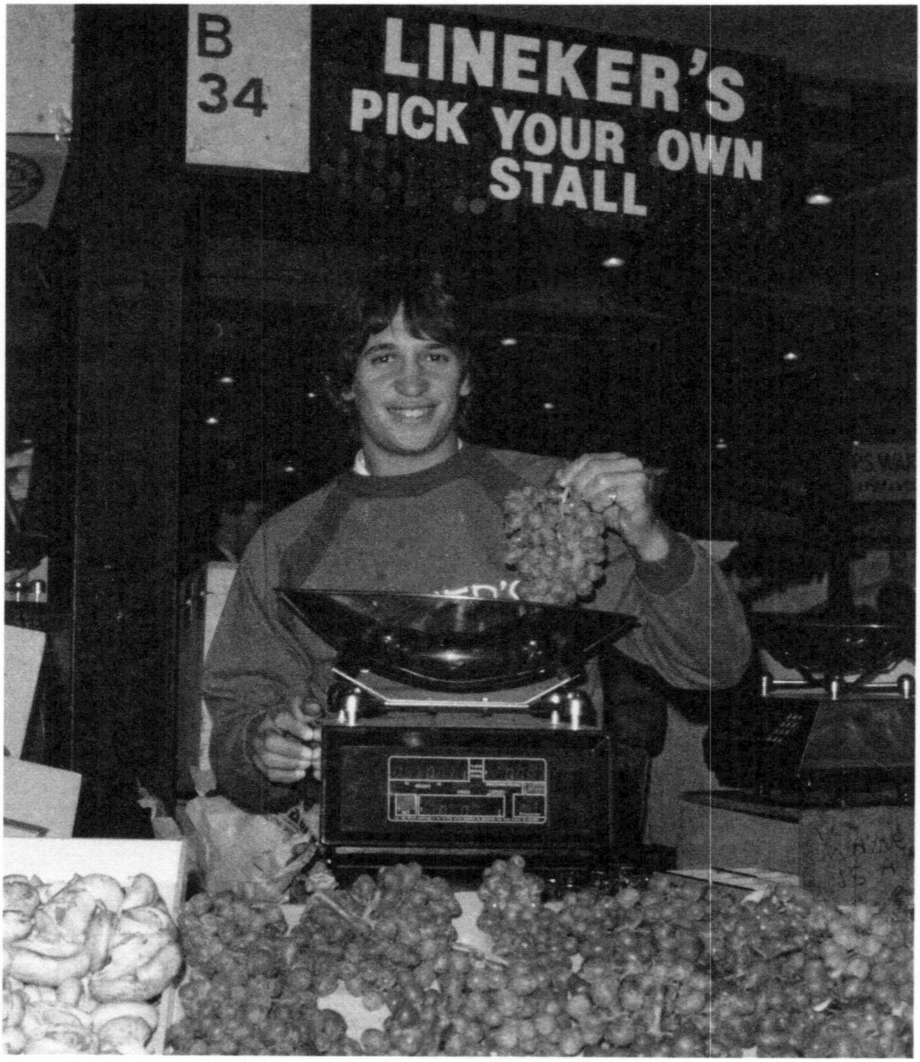
B
34
LINEKER'S
PICK YOUR OWN
STALL

1

ON THE MARKET

1960–1968

*'He concentrates far too much on football.
He'll never make a living doing that.'*

A swarm of bodies jostles for superiority. Shimmying this way and that to get space, arms in the air, trying to gain attention. Getting in front of your rival makes all the difference in this game.

But this isn't a crowded penalty area, the hunting ground for any livewire striker. This is Saturday morning at Leicester Market, a place where perfect timing and a nose for a good position are crucial for being served when demand is high.

Even nowadays, when many of the traditional fruit and veg stalls that were the focus of the market's hustle and bustle in its heyday have been replaced by stands selling phone cases and cheap bags, there's a special knack for getting noticed at the busiest times. A dash for room, a flash of eye contact and a ruthlessness to get your order in first.

It was perhaps here, beneath the translucent plastic roof and metal frames sheltering the sprawling marketplace, where one of England's greatest ever marksmen first witnessed the benefits of effective movement in tight spaces. Long before talk of England goalscoring records and TV stardom, Leicester Market was once Gary Lineker's world.

'The Lineker story is that they were three generations of market traders, although our business is now into its fourth,' explains Simon Reid, in between serving customers at his long-standing fruit and veg stall.

'Me, Wayne and Gary were all brought up together as kids and all worked together, their grandad, dad, me, and Wayne and Gary. The three of us were all born in the same room on London Road, in St Francis Private Hospital. Gary is a few months older than me and Wayne is a few months younger, so there's only 18 months between the three of us.'

Reid still expertly minds his family business, Len and Doreen Reid & Sons, under the roof of what was once the largest outdoor covered market in Europe. He's seen a lot of change since those early years as a kid, pitching in alongside the Linekers' family business in the next plot along.

Trade has dropped off as shopping habits have changed over the decades, but the same passion remains burning inside. 'Gary and Wayne may have gone on to do different things, but our market stall has seen them off,' Reid quips with more than a hint of irony.

While it's now part of Leicester folklore, there was a time when Lineker's Pick Your Own Stall was an integral part of the city's thriving market scene. And as a young Gary got to grips with the world around him after being born in November 1960, the stall was the centre of his family's universe.

Back then, the city's market was *the* place to shop and would always be teeming with customers as people flocked to the Linekers' stall to buy their potatoes, bananas and whatever else they needed for the week. It was a highly lucrative trade, with cash flowing constantly throughout the day, aiding a comfortable life.

First set up by Gary's great-grandfather, the trade was passed down generation by generation, with Grandad Harold – or Harry to those who knew him – starting his apprenticeship aged only 14, after being taken out of school to sample 'the fresh air of the market'.

The Lineker name became synonymous with the sale of fresh produce in the city over the decades, with Harry's son Barry taking over the reins himself when he came of age. As Barry's sons, Gary and Wayne were next in line to the family's fruit-and-veg throne and were exposed to the cut-and-thrust of market life from a young age. As soon as they were old enough, the brothers were called upon to offer an extra pair of hands during busy times and school holidays, replenishing stock and serving customers.

They witnessed the long hours and effort Barry would pour into running the market, getting up at 4 a.m. most mornings to go to the wholesaler at Freemens Common in the city to buy fresh produce, running the stall all day, then falling asleep on the sofa at night while trying to do the books. It might have taught a young Gary some valuable lessons about work ethic, but it certainly didn't sell the idea of a career at the market to him.

'It's a bit too much like hard work and at this time of year it's much too cold,' Gary told a January 1985 episode of *Football Focus*, filmed down at the markets. 'It's a great atmosphere down here, I used to enjoy it as a kid, working on summer holidays and Christmastime. It's a bit special, Leicester Market.'

It was an open secret from a relatively young age that Gary didn't see his future working at the market. Instead, he followed various sporting pursuits and dedicated himself to keeping fit and honing his talents. Wayne was the same and could rival Gary's physical prowess, but it was clear to everyone that the younger of the two brothers was much better suited to life on the stalls, regardless of their respective sporting potentials.

'Gary was not what I'd say as being cut out to be a market trader, he was way too polite and very softly spoken,' remembers market operations manager Rob Manley, who started his working life on a stall under the stewardship of the Linekers' family friend, Brian Pinkney.

'When you're on the market, you need to be a bit of a character, and Gary wasn't like his dad in that sense – but Wayne was. Gary was very softly spoken, he wasn't sort of "Alright sweetheart, how you doing?", that cheeky sort of thing. He was very quiet and unassuming, and he wasn't down here that much.'

While Gary might not have relished time at the market in quite the same way others in his family did, that didn't stop him being drawn like a moth to a flame when his dad's fellow traders came round for one of Barry's weekly card schools. Hosted every Friday night at the Linekers' home, the game would include several market stall owners and other prominent people from the Leicester scene, including much-loved crooner Engelbert Humperdinck.

The group would sit down to play a game of 10-card Kalooki on a Friday night and regularly not come back up for air until the early hours, with games sometimes encompassing most of the weekend. Barry's wife, Margaret, would keep the guests fed by making copious amounts of sandwiches and cooking meals, while Gary would sit behind his dad, soaking it all in until he was sent to bed. If Barry was doing well, he'd give his son what he called 'watching money', regularly in the shape of a pound note.

The games were sacred, with players dipping out for scheduled naps to ensure there were always enough people at the table to keep the game going. In fact, one of the only times when Gary can remember a break in play was to watch England face West Germany in the World Cup quarter-final in 1970.

'I'd sometimes stay there [at the Linekers' house] on a Friday night and these boys would start playing cards, then I'd come back on a Sunday night and the school was still playing,' Reid recalls. 'There were six or seven guys in the school and they all sat out and had a sleep at different times, that's how they kept it going for so long – it was massive.'

That sense of competition was constant and probably part of why Gary was so drawn to sport. Having a brother so close to him in age also helped, with Gary and Wayne regularly playing different games in the garden – often using toilet rolls for goalposts and shining lights out of the windows to act as floodlights to keep matches going after dark in the winter. They weren't always competitors, though, and earned a reputation as teenagers for being cricketers of high regard.

'Gary and Wayne used to open, one and two, for Clarendon Park when they were 15 years old and get hundred starts,' says Reid. 'That was the top men's team in Leicestershire, that's how good they were. I used to see them play a lot, and watched Wayne and Gary play at Caldecote, their junior school in Braunstone, and a few other times too.

'They were both very competitive. I used to play a lot of squash and played for the county, and once played Wayne in my club and beat him 6–0. I played him again three weeks later and he beat me 6–0. He couldn't not be good and had to get himself to that level, that's just how they both are – just total sportsmen.'

There was no question that that was the case for Gary. He was naturally good at a wide range of sports and seemed to excel at everything he tried his hand at. He was captain of Leicestershire Schools' cricket team from the age of 11 through to 16, was Leicestershire Schools' 400m champion, and always stood out on the football pitch.

One sport Lineker didn't have a natural cadence with was rugby, due to his slight frame, although his rapid pace would still have been an asset on the wing. After the family moved out of Leicester to Kirby Muxloe on the outskirts of the city, Gary was on a collision course with a new school that played rugby instead of football – until his dad stepped in.

Barry recalled his own experience of playing at a rugby school in his youth and, recognising Gary's potential as a footballer, he moved his son in with his grandmother so he could attend City of Leicester Boys' Grammar School and play football. Six months later, the entire family moved back to live more centrally.

It was the first big indication that the Linekers had seen the potential in Gary's boots. He'd always been smart, with a talent for English and maths – with the exception of algebra – but it was clear that getting good academic results wasn't the only priority.

'I wasn't a great lover of school, but City of Leicester Boys was a good school and a good sporting school,' Lineker later told the *Independent* in an article about his education in 2010. 'There were some good teachers and I got on with the teachers in the subjects I preferred, such as English and maths.'

Lineker recalls getting two As in his O-levels – one in maths and the other in English – while also picking up a high grade in geography, but only picked up a couple of Ds in science. Still, that was better than in history after being ungraded after having 'a teacher who seemed hell-bent on converting us to communism'.

'If I'd known how difficult it was to be a footballer, I'd have worked harder at school,' Lineker continued. 'I did okay, but my mind was elsewhere. My last report said something along the lines of: "He concentrates far too much on football. He'll never make a living doing that."'

Lineker wasn't unfamiliar with people underestimating his physical prowess, though. Perhaps it was his short and slight frame, or his shy and self-deprecating demeanour, but on first glance, it wasn't clear what a formidable competitor he was. That said, as childhood friend Simon Reid tells, anyone who went up against Gary would usually find out the hard way that he wasn't easily beaten.

'We used to be massive followers of Leicestershire County Cricket [CC] in the 1970s when Leicestershire were the best team in the world and Margaret [Lineker] used to take us to the finals at Lords,' Reid recalls.

'When we were waiting for the winning run to be hit by Leicestershire, we used to gather at the ropes around the ground and run on for the stumps. Three years running, Gary got these stumps because he was 10 or 15 seconds quicker than the other kids. But one year, I can remember we were playing Surrey and we were all there at the ropes, along with a West Indian boy to the side of me. He looked at me and said, "The stumps are mine, man, they're mine." And I said, "They're not, pal." He said, "You're not getting them." And I'm like, "I'm not, he is," and pointed at Gary. When the winning run was hit, that's how it turned out and Gary was there 10 minutes before the other lad.'

That speed to the stumps was possibly the biggest threat to Lineker's football career. Making sure nobody got his wicket and having fast reactions with bat in hand meant the possibility of playing cricket professionally was something Gary could easily have entertained if he'd wanted to. The question was whether he would be drawn to the crease or the football pitch.

Lineker's great timing with the bat in his hand and pace between the stumps meant he was marked out as having the potential to become a professional cricketer. He loved playing and watching the game, and was a big fan of Leicestershire CC batsman David Gower, who went on to captain England.

The summer cricket season segued almost perfectly with the winter football schedule, so Lineker found it easy to juggle the two, as several youngsters who had a talent for both sports did at the time. Although if he was going to take one more seriously, he was aware he'd have to make a choice to focus on it rather than the other.

And as the runs kept flowing, so did the goals…

2
EARLY INSTINCTS
Aylestone Road, 1968–1976

'It's become a bit of a trivia question: What was the first goal Gary Lineker scored at Filbert Street? The answer is that it wasn't for Leicester.'

Barry Lineker stormed on to the pitch and grabbed his son. Surprised to see his father there next to him, Gary stopped in his tracks and looked, unsure what was coming next.

The young striker, fresh from yelling at the referee following a string of offside calls, was about to become the subject of his own verbal storm, his father set to give him a public dressing-down that would stay with the future England captain for the rest of his playing career. It wasn't just the humiliation of being told off with his friends all stood agog around him that stuck with Gary, though. Barry's message was clear and firm: don't ever show such disrespect to a match official again.

'Everyone knows the biggest thing about Gaz was that he never got booked in his career,' says Simon Reid. 'Well, he told the story at his dad's funeral about that time when he back-chatted the ref and his dad went on the pitch, got him by the scruff of his neck and threatened him. He said, "You ever speak to a referee like that again and you'll never play football again," and Gaz kept to that.'

The impromptu life lesson was one of many that Gary would take from his time playing junior football in the suburbs spanning his hometown, Leicester. The 1970s wasn't a time of flashy academies and preened pitches that would tailor talented young players into first-team footballers.

Instead, Lineker and his band of cohorts were playing on bumpy council pitches and uneven surfaces against a whole manner of kids within the age group. Forget carefully curated training sessions and fixtures organised by professional clubs; young hopefuls had to stand out on their own accord. But often the cream still rose to the top.

'He really was a good prospect. From about the age of eight, he [Gary] had the knack of scoring goals,' said Lineker's first school football coach George Sim in an interview with the *Leicester Mercury* in September 1990.

'I think he had a good grounding in football and I hope that has served him well. But every sportsman is a product of a great number of influences and I wouldn't seek to gain credit for his success.'

Sim wasn't wrong. The PE teacher at Caldecote Junior School may have been one of the first coaches to have the pleasure of working with Lineker at such a tender age, but there were a host of figures queueing up to offer advice and keep the youngster focused.

While dad Barry may have been on hand to dish out scoldings for ungentlemanly behaviour in the face of questionable refereeing decisions, it was arguably grandfather Harold who provided more sage football advice from the family's perspective. Harold had been a promising player himself back in the 1920s, a nippy winger who earned rave reviews playing for Leicester Schoolboys – once being hailed as the star of the 1925 side that got through five rounds of the English Schools FA Shield before losing to West Ham in a replay.

Just like his grandson several decades later, Harold's pace was what initially stood out to anybody who saw him play, as he wreaked havoc up and down the flanks. He was almost always the fastest player on the pitch and had the delivery to match, although it wasn't until much later in life that Harold realised how much potential he had had to make it as a Football League player himself.

After leaving school at 14 to work on the market, Harold's playing opportunities changed – albeit he still played for the British Army football team – but he retained strong connections with the city's sporting fraternity, particularly at Leicester City. Upon seeing the talent Gary had as a child, Harold was keen to see his grandson flourish. And he did.

Before his 10th birthday, Gary was already playing above his age group for Caldecote Juniors and was regularly scoring three or four goals per game for the under-11s. It pinpointed him as one of the region's top young players and he was soon following in his grandfather's footsteps to represent Leicestershire Schools and take advantage of the opportunities that that presented.

'One of the teachers at Caldecote School, Jim Riley, took the Leicestershire Schools county side and that's how Gary got into the team at first,' recalls Bob Stretton, who went on to manage Gary at junior side Aylestone Park.

'It was just at the time when youth football was taking off on a Sunday, and Schools football was starting to, not lose its flair with the kids but wasn't as big because the teaching staff didn't want to give up their Saturday mornings. They started playing on a Sunday instead, so Jim Riley took the team to Aylestone.'

Situated on the south side of the city, Aylestone Park Football Club enjoyed decent links with the city's local authorities and was in the process of moving to a new private ground to help elevate the club's facilities as Lineker's age group was emerging. The affiliation with Riley and Leicestershire Schools would only enhance that further, and police officer Stretton became the beneficiary as a newly qualified FA coach.

'Going back to my early police days, the police constable had this idea of us getting involved in the community and said, "If any of you want to get a coaching qualification and start a kids' team on your respective estate, I'll give you a week off to get your coaching badge." So everybody said, "Go on then, just this once,"' smiles Stretton, remembering his good fortune.

'We all started these teams up, but it wasn't for any other reason than wanting to get involved in the community. When Jim Riley said, "I've got the Leicester boys on a Saturday and I can't do a Sunday, do you want to take them on?" I said, "Yeah, alright then, it's a ready-made side." I hadn't realised how good they were.'

Stretton has since become an Aylestone club legend, taking a long string of junior sides under his wing over the decades, but the first cut was the deepest. Lineker was one of a cluster of players within that team with enough talent to get noticed, with several going on to become Leicester City apprentices after cutting their teeth with the Park.

'They were all good players, a team of really good players,' Stretton says. 'We were the best football team, but we used to play against a team called Wadkins, which was run by a sergeant, and he'd got all these big lads together that used to kick you off the park.

'In that first year, we got to the Eddie Plumley Under-11s School Cup final that was played at Filbert Street, Leicester City's ground at the time. It's become a bit of a trivia question: What was the first goal that Gary Lineker scored at Filbert Street? The answer is that it wasn't for Leicester, it was in the Eddie Plumley Cup final in the early '70s.

'We had such a good team. We had John Parsons, an England Schoolboy, in the side, and six of that team signed apprentice. It was just one of those teams that fell together, you get them like that, and they really liked playing with each other. It was just one of those things and you let them get on with it.'

A photo of that team still hangs in the corridor connecting Aylestone Park's clubhouse with the dressing rooms, with newcomers regularly challenged to pick out Lineker from the line-up of players. The customary introduction is usually followed by a who's who of the other less-famous faces in that team and an appreciation for those lads who at one point were considered to have had more of a chance of making it big than their teammate.

One of those players was Mick Duffy, a big strapping forward who was Lineker's polar opposite. They may have looked like chalk and cheese, but Duffy and Lineker got on famously, and built a chemistry on and off the pitch that helped them both enhance their reputations in equal measure.

'I met Gary at 10 when we used to train together and we became best mates through the period from ages 10 to 22,' says Duffy, who spent three seasons at Leicester City before joining FC Saarbrücken in Germany.

'Me and Gary played together in the schools team, but when we got to 11, we started playing together at Aylestone Park – we were the best team in the county by a stretch. We were going round the county beating everyone in those days, we were that good.

'Me and Gary were playing up front together and we were a good pair and had a good relationship, that's just how it was. He had pace, I didn't, but I could dribble the ball and use both feet. Our talent came together and it wasn't that one of us had more talent than the other, it worked together as a relationship.'

Stretton takes it one step further and credits the understanding between Lineker and Duffy for more than just a platform for the duo to show off their talents. The way he remembers it, those early days playing in that junior team helped Lineker to learn and develop his instinct of reading where a ball would drop in a busy penalty area.

'Lineker was always a poacher, but Mick could hit a ball,' continues the former Aylestone Park boss. 'Mick could use right or left foot, he was a really gifted player – not that quick in terms of passing or whatever, but he could hit a ball from 20 or 30 yards and in those youth days, he'd hit a ball and it would come back off a post, a bar or a player and Lineker would nip in. That's how Gary learned his skills and he adapted to that style of play superbly. He used to say 90 per cent of his goals were scored from inside the six-yard box and it was true for us too.'

Despite his unerring ability to sniff out goalscoring chances on a regular basis, Lineker didn't stand out as a player who would definitely make it as a professional in later life. Gary's instincts were impressive but, flanked by teammates who were also bristling with potential, the attention often fell elsewhere – particularly on to Duffy, whose name is still revered by those familiar with Aylestone Park folklore as a precocious talent who never reached his full potential.

'Me and Gary had different styles,' laughs Duffy, expertly batting away a claim he's heard several times. 'I could use either foot, and that helped, but he had pace that I didn't, although I probably had more ability. It's difficult for me to say if I was a better player than him, but he won the Golden Boot in the World Cup and I didn't, so that probably tells you a lot.

'Maybe at 16, we were on par or I was technically a little bit better at the time, but there wasn't a lot in it and I don't ever think I was a better player than him – we were both good players.'

If urban myths about Lineker's credentials compared to Duffy's as a youth prevail several decades on, so does another rumour that still rattles around his former haunts. Namely that Gary wasn't even the best footballer in his family as a kid, although the credibility of the claims appears to waver depending on where they're coming from.

'In my opinion, Wayne was the better player [of the two Lineker brothers],' says Leicester Market's Rob Manley, who saw them both play in those early days. 'I've always said it that Wayne was a better footballer, and that Gary was a better cricketer than he was a footballer.

'Wayne was a forward, too. He'd put the work in and would cover the ground, every blade of grass, but Gary wouldn't. Wayne would be happy to drop right the way back to the other side of the halfway line, but not so much Gary – he [Wayne] was a better all-round footballer.'

'Wayne was a more skilful player than Gary,' family friend Reid concurs. 'Gary had the speed and the dedication to be a footballer, but Wayne was a better player – although he was, like, in the market bar having a brandy and Babycham at 15 and chatting up girls, which was what made the difference.'

Not that Duffy agrees. 'Wayne had nowhere near the talent of Gary,' Duffy scoffs. 'I've heard this story a million times and it's rubbish. Gary Lineker was a far superior player than his brother and he proved it in his career. I don't know if that rumour was started by Wayne saying it, but it's not true.'

With so much talent on their books, it was no surprise that Aylestone Park's crop of promising young starlets soon captured the attention of Leicester City's scouts, particularly Ray Shaw, who would make regular pilgrimages to watch Stretton's side. Shaw was friends with Gary's grandad, Harold, and upon his first visit to see the team of 12-year-olds, asked him who the tiny striker playing up front was. Harold proudly answered that it was his grandson.

Lineker's reputation had already marked him out as a player who rarely missed his chance and so it proved, as he scored almost immediately after Shaw had first spotted him – and showed enough throughout another goal-laden display to earn himself a trial. Naturally, it wasn't long before Lineker, Duffy and a handful of other Aylestone players were invited to join Leicester City's junior side, Leicester Beavers, for training twice a week at the club's Belvoir Drive training ground.

'It wasn't an academy in those days, it was a stone pitch at Belvoir Drive,' recalls Duffy. 'We used to go there training every Tuesday and Thursday, although I couldn't afford to go as regularly because I was from the poor side of town, whereas Gary was from the posh side of town.'

With so much football to play, Lineker's goals were starting to get him noticed. One season, he netted more than 200 goals for his school and club – including 161 for Aylestone at an average of four goals per game – and was rewarded with a small article in the *Leicester Mercury* hailing his exploits. The goals were flowing freely, with Lineker scoring 12 in one game, and chalking up a 10 and a nine at other times too.

It was a rarity for Lineker to find too much resistance when it came to adding to his tally, especially with Aylestone routinely trouncing sides across the county. Leicestershire Schools' runs in the FA Schools Cup provided more of a test, with one run to the quarter-finals ending with defeat to Liverpool at Anfield. That success didn't stop Lineker from making a brief defection, though.

'When he was about 14, he became a bit disgruntled and moved to Syston Town Juniors for about four weeks until his dad rang me up and asked if he could come back,' Stretton recounts. 'I can't remember why he was disgruntled, but kids would leave because of domestic circumstances, such as moving house, moving schools or whatnot. He clearly missed playing with the lads he'd got round him; they were all mates and they all just clicked.'

Temporary blip aside, Lineker continued to plunder the goals throughout his teenage years. Inevitably, his prolific record meant interest in him was high as he moved closer to his 16th birthday. By then, several of the other traits that characterised the future England captain had started to shine through, even if he still carried that childhood shyness.

'He was very quiet; he had no aggression. I think that came from the fact that the bigger lads in the team were the ones who dished it out a little and he didn't need to,' explains Stretton. 'But he was so quick in that penalty area. He capitalised on his skill and like all the great players, it was a fairly unique skill, where 50 or 60 per cent of it is up in your head.'

Despite having been affiliated with Leicester City for several years as part of the club's junior Beavers team, Lineker wasn't short of options to sign elsewhere as his thoughts turned to a full-time career in the game. It was time to make a big decision.

3
CITY BOY

Leicester City, 1976–1981

*'I remember thinking at the time
that Gary nearly didn't make it.'*

The trip back home from Wembley was almost too much to take. Three generations of the Lineker family had been left dejected by what they'd just witnessed, but none more so than eight-year-old Gary, who couldn't keep the tears from his eyes.

The Linekers had been at England's national football stadium to see their beloved Leicester City take on Manchester City in the 1969 FA Cup Final, the Foxes' fourth attempt at lifting the famous trophy. And just as it had ended on each of the previous three occasions, they were returning to the East Midlands empty-handed after a spirited-yet-fruitless display, losing 1–0 to Neil Young's first-half strike.

Cramming into Wembley's packed terraces would have been an intense experience for even the most hardened fan, but for a youngster witnessing a reported 100,000 supporters bunched in for a game of such magnitude would have overloaded the senses. The stadium was teeming with people waving flags and holding up banners of different hues – Leicester's royal blue contrasting with Manchester City's lighter tint. Passionate cries for 'City' were reverberating around all four corners of the stadium.

Neither side were serial winners at this stage, so the occasion was tinged with a sense of opportunity, an energy filled with anticipation of long-awaited victory. The alternative, as the Linekers' Leicester cohort discovered, was bitter disappointment at a chance to dance down Wembley Way as winners. Another shot at immortality passed up.

This was Gary's first experience of watching Leicester on such a big stage, having been too young to join the family trips to see the team play in the 1961 and 1963 finals. Naturally, the upset of defeat was even tougher to take for a young child, with the heartbreak of the loss aching all the way back to his hometown.

There'd been tears. But they'd been tears of love that confirmed what would become a lifelong passion. The first cut is the deepest, after all.

Leicester City was in the Lineker family's blood. Harold had been a season ticket holder as far back as 1921 and had passed the baton down to each generation since. So, aged six, it was Gary's turn to make his first trip to see the Foxes play at their Filbert Street home, joining 39,000 others to see them lose 2–1 to a star-studded Manchester United side including George Best, Bobby Charlton and Denis Law.

Defeat hadn't put Gary off and he was soon hooked by Leicester's entertaining style of play. They may not have been the biggest and most successful club about, but they were his club. So when the time came in 1978 for a teenage Lineker to choose between signing as an apprentice for the Foxes, or for Celtic, Leeds or Chelsea, who all reportedly showed an interest, there was only one decision to make.

Lineker's first contract was worth £16 a week, plus an extra £5 for his mum to cover living costs because he was staying at the family home instead of in digs like many of Leicester's other apprentices, although Margaret would hand the envelope containing the fiver straight back to her son to add to his kitty.

Gary was a homebody and never had any inclination to fly the nest as soon as he was earning. He was happy living at home and stayed there right up until his move to Everton as a 24-year-old, telling the *Leicester Mercury* in November 1980, 'I've never thought of getting my own place. I can't cook and my parents let me do what I want.' Not that Gary was much of a hellraiser, anyway.

'People always ask if I have stories about Gary because I knew him in his teenage years when things might have been more chaotic or interesting, but they're not,' says fellow Leicester youngster Mick Duffy. 'When we were both 17, we were playing first-team football for Leicester and we were going out at night clubbing, but he had no airs or graces. It's not like I've got stories that could get Gary in trouble, because he was strait-laced.

'From the age of 10 to 22, Gary Lineker didn't get up to anything because if he did, I would have known. We went out together and even met girls in twos, there was nothing on him, he didn't upset a girl, he didn't have hidden secrets. He was Mr Nice Guy.'

It was just as well, really, because Lineker had a lot of work to do as an apprentice. He might have been scoring goals for fun for Aylestone Town and Leicestershire Schools, but the young striker was a long way from being ready for the cut and thrust of the Football League when he first signed forms with Leicester.

Standing at only 1.68m (5ft 6in) and weighing 57kg (9 stone), Gary was a late developer and has spoken on several occasions since about how he didn't go through puberty until much later than a lot of his peers. Bulking up was crucial to any hopes of an ascension to the first team and he was soon put on a protein-heavy diet of steaks and bottles of milk – alongside a routine of two or three hours' weightlifting a day – to help him grow bigger. That combination of nature and nurture got results, with Lineker gaining 7.5cm (3in) in height and 12.7kg (2 stone) in weight in those early days at the club.

That development was crucial for both player and team. The season before Lineker signed on as an apprentice, Leicester had been relegated from the First Division and so making the most of their talented crop of youngsters was a key part of their strategy to stabilise in the second tier.

New manager Jock Wallace had big ambitions for his band of youngsters and while most within the club had highest hopes for midfielder Andy Peake and another young forward, Dave Buchanan, Lineker knew there were first-team opportunities on offer if he could step up. Wallace could clearly see his potential too.

'When I first arrived at Leicester, I got a couple of games with the reserves and me and Gary were playing together,' recalls Scotland international Ian Wilson, who joined Leicester as a 21-year-old in 1979.

'Gary was 18 and played on the right wing – with his pace, Gary was a threat at that young age – and I played in midfield alongside him. Jock Wallace was at the game and was just trying to get me settled, and popped round to see me after the game and asked, "How do you think you did?" His next question was "Did you see anyone who caught your eye?" and I said Gary. Jock said, "I hoped you would say that; we've got big things planned for Gary."'

Wallace wasn't the sort of manager to put his arm round the shoulders of his players to inspire them, even if they were a relative babe in arms. A former goalkeeper who had spent most of his years bouncing around the lower reaches of the English and Scottish football pyramid while serving in the military and working in the local pit, Wallace had the air of a no-nonsense leader who spoke with as little ambiguity as possible. Discipline was a key trait Wallace demanded, no doubt a symptom of his time in the Army doing stints in Northern Ireland and the jungles of Malaya, off the coasts of Malaysia and Singapore.

Born less than 16km (10 miles) east of Edinburgh, the Leicester boss cut an impenetrable figure, with a neck as thick as the broad Scottish accent he barked orders in. For a youngster who had spent his entire life living within Leicester's city limits, Lineker needed a trained ear to understand what Wallace was saying – and listen he must. This was a man who had transformed the fortunes of Rangers in his six years as manager at Ibrox, winning the Scottish league title in 1975 to bring the Gers their first championship success in 11 seasons, while ending Glasgow rivals Celtic's dominance in the process.

League glory in 1975 was only the start, with Wallace leading Rangers to the Scottish treble in two of the next three seasons before abruptly resigning in the summer of 1978 and resurfacing at Leicester. Glasgow's loss was the Foxes' gain and while Wallace may have brought a brashness that sometimes struck the fear of God into his charges, there was undoubtedly method to the madness.

Nobody was safe from Wallace's boisterous approach, with Lineker regularly telling the tale of how the formidable Scotsman angrily pinned him up against the dressing room wall at half time during one reserve team match. A shy teenager with the look of an innocent choirboy, the young striker had scored a first-half brace, but far from earning Wallace's praise, Lineker found himself being picked up by the scruff of his neck, told to elevate his performance and summoned to the manager's office the next morning.

After enduring a sleepless night worrying about what Wallace was going to say, Lineker arrived trembling in the office to be greeted by a more amiable individual, who went on to explain the importance of keeping his feet on the ground in the good times. Far from the reprimand Lineker feared, Wallace talked about how his protégé 'had a chance' to make it if he remained focused and avoided the temptation of going out drinking before matches.

This was Wallace's way. It might have sounded terrifying, but it created a group ethic that brought Leicester's youth players together and would later benefit the first team as they were drip-fed into the starting XI.

'Jock did seem to bring a lot of youngsters through,' says Peake, who broke through at the same time as Lineker. 'Maybe Jock's mentality was that if he brought us through, we'd play for him, like "Oh, he's the boss, he gave us our chance" – that sort of thing.

'He was brilliant, Jock, and a fantastic manager. I always used to say to people, "You've never had a rollicking until you'd had one from Jock Wallace." He probably taught Alex Ferguson everything he knew. He was a hard, hard man, but a fantastic man and he had a heart of gold – if you were one of his lads, he'd back you to the hilt. He'd be hard on you, put people against walls and take the heads off people, but he was a fantastic manager.'

Life inside a football dressing room in the 1980s was an unforgiving place for more than simply a ferocious manager. Senior pros were there to be respected and there was a clear hierarchy among the players, with anyone who stepped out of line soon finding out about it.

For an apprentice like Lineker, they were the bottom rung. The sprat at the bottom of the food chain. And all too readily devoured by the older players if they so pleased. The apprentices would be given any number of unpleasant tasks in service of the first team.

Lineker's allocated job was to clean the first-team dressing room after training and lay out the kit before the next day's session. At that time, players were only supplied with one set of training garb, so throughout the week the young apprentice had to scoop up the discarded clothes off the floor, put them on wrought-iron hangers and place them in the neighbouring drying room ahead of the next day. By the end of the week, the stench that would emanate from the kit that Lineker was knee-deep in was dreadful, really testing his mettle to maintain the standards that were expected.

That also meant Lineker keeping his mouth shut, regardless of how many quips would enter his mind. By now starting to release the shackles of shyness that had always surrounded him, Gary would sometimes find those one-liners bursting to come out.

'Gary was always happy to be part of the banter once he got his confidence and earned his wings a bit,' explains winger Winston White, a senior member of the side at the time. 'As an apprentice, as he was at the time, Gary had to be careful because he couldn't cross that line, but you could see he had the potential to have a sense of humour and be part of that banter. That was overridden by his ability to want to learn and want to get a professional contract.

'The world has changed and you don't get apprenticeships any more, but back then if you were an apprentice and talked out of turn, oh my god, wow, you'd be hung, drawn and quartered in the verbal sense because you were told what to do and barked at.

'Gary was treated no differently as an apprentice. He wasn't a golden child or anything; you did your apprenticeship – that's how you earned your bones. He took it like a man and got on with it, and that's one of the reasons he had such a great career – because he was willing to do what was needed to be done to make it as a pro footballer.'

Those hard yards eventually paid off on New Year's Day 1979 when Gary was handed his debut for a home clash against Oldham Athletic. Outside of the club, Lineker was still a relative unknown with his own fans, to such a point that he didn't even appear on the programme being sold at Filbert Street for the match.

As the several thousand hardy souls filtered through the tight metal turnstiles for the match, foggy heads inevitably still lingering from the previous night's exertions, they could have been forgiven for sharing puzzled looks at who the slight, gawky-looking imposter with the long mop of brown hair was. Even when the name Gary Lineker was announced across the muffled speaker system as the starting XI was read out, only the most ardent of Leicester followers would have successfully identified him.

Wallace had named the 18-year-old as his right-winger for the match, deeming him too lightweight to cut it as an out-and-out striker at senior level. But what Lineker may have lacked in physicality, he made up with in pace, clocking a 10.5-second 100m personal best – making him a full-back's worst nightmare. This was no day for a summertime athletics meet, though, with a winter chill hanging alongside the stench of tobacco smoke and fried food rising up from the surrounding stands.

Lineker wasn't the only one of his young cohort to be given a debut for the Oldham game, with hot property Buchanan starting in one of the striking berths. And it was the Geordie who shone out of the two youngsters, bagging the first goal in Leicester's 2–0 win. Far from grabbing his opportunity, Lineker struggled to make the impact he'd hoped in his maiden appearance – not only being outshone by Buchanan, but also remaining relatively anonymous. When Wallace named his next side for an FA Cup third round tie with Norwich City five days later, Lineker was nowhere to be seen.

It remained that way until April, when Gary received a surprise Easter call-up to come back in from the cold. Lineker was at the family home when he received the SOS from Wallace asking him to join the squad for an away match at Preston. The first team were already in the North West to visit Oldham, but with injuries taking their toll, Lineker, Duffy and another youth prospect, Neil Grewcock, were asked to travel up.

It was Duffy rather than Lineker who was originally slated to start the match against Preston, but a stroke of misfortune for the fellow Leicester native opened up the chance for his mate to take centre stage.

'In those days, it was 11 players and one sub. We were going up north, Gary was sub and we had a 13th man,' Duffy remembers. 'We were travelling up and I didn't feel very well. I was starting to come down with something and I explained to Jock Wallace and he changed the team, put Gary in my place and the 13th man became sub. We lost the game 4–0, but Gary Lineker was man of the match when originally he wasn't playing. That particular night, I was thinking, "You lucky sod."'

Lineker's performance was a glimmer of promise in that Preston debacle and Wallace decided to give the teenager another opportunity from the start for the home match against Crystal Palace a few days later. With Leicester battling against relegation from the Second Division, Lineker then kept his place for a crucial away visit to Notts County. It was his best run in the team and at such a crucial time of the season, although Lineker batted the attention away in what would become trademark self-deprecation.

'My only target for this season was to get into the reserves if I could and I wasn't even sure I would make that, but I'm thrilled to have made a first-team breakthrough,' Lineker told the *Leicester Mercury* on 28 April 1979. 'If anyone had suggested I would be playing for the first team by now I would have told them they must be joking, but it has happened nonetheless.'

The trip to Meadow Lane would be a significant one. For Leicester, the 1–0 win they secured in Nottingham – their first in eight games – would go a long way to securing their survival, but for Lineker his winning goal would be his first for the Foxes. What made it even more special was that it was Lineker's old pal Duffy who provided the assist for the big moment.

'I came on at half time, it was 0–0 and it was chucking it down with rain,' says Duffy. 'I remember coming on the left side of the pitch, dribbling it and hitting a left-footed shot, but it went across the goal and the keeper missed it. It was going by him and Lineker came sliding in in the rain and slid it in. He went in there too, along with the keeper.

'I always say it was going in and that he stole my goal and my career, and we have some banter and a bit of a laugh about it because he says it was going wide. That was his first goal and the rest was history. Once he'd got his first goal against Notts County and we stayed up, that more or less started his career.'

A draw a couple of weeks later in a fiery encounter with Sheffield United at Bramall Lane meant Leicester stayed up. It was particularly notable because by then, Wallace was regularly playing a team full of youngsters and was trying to mould them into a hard-working side that was difficult to beat. The time was now for many of those starlets to make their mark with Leicester, and Lineker wasn't about to let that chance go by.

'After we made our debuts that January, we were kind of in and out of the team for the rest of the season, then we went abroad on a pre-season tour to Finland and Sweden for about three weeks,' says Peake. 'Gary got to the end of the previous season, had a few weeks off, went back for pre-season and he almost kind of developed during that tour. He'd gone from "He's all right" to "Blimey, this bloke's got something."'

Lineker may have made a step up in his own performance, but that didn't mean he'd be guaranteed a starting place in Leicester's side – especially in his preferred position as a striker. Wallace wasn't about to settle for another season near the bottom of the table and had spent money to bring in forward Alan Young to boost his side's firepower.

There was also Wallace's gruelling pre-season regime to contend with. Replicated from the Scotsman's successful spell as Rangers boss before joining Leicester, Wallace would send his charges on long runs up and down sand dunes, showing no let-up even when players became so tired they were being sick or feeling faint. When training sessions were held nowhere near a beach, a coastal location was substituted with the sand and gravel of Wanlip Quarry in Birstall to the north of Leicester.

Gary didn't shirk the challenges thrown his way, but still found himself in and out of the first team during his second season, deputising when his more senior colleagues were unavailable. It meant he kept flitting between sides, sometimes slotting in as an auxiliary winger or striker in the Second Division, or increasingly as the focal point of the reserve-team attack. But wherever he played, Lineker's golden touch in front of goal was starting to shine ever brighter.

'I played with a few terrific goalscorers and they have an extraordinary ability to get into the right positions,' White picks up. 'They figure out very quickly that you need to be between the goals, and the nearer you are to the goalkeeper, the better chance you've got of scoring a goal – as long as you're onside and all that – and I think Gary probably got that a lot quicker than most.

'People talk about Jimmy Greaves, who was another who was a fox in the box, and he could also score goals by dribbling past three or four players, but Gary wasn't that sort of player. It's football intelligence, that's where he excelled. A lot of us wanted to score goals like Gary, but we didn't pick it up as well as he did.

'I played with him a few times and, if we lost a game 3–1 or 3–2, he'd always score the one or two, so before you knew it, he was top scorer in the reserves. That's how you build your credibility and your confidence. If I knew the exact science of it, I'd coach it to people, but it's an art form that players pick up very quickly.

'Gary was one of the closest things to Gerd Müller, the great German striker, in that he had this amazing ability to figure out the percentages of the ball falling in that position and it's no coincidence that, if you look at a lot of the goals Gary scored, he was stretching out with every sinew of his body and just getting a toe to it to steer it into the corner. That's an art, a scientific approach that I'm not sure most people could break down.'

Lineker may have been starting to demonstrate the talents that looked as though they'd carry him to a professional career, but there were still plenty of lessons for the livewire striker to learn. Not least that his breakthrough as a first-team player, albeit on the fringes of the team, would mean greater notoriety within the city and that even the most innocent of social activities had the potential to land him in hot water.

'We'd gone out one night and met these two girls we'd seen previously,' Duffy recalls. 'We arranged to meet them for a drink on a Thursday and I remember getting up for training on the Friday at Belvoir Drive and Ian MacFarlane, who was the assistant manager, came into the dressing room and said, "Mick Duffy, Gary Lineker, get back to the ground, Jock Wallace wants to see you."

'We thought "Oh my god," if Jock wants to see you, you're at death's door and you're petrified. We went back to the ground and I said to Gaz, "What have we done?" and he said, "I don't know, let's see what he's got to say." The father of one of the girls had rung Jock Wallace up and told him that we'd been out the night before and got drunk, which wasn't actually true.

'Jock laid into us massively and asked, "Did you go out last night?" I couldn't look at Gary because Jock Wallace was looking at us, so we didn't know what each of us was going to say. Jock Wallace stood there like a mountain over us and said, "Did you go out last night?" I said, "No" and Gary said the same, and we lied. Jock Wallace stood there and said, "OK, I believe you. If you didn't go out, you didn't go out, but if I find out you did, your careers are over." I didn't realise at the time, but Jock knew and it was him telling us off and making a point because he believed the guy and had checked. He let us off, but I remember thinking at the time that Gary nearly didn't make it [because of the incident].'

Lineker wasn't one for letting his new-found status as a professional footballer go to his head, so he needed little guidance to stay on the straight and narrow. He remained the same softly spoken, well-mannered local boy he'd been before his Leicester breakthrough and wasn't about to get ahead of himself. He still remembered those cold, early mornings at Leicester Market and realised he needed to properly establish himself as footballer to avoid going back there.

He'd have to be patient to get his chance again too, with new signing Young scoring six in his first seven Leicester matches. It wasn't until the end of October and the 13th league match of the campaign that Lineker got into the first team. He then scored a brace against Sunderland in a 2–1 win at Filbert Street, before playing in the next nine matches, in which the Foxes lost only once, putting themselves in the thick of the promotion race.

But after an FA Cup replay defeat to non-league Harlow – a match Gary played in despite having a fever because he was too scared to tell Wallace he was unwell – he found himself back in the reserves. Lineker made fleeting returns to the side, but despite playing in the 2–1 victory against Charlton that clinched promotion, he couldn't hold down a regular starting place.

The season had undoubtedly been a success for Leicester, as they won the Second Division title. Wallace had created a side with a high work ethic and had shed the tag of 'exuberant entertainers' that mavericks such as Frank Worthington and Keith Weller had bestowed upon the side. Wallace's side, which was known as McLeicester City due to their high number of Scottish players, wasn't without its flair, but they had more steel.

Lineker had made 19 appearances in the promotion campaign but was clearly considered too green for the First Division – playing in just nine games and scoring twice as Leicester's youngsters struggled to deal with the higher standard and came straight back down.

'I'd say we probably went up a year too soon,' admits Peake. 'If we'd missed out on promotion that year and then gone up the following year, we'd have been better prepared for it, and we were still quite young. It's a big jump into that First Division and playing against the likes of [Kenny] Dalglish and [Graeme] Souness at teams like Liverpool. Had we missed out then got promoted, I don't think we'd have had that yo-yo, we'd have stayed there.'

Relegation provided an opportunity for Lineker once more. Aided by Young's suspension for the first three matches of the campaign, the now 20-year-old forward started and scored in the season opener against Grimsby, and contributed as Leicester won the next two. But when Young returned, Gary's run in the team ended.

He'd made an impression, but despite coming off the bench to score a late equaliser against Crystal Palace and Leicester's patchy form, first-team opportunities were scarce once more. Although he was now firmly on Wallace's radar.

'We've had to bring him on gradually over the year and it's beginning to pay off, mainly because of the boy's attitude to the work we have put in,' Wallace told the *Leicester Mercury* in September 1981.

'He has had a lot of setbacks in that time – being left out of the team, being switched to different positions – but each time he has learned from it and has never gone under a cloud. If all players were like Lineker, with his enthusiasm and enjoyment of the game, then it would be great to be a manager.

'I said last season that it wouldn't be long until he came through and so it has proved... Lineker's recent success might come as a surprise to some, but not to me. I have long admired the boy's character and I'm delighted to see the game going so well for him.'

These were promising words, but Lineker wouldn't get another start again until November, and only because Young was ruled out for six weeks due to having a cartilage operation. That was all the time the future England man would need, as he scored two in his first start back against Charlton to kick-start a run of seven goals in his next 11 matches. By the time Young returned from injury, Lineker was now a must-pick to partner his more experienced teammate.

'You've just got to keep playing, trying to improve and take it all in your stride,' Lineker remarked to the *Leicester Mercury* in November 1981. 'I just don't let it get me down and I fought my way back by showing the right form.

'I was very disappointed when I made way for Alan Young earlier in the season. It's very difficult competing with big money players for your place in the team. I prefer playing through the middle and I'm looking forward to an extended run. However, I didn't want to get my chance because of another player's injury.'

After years of plugging away and honing his talents, this was Lineker's moment to show he could perform on a regular basis as the main striker for a Leicester team that still had an outside chance of launching another promotion push. And he wasn't about to let it pass him by.

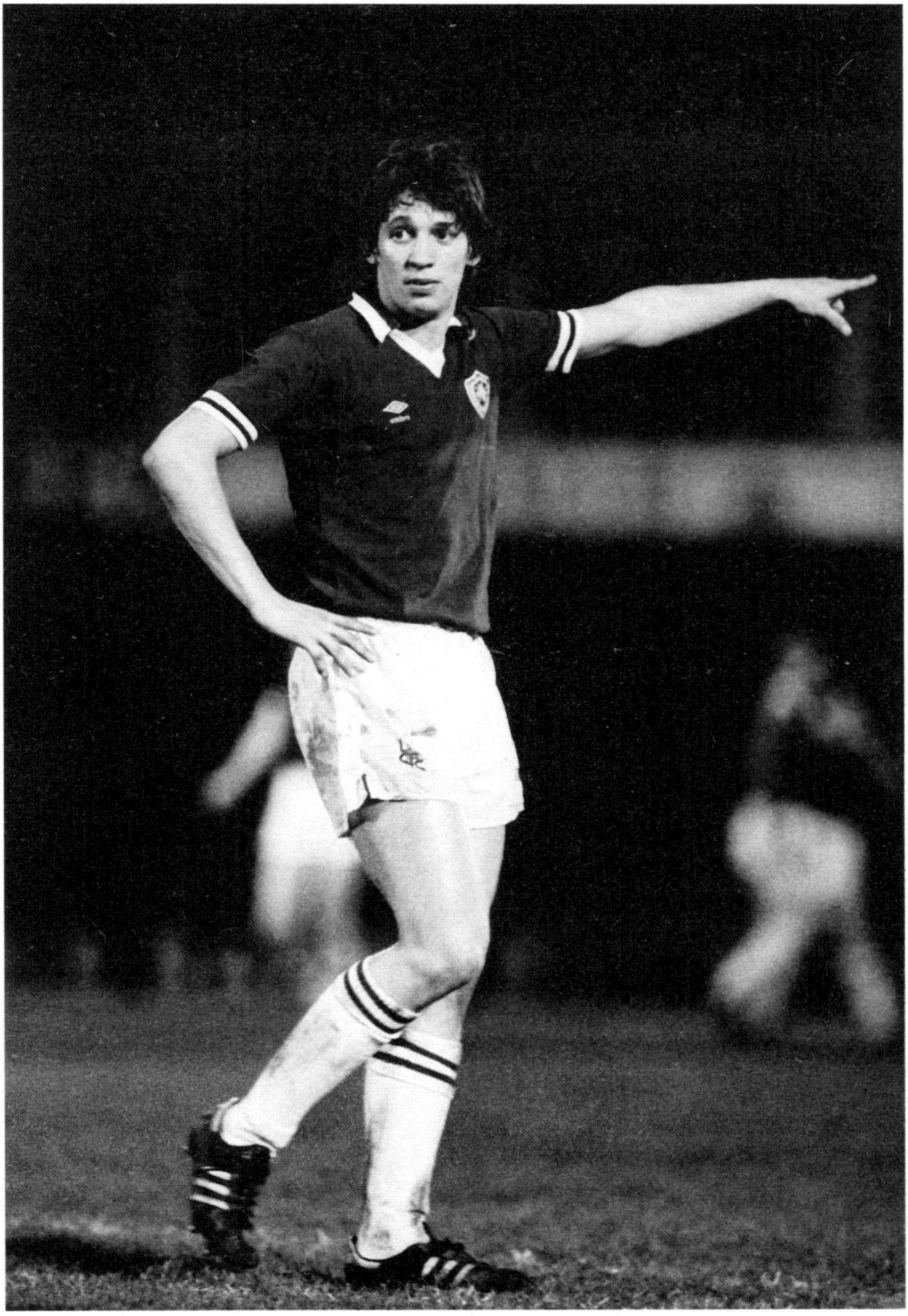

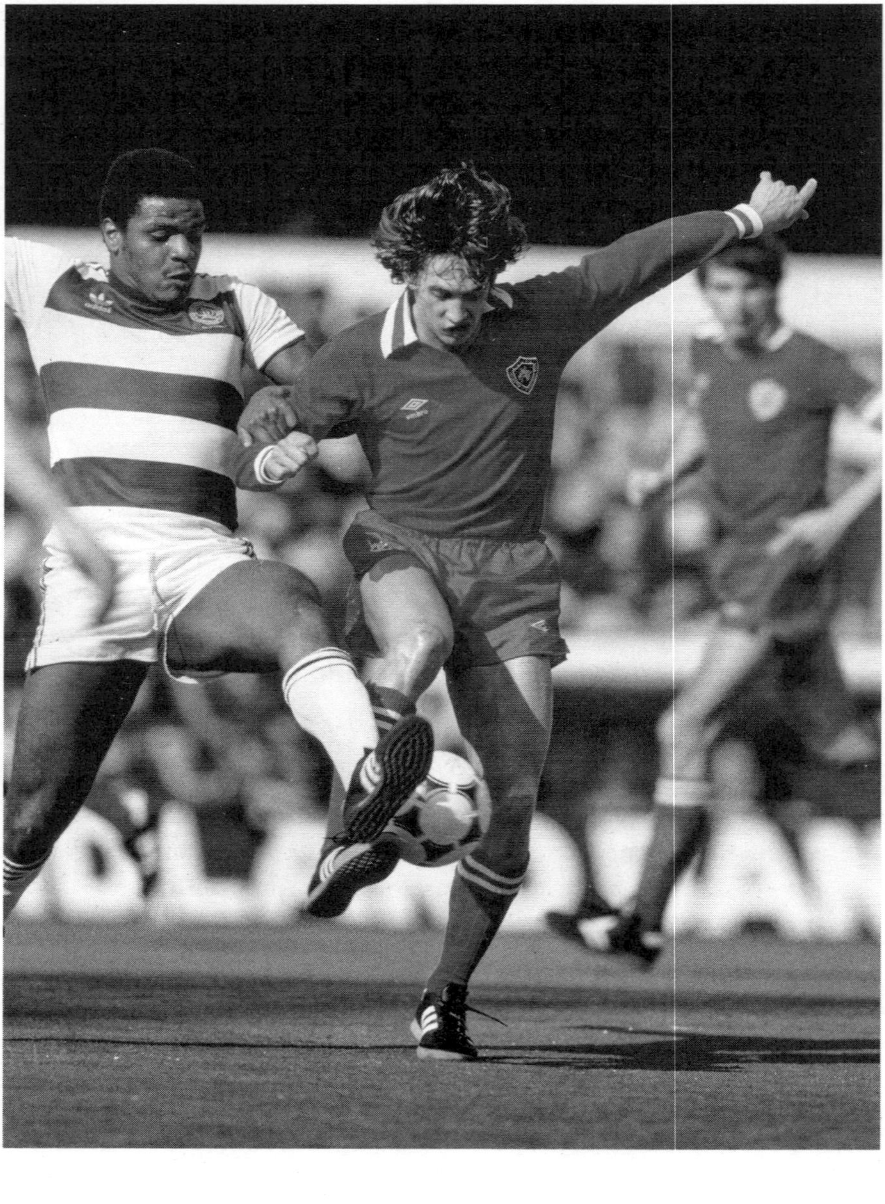

4

BIG BREAK

Leicester City, 1982–1984

'I don't feel like a superstar at all, I just feel normal.'

The news had rocked the city of Leicester. After four years in charge, Jock Wallace had stood down as manager, taking everyone by surprise. While many Leicester fans may have hoped for better than the eighth-place finish that meant they failed to bounce back to the First Division at the first attempt, there hadn't been an expectation that the Scot would leave.

Wallace was still a firm favourite with supporters with his inimitable manner and ability to marry a squad bursting with exciting young talent with experienced old-stagers to create a team that had the potential to mix it with the bigger sides on their day.

The Foxes had been in the promotion picture until late in the 1981/2 season, with Gary Lineker's 17 league goals keeping them within striking distance of the top three until four defeats in the last six matches saw them fall five points short. That disappointment had been tempered by a run to the FA Cup semi-final, where they lost 2–0 to eventual winners Tottenham in front of more than 46,000 people at Villa Park.

As Lineker first set eyes on the distinctive large brick staircase that greets visitors to the Holte End, he was filled with hope that this would be the day he'd go some way to putting those childhood memories of 1969 FA Cup despair behind him. Leicester hadn't reached an FA Cup Final since and while a Spurs side boasting Glenn Hoddle and Ossie Ardiles among their ranks posed tough competition, there was still belief the Second Division side could win. While Tottenham's quality eventually told, the hope that had abounded among the Leicester faithful before kick-off highlighted what Wallace had created.

The cup run was also memorable for a hectic quarter-final clash with Shrewsbury Town that Lineker later described as his favourite ever game at Filbert Street. The Shrews had come from behind to lead 2–1 when goalkeeper Mark Wallington had to be taken off due to injury and, with no replacement on the bench, striker Alan Young donned the gloves. But when Young himself then had to be taken off, Leicester were forced to temporarily play with 10 men – and a third goalkeeper of the day in the form of winger Steve Lynex, before Young made an unexpected return – but still found a way to get their noses ahead to eventually win 5–2.

Lineker had scored the home side's fourth that afternoon. This, added to his strike against Southampton in the third round, meant he ended the season with 19 goals in all competitions. The season had represented a real breakthrough campaign for the 21-year-old and he was being discussed as a serious contender for the Midlands Football Writers' Young Player of the Year award, before being pipped by Coventry's Danny Thomas.

The concern was that Wallace's sudden departure might derail Leicester's progress and have a knock-on effect for Lineker too. The Scot, who had decided to leave the club to move back north of the border, had built a united group with players loyal to him due to the opportunities he'd given them.

Former Coventry City boss Gordon Milne was a more than competent replacement, but any swap in the dugout was expected to herald a changing of the guard.

'Jock was popular with the fans and the thing when I went there coming from Coventry was that they're local rivals in a way,' recalls Milne. 'I knew Jock and I was quite friendly with him, and I'm from Scottish parents, so the big, aggressive, noisy Scotsman was part of what I was brought up with as well.

'Jock had a certain style of working, playing and training, which was his character, and the players played for him – he was popular with the players and fans. It was a shock when he left, he left just out of the blue, it was a bolt and a big problem for the board at that time, so he was a difficult act to follow. But that's what I did and that's where we went.'

Milne knew he'd have to put his own stamp on the side if they were to get anywhere near their ambition of getting back into the First Division. There were some natural clashes, such as the abrasive Young, who was a staunch Wallace disciple and struggled to adapt to the managerial change.

Young would be one of the first to exit, moving to Sheffield United. But it turned out that Milne already had a replacement who was coming in to the club that summer in the shape of Alan Smith, a strapping young forward Wallace had plucked from non-league Alvechurch. If Lineker needed a new partner to lead the line with, Milne appeared to have stumbled on the perfect match.

'The way Jock had put it [before leaving] was that it didn't seem as if I'd get much game time to start with because I'd come from non-league and he said I'd have to learn my trade in the reserves for a couple of years before pushing for a first-team place,' Smith explains.

'Jock did put younger lads forward, but the dressing room was full of Scottish lads when I got there and it was one of those things that Gordon came in and cleared out a lot of players. I was one of the new players and got a chance.

'It all turned round for me one day in pre-season when the first team and the reserves were playing Northampton in a friendly on adjoining pitches. I was playing for the reserves and Gordon Milne whistled over and said, "Alan, we want to you come on in the second half for the first team." I was playing with Gary up front and I got a hat-trick in that second half. From then on, I was training with the first team and I started the first game of the season up with Gary – it happened pretty quickly.'

Smith was almost exactly two years Lineker's junior and was still deciding if professional football was for him. As a university student studying modern languages at Coventry Polytechnic, the new 19-year-old striker whom Milne was integrating into his Second Division team remained convinced education was his long-term career plan.

Yet here he was being thrown straight into the first match of the 1982/3 season alongside Lineker for the visit of Charlton. The pairing only had a combined age of 40 – a far cry from Wallace's first-choice picks of Young and Jim Melrose at the beginning of the previous campaign – but Milne had spotted a spark he wanted to cultivate.

'With Gary and Alan, they were both young kids, but as a combination of players, there was something together that kind of married and I liked that idea,' Milne explains. 'When you look back now, you think it had to be obvious with the careers they both had, but when they're young, trying to get that chemistry, there was that combination. There was material to work with.

'The former national coach of [West] Germany, Jupp Derwall, whom I met when I worked in Turkey, once said to me, "There are good players, but the great players have something different." And I said, "What's that, Jupp?" and he said, "The great players have intelligence." And when I look back now, Alan Smith and Gary Lineker were both intelligent lads and that's stood the test of time.

'Forget their football ability; you can have some good players and great players who are thick, they'll nod and say they understand you, but don't take on what you've said or listened, but they were two intelligent lads. Mentally, they were on the same wavelength and then technically things developed.'

It was impossible to know at the time, but the Lineker–Smith axis would eventually become one of Leicester's most famous strike partnerships. Smith was 1.9m (6ft 3in) tall, selfless and worked hard for the team, and played a key part in his speedier and more goal-hungry accomplice's progression. It was all very natural and while Milne had spotted something between them, this wasn't a time for painstaking hours on the training ground choreographing moves.

'I don't remember having to work too hard on the relationship,' admits Smith. 'Gary would naturally hang on the last line of the defence, looking for that half chance to put the ball over the top. I naturally played with my back to goal – if it was played in the air, I'd flick it on or hold it up and put it out wide to Stevie Lynex. But Gary was the poacher, he was always the man looking for a chance and our respective styles did click pretty naturally. We didn't have to put too much effort into it.

'It was a big step for me between non-league and the old Second Division, so I was still learning my trade and learning the game. Gary was relatively young at this stage too, so you do various drills, shadow play, attack against defence. All the time, you're working with each other and working out what each other likes and the moves each other wants to make. It's kind of a natural thing in training and in matches.'

A Smith did get on the scoresheet in the season's curtain-raiser against Charlton, but it wasn't Alan. Instead, it was Scottish midfielder Bobby who scored Leicester's only goal of the defeat, although Alan Smith, Lineker and Melrose were on target in a 3–1 win at Rotherham a few days later.

Success against the Millers was Leicester's only victory of the opening four matches as the feared dip which began after Wallace's departure appeared to take hold. Milne continued to rejig the side, with Smith being dropped to make way for new signing Tommy English, who had played for the new manager previously at Coventry, while Melrose became the latest player to leave Filbert Street.

Lineker knew his form from the previous season would not make him immune to Milne's shake-up, saying in an early season interview in the *Leicester Mercury* that he needed to 'start to prove himself all over again' and he had to 'make an impression on him by playing well'. And despite Leicester's disjointed start, that's exactly what Lineker did – netting 12 goals in the opening 14 league matches.

The local boy's goalscoring form was one of few bright sparks in a tricky first few months of Milne's reign, with the promotion hopefuls only picking up six wins from their first 18 matches in all competitions under Milne by the end of November. The transition was going to take time.

'Anybody who had gone in there would have been thinking they needed to change it and with Jock leaving, it had to,' says Milne. 'Jock had gone, and it wasn't as if he'd had the sack: Jock left them [Leicester], and the fact that change was in the air was just the way it was.

'There was an older brigade, good players like Eddie Kelly, Youngy and that group, but it took time to move them gently out and give the others a go, while searching for different combinations of players. We started crap, terrible and then with about 15 games left, we never lost again.

'The young pros were feeling their feet and it's easy to look back and say, "It's natural, that," because of how they turned out. But for all those lads, it took time for that to come together and really in a way, once it started, it worked for itself. That wasn't difficult to manage.'

After that difficult start, Leicester only lost four times from the beginning of December onwards and, as Milne points out, they didn't lose a league match from mid-February – steaming through to take the third automatic promotion spot and secure a return to the First Division. Lineker had scored 26 goals, smashing his tally from the previous season and beating his personal target of 20.

He put a large part of his personal improvement for his goalscoring record down to Milne's style of play, telling the *Leicester Mercury* that the 'smoother build-up meant I was seeing more of the ball'. That may have been the case, but it also coincided with him blossoming into one of the Football League's most-feared marksmen.

As the side's chief goal threat, Lineker was now undoubtedly Leicester's box-office star. A hometown wonder who combined being a matchwinner with a choirboy-like charm and politeness that made him appeal to men and women of all ages in equal measure.

'Well, it doesn't feel like I thought it would,' Lineker told the *Leicester Mercury* when asked about his new-found stardom in December 1982. 'When I was a lad watching Allan Clarke and Frank Worthington knocking in goals, I thought professional footballers were superstars. They seemed untouchable, unreachable figures, the kind of people fans would swoon over. I don't feel like a superstar at all, I just feel normal.

'At first I found it a bit uncomfortable when people recognised me in the street. I used to be shyer than I am now and when people I didn't know started pointing me out and speaking to me, I was a little bit embarrassed. I can cope with it now and I don't really mind people praising or criticising me.'

He would have to get used to it. The pressure of the Second Division and being recognised by your own fans was one thing, but stepping up to the top flight where he'd be known on an even greater scale would be an entirely different challenge.

Fame wouldn't change him, though. Aided by living in the same city he'd grown up in, Lineker kept many of the old habits he'd had in his younger years, wasn't a big drinker and retained the friendships that served him well previously – meaning he wasn't easily led astray and wouldn't put himself in situations he wasn't comfortable with.

'He liked playing snooker, he liked playing cricket, and he seemed to be in control of whatever he was doing,' Milne explains. 'It was obviously his choice whatever he did and wherever he went, he wouldn't go somewhere he didn't want to go or do anything he didn't want to do, without being snobbish or anything. If you asked him to do something, like "Gary, we're going to the hospital today" and presented it to him, then he'd do it. He wasn't difficult to handle at all, but he was focused on what he did – and whatever he did, he put his heart and soul into it.'

Almost without fail, there was one place in particular where Lineker could always be found after training. 'At the end of training, he'd go off and play snooker at Willie Thorne's Snooker Hall,' says Smith. 'He was really into his snooker. Some of us would go and play golf, but he wasn't into that at that stage, although he took it up later.'

Lineker was a dab hand with a cue and has since spoken about racking up several centuries in his time at the green baize. He had a good teacher in fellow Leicesterite, Willie Thorne, the moustachioed former world number seven snooker player, who was a big friend of the striker's. Lineker claims to have taken the odd frame from Thorne in the past and was well known for travelling around the UK to watch his mate in action at several major tournaments.

After winning promotion and finishing as the Second Division's top scorer in May 1983, Lineker followed up that success by being part of the team that won the Leicester Inter-League Trophy for the Wille Thorne Snooker Club, despite losing his two frames in the tournament.

'I'm not sure he'd say it, but I think his first love was playing snooker,' adds former Foxes winger Kevin MacDonald. 'He was very big mates with Willie Thorne and snooker was probably the release for him from the pressures of being the number-one striker at Leicester.

'He was still sociable. If we went out as a group for a drink after a game, he'd be there and then we'd split up into different areas and friends – some had girlfriends, some didn't. He was still very sociable in a team environment and you have to be whether you drink or not. There were quite a few others who didn't drink at all, but they realised that part of becoming a team and being together was turning up.'

Like all of the players, Lineker had stronger bonds with some of his teammates than others, with Andy Peake – another one of the local lads still in the side – regularly joining him to play snooker and going on holiday with him too. Without exception, his former teammates talk about Lineker's quick wit and how nice he was, although only a handful of them spent too much time with him outside of a football environment.

'He [Lineker] would have to allow you to come close to him and you would never manufacture that yourself – I'm talking about teammates or anybody socially,' Milne expands. 'He had his mates and was a great mate, so when he was with the lads, he liked to be with the lads – and nobody has a bad word to say about him. But he didn't mix in a way of being pals with everybody, or this, that or the other.'

If there's one way to ingratiate yourself to your teammates, it's by scoring goals. Lineker had missed the final two matches of the promotion campaign due to a knee ligament injury he sustained in a draw against Leeds at the beginning of May, but his impact had already been huge.

Leicester had gone up with a free-scoring swagger that wouldn't have gone unnoticed by the teams in the top tier. Lineker had topped the goalscoring charts, but he'd been ably backed up by Smith and winger Steve Lynex, who weighed in with a fair share of goals themselves. That sort of firepower made the Foxes a dangerous proposition for opponents because they could carry a threat against anyone.

As part of winning promotion, Milne had shaped the squad and centred it around young, hungry talent that excited the Filbert Street crowd. Naturally, that meant there was a growing interest in their players and while they each played their part, there was an understanding that Lineker's goals were crucial to them showing up well.

'If you don't score, you don't win games, then you don't ever get promotion. Gary's goals helped our status because we were predominantly young footballers and there was a lot of interest in our players at the time,' says MacDonald.

'The big thing about Gary was that any player who was within 12 yards' width of the goals and the six-yard box knew he'd be there and if you got the ball out into those areas, he'd make it with the change of pace he had. As he got older and better, he developed this knack of always being on the front foot, looking to be the first person to make the movement rather than allow the defender to force him into a situation he didn't want to be in. Gary would be the one who was forcing and taking positions they were uncomfortable in.'

'It's difficult to teach that knack,' Smith adds. 'You could practise your finishing and you could improve on that, but I suppose it's getting into those positions. And even when you do, making sure you stay relaxed, you've got a clear head and don't tighten up. What Gary had was the instinct of where to position himself and where to be when the move was building up, anticipating mistakes – it's having that sharpness of thinking in the box.'

Fleet of mind and foot, Lineker was a teammate's dream and could always be relied upon to make the smart runs and pop up in the right positions at the right times. For a midfielder whose job it was to provide ammunition to the front line, working with an intelligent striker who had an innate understanding of what was required of them made their job much easier.

'It's hard to say what it was, [but] Gary and I had a really good understanding,' says Peake. 'I didn't really have to look; I knew if he wanted the ball to feet without looking or I knew if he wanted me to turn them around using his pace. He was a clever player and as a midfielder, very good to play with.

'Gary almost recognised when the midfielders received the ball that we'd only got one touch and he'd just go. He knew whether to show or spin, and he was just an intelligent player. It's a bit like when he was in front of goal and having great chances and putting them away – he almost knew where the ball was going before it even went there.

'If the ball went into Gary's feet, he did the simple thing: he'd hold it up and lay it off. He wasn't one for fancy turns, he wasn't that sort of player; he'd hold it up, play it off, then spin – he had great pace and knew how to use it. He wasn't one for getting it, nutmegging someone, beating three men and doing a twirl on the ball. He understood the team wanted him to hold the ball up and not give it away; he was very good at that.'

The big question was if Lineker would be able to replicate his second-tier form in the top flight. The hometown lad was understandably pinpointed as a key factor in the Foxes' ability to be competitive against better opposition, although many who had watched him tear up defences during the promotion season felt they'd seen enough to warrant a belief he'd make the jump comfortably.

'It's impossible to gauge City's chances without concentrating on Gary Lineker,' wrote the *Leicester Mercury*'s Bill Anderson ahead of the new season. 'This local product's scoring rate made it [promotion] all possible and so much will depend on him this time. Perhaps his pace, which electrified Second Division defences, will meet stiffer opposition in the top flight, but the goal touch – once achieved – is a hard habit to lose.

'In the early stages of the season, City's habit will be to look for him with long passes at every opportunity. This may play into the hands of the enemy, but Lineker's supply of goals shouldn't suddenly dry up.'

Despite Anderson's belief, Lineker and Leicester struggled to take to the First Division quickly. If their start to the previous campaign had been sluggish, their opening to the 1983/4 season was more or less stationary.

The Foxes lost eight of their opening nine league matches, drawing the other with Stoke. Despite the buccaneering style that got them promoted, they only scored six goals in that time – four of which were netted by Lineker – and looked unable to handle the higher standard. Another immediate relegation, just like they'd suffered under Wallace three years previously, looked on the cards.

Part of the reason for their struggles was the absence of Smith, who was out injured for the start of the season. Lineker wasn't afraid to give his assessment in the *Leicester Mercury* on 12 October about where he felt the side needed to improve: 'We will end our bad run when we stop giving goals away at the back, it's as simple as that. The key lies in the defence, not the attack, and I will just keep on doing my job as best I can.

'I do prefer playing with a big partner in attack, moving on to knock-downs, being the runner for the target man and the manager is looking at possibilities. Once Alan Smith is back to full fitness then that should help, but there is no way I consider myself a one-man band.

'I am the only one who is scoring at the moment, but the rest of the team are still making chances for me. However, it can be a bit soul-destroying to see goals being given away at the other end when you have worked so hard to get it in the opposition net.'

Ironically, Lineker didn't score again for another six weeks after giving that interview. Although he was proved right in his assertion that tightening up at the back would make the biggest difference, with two clean sheets resulting in much-needed points and a first league win of the season against Everton at the end of October. By now, Smith was back too – scoring against the Toffees – and the hallowed pairing were plugging away to rediscover their groove.

'It was a big step up, playing against the likes of Alan Hansen and Mark Lawrenson, European Cup winners,' remembers Smith. 'As a partnership, we just kept doing the same things and it wasn't like we were trying anything different because it was the top division. What we did do was good enough for that level of football and it worked. We both had to step up our game a little bit, but as a partnership, it was one of the most effective out there.'

The duo's thirst for improving was a key part of their progression. Since Lineker had arrived at Leicester as an apprentice, his modus operandi had been to understand where and how to improve his game, with much of the motivation to do that coming from within. That approach had served him well to outlast other young players who initially appeared to have more promise than him, and that wasn't about to change now he was in the First Division. And that meant giving him the leeway to work things out in his own way.

'With Gary, it was a question not so much of tactically working on the training ground with him, but talking about ideas and showing him, because he was intelligent and a quick learner,' Milne explains.

'As a student, he wasn't that enthusiastic. He didn't like training and I'm being polite there, but he listened. Some players would just nod and couldn't repeat what you'd said and weren't paying any notice, but he took on board what he thought was helpful to him and he'd try to do it. If he didn't like it, like he didn't enjoy training, he was hard work, impatient and would say, "What am I doing this for?" He didn't like five-a-sides; he liked shooting and enjoyed scoring goals.'

That might not have worked for some managers. But Milne recognised Gary's natural ability and knew that forcing him to do what didn't come easily to him wasn't going to get the best results. After all, Lineker's goals would be crucial if Leicester were to stay up.

'John Mcvey was the physio at the time and occasionally on a Wednesday or Thursday when we were doing some technical work, he'd come and say, "Gordon, Gary's not feeling too well this morning,"' Milne says with a smile. 'It'd be pissing it down with rain or something and he'd say, "If I were you, there's a game on Saturday and I wouldn't risk it." By Friday morning, I'd say, "John, by the way, how's Gary?" and he'd say, "Oh, he's fine, he's spot on."

'Having a physio who understood the game was vital because players sit on the treatment table and will talk to him, and they listen. A good physio would feed back what he thought you ought to hear. Consequently, with Gary, he'd say, "He's perfect, you've handled him perfectly this week and he's raring to go" and that's music to your ears on a Friday, even if he's missed the training session and all the technical work you were doing.'

It was hard to disagree with Milne's approach. A reportedly disgruntled Lineker did sit out of a 1–1 draw with Manchester United in mid-November due to a disagreement about his recovery from an ankle ligament injury and while speaking out allegedly nearly led to Lineker losing his place on the bench, he came back raring to go.

Upon his return, the hotshot striker scored four in the next six matches, with Leicester winning each of the games he netted in.

He then got a hat-trick against Notts County in January as the Foxes went on a run of one defeat in 11 games to ease their relegation worries. 'When things aren't going well, you've got to make sure you don't get down,' Lineker told the *Leicester Mercury* afterwards. 'In the same way when you're getting goals, you mustn't get carried away.'

Lineker had his mojo back and it was no coincidence it was at the same time as his team. Leicester lost as many matches in the last 25 games of the season as they did in their first eight and were soon zooming up the table. In fact, it was only four defeats in their last five games when safety had looked more secure that meant their record wasn't even better.

A 15th-place finish represented a successful season in that part of the East Midlands, with Lineker's 22 goals putting him second in the First Division top scorer's chart. Only Liverpool's Ian Rush, who netted an impressive 32 times, was ahead of Lineker and he'd outscored a host of more experienced top-level strikers, including England striker Tony Woodcock and Barcelona-bound Steve Archibald.

'We were always looking below us to make sure we were going to escape relegation, rather than above us,' says Smith, who bagged 15 himself that season. 'We were a team that could score goals. We'd let them in at times as well, but if you're knocking them in a bit – even if it's not you – the pressure is off a bit. If you're winning the game, all is well.

'It was a good atmosphere and team to learn your trade in. It was an attack-minded side under Gordon [Milne]; he'd been in the Liverpool side that played under Bill Shankly and was very much a footballing manager. He was a great manager to learn and train under; I'm sure Gary would say the same thing. The partnership flourished against the better standards and that's when Gary was really making a name for himself.'

Smith wasn't wrong. Now Lineker had proved he could cut it at English football's top table, he was on the radar of England boss Bobby Robson.

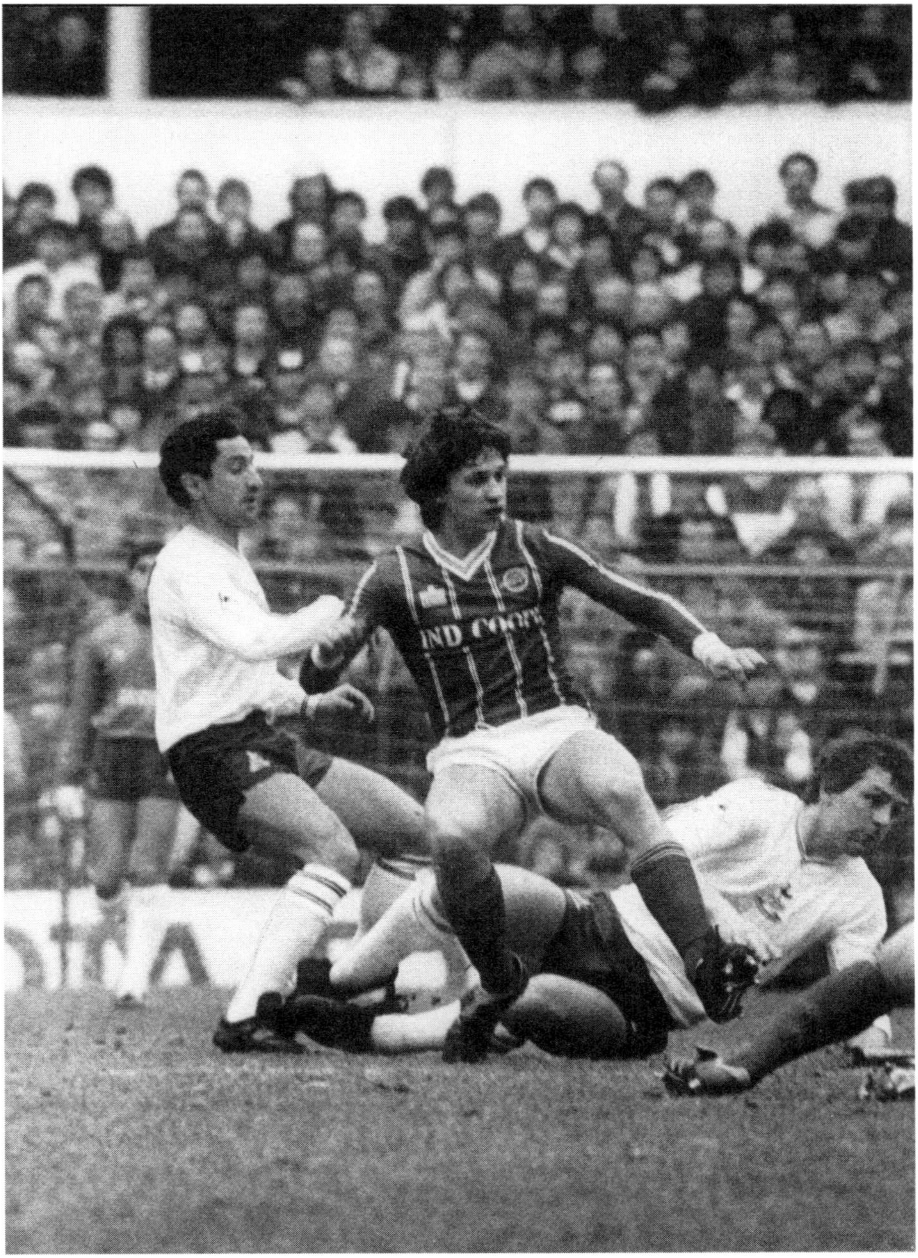

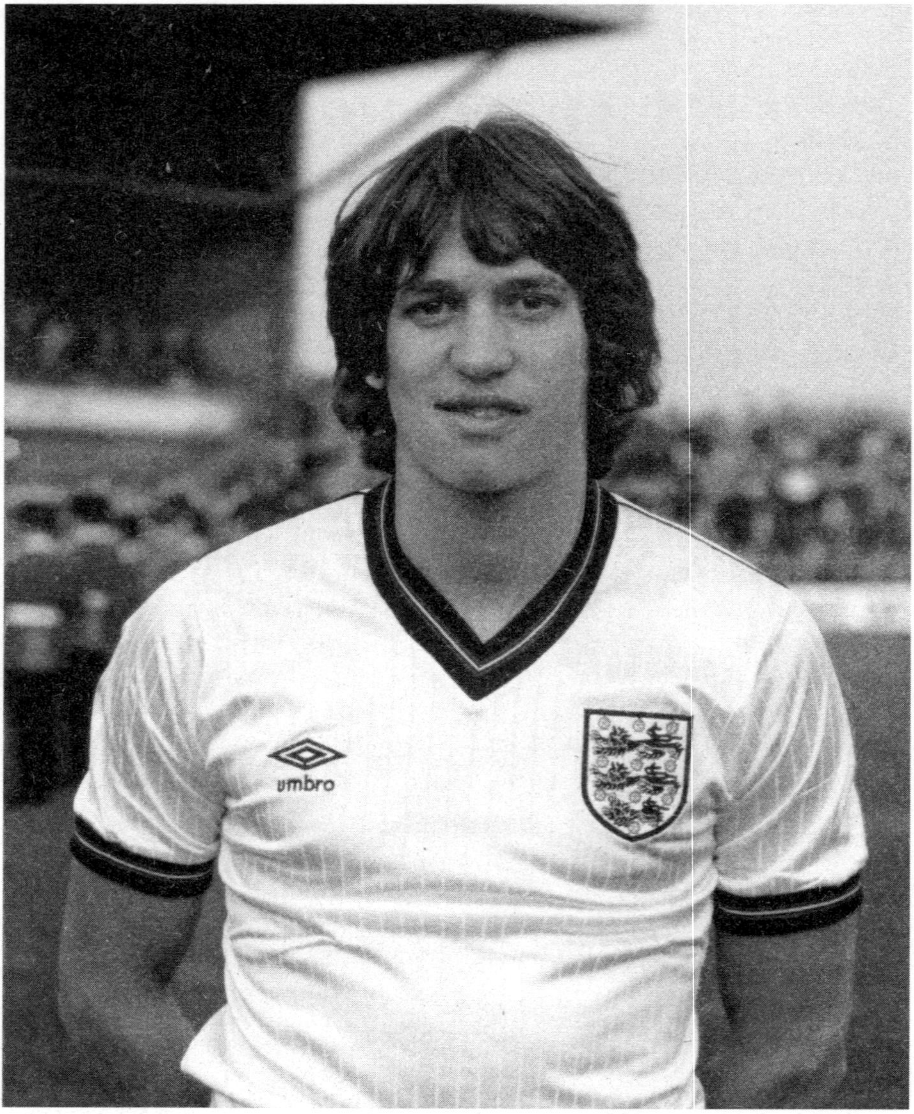

5
CALL-UP

England, 1984

*'I have an England cap now and they
can't take that away from me.'*

The phone was ringing in the Linekers' family home. After a few shrill bursts, Gary's mum Margaret picked up the receiver to be greeted by Leicester manager Gordon Milne's northern tones. The two exchanged pleasantries, but it was Gary whom Milne wanted to speak to. He'd received some news and he instructed Margaret to get hold of her son immediately. This couldn't wait.

Margaret knew exactly where to find Gary. The striker was sitting in the front room, kicking back and taking in the action from the Monday afternoon session at the World Snooker Championship on TV. The mesmeric green baize had drawn him in, with the two-week tournament well under way at the Crucible in Sheffield and his good friend Willie Thorne in action against Cliff Thorburn that day, Lineker was set for the evening. Or so he thought.

Upon being told by his mum that Milne was on the phone, Lineker eased himself up out of his chair, wondering what he'd done to warrant an urgent call from his manager. The 23-year-old was like a schoolboy being summoned to the headmaster's office, brain whirring, pondering what the problem could be. He tentatively picked up the receiver, before addressing Milne. 'Er, hi boss, everything OK?' Lineker asked in soft tones. 'Yeah,' Milne replied. 'Get a bag, pack a toothbrush, Bobby Robson's been on.'

Lineker's mind quickly caught up. Far from having done something wrong, Robson getting in touch could only mean one thing: an England call-up. His 22 top-flight goals during the 1983/4 season had naturally meant his name had been suggested as a possible pick for the Three Lions in the future, but after initially missing out on selection for the Home International against Wales on 2 May 1984, any hopes of receiving full international honours had been put on ice. Yet after Sampdoria forward Trevor Francis was forced to pull out of the squad, it was Lineker whom England boss Bobby Robson wanted as his replacement. The snooker would have to wait.

After thanking Milne for letting him know, Lineker sprang into action. Never slow off the mark, he dashed upstairs, grabbing the basics from around his home, before jumping in his Fiat to head to the training ground to pick up his boots. From there, he was straight on to the motorway and hotfooting it to Wrexham, a maelstrom of nerves and excitement, to join up with the England squad.

'I think Bobby Robson had to go through the phone book before he got to me,' Lineker told the *Leicester Mercury* self-deprecatingly upon hearing the news. It didn't matter how or why; this was a dream come true.

The call-up had come at such short notice that his family struggled to make arrangements to be in Wales to see what could have been Gary's first cap. Dad, Barry, spoke to the *Leicester Mercury* about his disappointment at not being able to leave the fruit and veg stall to be there, but admitted, 'I still haven't come down really; the news came out of the blue.'

That was true, but Lineker being noticed by the England hierarchy was no real surprise. He'd top-scored in the entire Football League to help fire Leicester to promotion from the Second Division the previous season and had eventually taken to the top flight in similar form. After City had found their feet at the higher level, the goals had started to flow for their star poacher, with his pace and direct running marking him out as a thorn in the side of any top defender. Not to mention finishing the season as the top flight's most prolific Englishman.

It's true that some of Lineker's play was green in places – that was to be expected after only one campaign in the top flight – but the rate at which he was improving, and regularly getting on the scoresheet, meant he was a player who had the potential to get goals at international level.

But back in the 1980s, it often took a little bit longer for players to get the chance to show what they could do, and perhaps Lineker's lack of all-round play still left question marks over whether he was the finished article.

'I like artistic players and as much as I like Lineker as a person, I wouldn't have paid to watch him,' admits decorated sportswriter Patrick Barclay. 'As a goalscorer, he wasn't as fruity as let's say Jimmy Greaves or in a later era, Robbie Fowler, who could finish with this flourish and style of a number 10. Gary was not that; he was ultra practical, a great striker, but one whose talent was in geometry and instinct and finding the way to goal, rather than élan or style of finishing.

'Lineker was 23 before he was given his chance with England. Selection for England was a little bit more conservative then, and there was the infamous case of Ron Greenwood and Glenn Hoddle, who stroked in a belter from the edge of the box and promptly got dropped. Selection for England was a little more conservative in those days than it is now when they think absolutely nothing of chucking in someone who has only had 12 games in the Premier League.'

Lineker may not have been Robson's first pick for England's frontline, but when it emerged that Francis would need a late fitness test for the Wales match, the Three Lions boss decided it was time to take a closer look at the Leicester hotshot.

'We want to give it as much time as we can, but if Trevor isn't fit then that would leave us with only three forwards,' said Robson, as reported by Aberdeen's *The Press and Journal* ahead of the match.

'I decided upon Lineker because, although he has no international experience, we have been following his progress very closely.'

England needed the cover, with Francis's late withdrawal becoming the eighth of Robson's original squad of 20 to pull out. Lineker was installed on the bench, but with an inexperienced side taking to the Racecourse Ground pitch to face Wales, there was every chance he'd get to win his first cap.

Lineker's future Tottenham teammate Paul Walsh got the nod up front to collect only his fifth cap, while defenders Mark Wright and Terry Fenwick made their international debuts. It was an inexperienced side, but one that promised opportunity for the new England hopefuls.

It was a Wales debutant who would grab the headlines, though, with Manchester United's 21-year-old striker Mark Hughes scoring a header to break the deadlock. It was no more than the hosts deserved and as England failed to lay much of a glove on their opponents in response, the prospect grew of Robson throwing on another forward to salvage the game.

Lineker was off the bench and warming up down on the touchline in preparation for his big moment. However, when his manager's call for extra artillery support finally came, it was AC Milan's Luther Blissett who was summoned, leaving Lineker to watch the remainder of his side's 1–0 defeat from the sidelines – not that he was too downbeat about it all afterwards.

'I just hope I get another chance in the future because once you get a taste of the international scene, you want some more,' Lineker told the *Leicester Mercury* days after returning from Wales. 'At least I got stripped and was ready if needed.

'I thought that if no goals had come by the last 10 minutes or so, then the manager might have thrown me in as an experiment. But when Alvin Martin got injured and Luther Blissett went on into attack as well, I realised my chances were slim. Still, at least I was part of the full England party and that is always something – and I have my number 16 shirt as a memento.'

A few weeks later Lineker got his wish, as his name appeared on the England squad list for the trip to Scotland. It was to be the final

Home Nations Championship fixture the Auld Enemy would ever play, with the tournament being retired at the end of the season – and with both sides still in with a chance of lifting the title with victory, the stakes were high.

This time, Lineker wasn't called up as a late replacement, so he joined up with the rest of the squad at their base at the impressive Troon Hotel in Scotland ahead of the Hampden Park clash. He was joined by a host of fellow newbies, who had equally high hopes that they would make their England bows during the camp, which also included a friendly with the USSR at Wembley a few days later.

'It was a massive thrill and excitement to team up with everybody,' recalls former West Brom winger Steve Hunt, who was among the clutch of uncapped players hoping to play. 'Gary and I were roommates for the match in Scotland. The other guys selected their rooms, but the newbies got put where we were told. I knew Gary previously from playing against him, but not on a personal level.'

The selection issues that had blighted Robson for the Wales match had shown no sign of abating. And with England's poor showing in Wrexham earlier that month, there was an appetite for further change.

Lineker knew he'd at least be on the bench again for the Scotland decider and with injury doubts hanging over the two strikers ahead of him in the pecking order, Blissett and Arsenal man Tony Woodcock, there remained a chance that he'd get the nod from the start. Blissett was having a back injury closely monitored by England's medical staff right up until kick-off and while it left Lineker in limbo, he showed no signs of the anticipation getting to him.

'My biggest reflection of sharing a room with Gary was what a good guy he was,' Hunt continues. 'He spent most of his time [in the room] on the phone back to his folks in Leicester – I think he was checking up on the fruit and veg stall back there more than anything else – but we got on well.

'He came across as such a family man and wanted to talk to his family back home – I wanted to talk to my family to a certain extent too, but he took it beyond that. He spent a significant amount of time on the phone to them, especially when we got to the room in the evening when we'd done our training sessions, team meetings and that. I remember it vividly.

'Gary was a little bit younger than me, so you'd maybe expect him to have a few more nerves than me. I was 28 years old, but you can't not have nerves if you're part of an England squad and could get your first cap.'

With Blissett and Woodcock suffering no further complications before the game, Lineker would have to keep waiting to see if he'd get his big moment as he settled on the bench for a second game running. In some ways it was a blessing in disguise, with a fervent Scottish contingent creating a blue-and-yellow cavern of noise before kick-off. Not even the large running track that wrapped itself round the pitch could cocoon England's players from the noise and jibes raining down on them.

Lineker at least had the sanctity of the substitutes' bench to acclimatise in. Although he had to watch on as, just as against Wales, England went behind once more, Mark McGhee heading in a Gordon Strachan cross to give Scotland the lead at 13 minutes. The Tartan Army went wild.

Unlike in Wrexham, England did have a response this time, Woodcock being allowed too much time and space to angle a powerful left-footed effort into the top corner from the edge of the area. The match was perfectly balanced at half time, with both sides realising a win could clinch the Home Nations crown, but that a draw would hand the chance for Northern Ireland or Wales in the other game. As the second-half minutes ticked away, both Lineker and Hunt were sent out to warm up in front of a baying Scottish rabble. There was no easy going on the debutants.

'It was, shall we say, a very passionate crowd, both on the way going past them on the bus on the way into the ground and warming up,' Hunt recalls. 'I think warming up was probably the toughest part because of the abuse and whatnot, but it was Scotland so you had to expect that.'

Then with 73 minutes on the clock, the moment came. Lineker was beckoned across by Robson and introduced into the action for Woodcock, who was struggling with a knock. The 23-year-old may only have had 17 minutes to make an impact, but he was now an England international. Hunt followed two minutes later for Mark Chamberlain and while neither debutant could make a decisive contribution to break the stalemate, it made for a happy room post-match.

'I was pleased for him and he was pleased for me, I remember a massive grin on each other's face because we'd got that cap,' says Hunt. 'It was just a massive thrill. I didn't want to come off the pitch at the end; I'm sure Gary felt the same.'

The draw meant neither England nor Scotland were left celebrating after the match, with Northern Ireland's draw with Wales elsewhere being enough for them to take the Home Nations title on goal difference. It was a bittersweet moment to be part of, but with the *Leicester Mercury*'s Bill Anderson reporting that Lineker's cameo wasn't 'long enough to make a vital impact, although he certainly didn't look out of place,' it was one the Foxes striker hoped would be the first of many.

'I can hardly believe I've gained a full cap,' beamed a delighted Lineker to the *Mercury* afterwards. 'It was never in my mind at the beginning of the season, especially after the first six games in our [Leicester's] disastrous start. I was simply delighted to be part of the squad for this match and, while there was a lot of talk about my chance, I knew from within that camp that it would have taken a lot more to start the game.

'Just before half time, I thought I might get on when Tony [Woodcock] complained of an injury. When he resumed in the second half, I felt my chance had gone, although I kept myself warmed. Getting on was tremendous.

'It was a terrific atmosphere and the pace of the game, on a greasy pitch, was a surprise to me at first, but I'm glad I didn't make a fool of myself. I realise I got a chance because a lot of other players were unavailable, but I have an England cap now and they can't take that away from me.'

Unfortunately, the chance to get further England caps wouldn't come that summer. After picking up an injury playing for an

England XI in a testimonial match for departing Tottenham manager Keith Burkinshaw, Lineker was ruled out of the senior side's match defeat to the USSR. It would also keep him out of the following tour to South America later that summer, where England would play friendlies against Brazil, Uruguay and Chile.

The Three Lions did beat the Seleção 2–0 at the Maracanã Stadium in a match made famous for John Barnes's wonder goal, but lost to Uruguay and could only draw 0–0 with Chile in Lineker's absence. England may not have been flying, but his misfortune did leave the door open for Mark Hateley, who had enjoyed a prolific season with second-tier Portsmouth and was one year Lineker's junior.

By the time the Leicester marksman was back fit by the start of the 1984/5 season, Hateley had leapfrogged him in the queue and more established internationals in Francis and Paul Mariner had returned from injury. This meant Lineker was out of the squad for the 1–0 friendly win over East Germany in September, was sitting on the bench for the World Cup qualifying trouncing of Finland in October, and then was left out entirely for the qualifier against Turkey in November.

Lineker would have to make do with a place in a 17-man England B squad for a match against New Zealand instead. If that privately smarted, Leicester's top scorer would be playing for the second string at the City Ground, the home of East Midlands rivals Nottingham Forest. Not that he showed any hint of disappointment.

'Bobby Robson left me on the bench on my last call-up for the seniors [against Finland] so the B squad looks just about right for me at the moment,' Lineker said in the *Leicester Mercury* upon the squad announcement. 'I'm just glad to be in at that level because there are a number of good players who have been overlooked this time. Just being among the names is a good thing for me.

'I accept I'm in the queue behind Trevor Francis and Tony Woodcock for the striking role [with the seniors] alongside the target man and if I had been down for the Turkey trip, I would probably have been sitting in the stand. So at least with the B international, I have a much better chance of playing ... and that means a much better chance of proving my worth for a step up.'

Even getting a start for the B team proved difficult with manager-for-the-day Howard Wilkinson opting for a front two of Blissett and Peter Davenport, the latter's selection pleasing the City Ground faithful as a Forest player. Lineker had to remain patient and only came off the bench for the final 15 minutes, replacing Davenport to chants of 'We hate Leicester' from the partisan Nottingham crowd.

Once more, Lineker didn't have much time to shine, but was on the pitch when defender Gary Mabbutt added England's second of the night to complete a comfortable 2–0 win. If the young striker was going to force his way into contention, it would have to be down to his club form.

'As far as my England future is concerned, I've got to keep scoring goals to keep myself in the reckoning because, as I found out in getting a cap back in June [sic], you never know what might happen,' he wrote in his *Leicester Mercury* column on New Year's Eve 1984.

'My main aim is to assert myself in the squad and I must realistically look on any appearance as a bonus. I've known what it's like to be involved in the international squad and it's something I want more of.'

Scoring 20 goals for Leicester by the end of February certainly helped and Lineker was back in the England squad for the qualifier with Northern Ireland, but didn't feature in lieu of Hateley, Woodcock and Francis – the latter coming off the bench in the 1–0 win. Yet only a month later, Lineker got his first England start, in a friendly at home to the Republic of Ireland.

Like clockwork, injuries to Woodcock and Francis provided the chance, but after waiting patiently for 10 months to get his second senior cap, Lineker wouldn't have cared. He was paired with target man Hateley, giving him a chance to stake his claim to be his long-term partner. Notably, winger Chris Waddle made his England debut that night, with the Geordie making the first of 52 international appearances alongside Lineker – nobody made more – to show manager Robson another combination with plenty of potential.

'The reward for a good performance is World Cup football and what greater incentive could there be than that?' Bobby Robson said in a pre-match interview. 'The two boys [Lineker and Waddle] are coming on at exactly the right time. They're at the right age, have been around a bit and are both having exceptionally good seasons.

'They know that if they can reproduce for me what they do at club level, they will have years of international football ahead of them, just like Mark Hateley, who grasped his chance when I gave it to him.'

Robson's words were prescient, with Hateley and Lineker looking on a similar wavelength throughout. But it was Hateley's replacement, Davenport – the man who started ahead of Lineker in the recent B international – who took control of some head tennis in the middle of the pitch to play a square pass to his new partner and allowed the striker to show what he'd been doing so effectively for Leicester.

Lineker had the freedom of Wembley to run through on Paddy Bonner's goal, taking two touches with the outside of his right boot to get the ball out of his feet before dinking a smart finish over the prostrate Ireland goalkeeper and into the net. As the ball bounced in, Lineker lifted both his arms triumphantly into the air, looking back towards his teammates with gritted teeth, before clenching his fists and bending down in celebration, shouting 'Yes!' It was a moment that unleashed a raw innocence in the 24-year-old's joy, for a moment not resembling an England international, but a young boy celebrating his first goal for a junior side. There was no doubting how much the moment meant.

The goal would prove to be the winner in a 2–1 England win, proving decisive as Liam Brady scored a late goal to put pressure on the home side at the death.

'The England game ... has given me the most memorable occasion of my life,' Lineker penned in his next *Mercury* column. 'I could hardly believe everything went so well and I hope it is just the beginning for me.

'I was told beforehand to go out and enjoy myself – and that's just what I did. I was surprised I wasn't very nervous at all and that helped, of course. Mark Hateley and I hit it off immediately up front. We had never played together in training because, with England, we don't do training as such or hold practice matches, so it was lucky we managed to combine as well as we did.

'Getting a full game and my second cap was a big enough thrill, but to go on to score what proved to be the winning goal was, to use a well-worn but very accurate expression, a dream come true.

'I'd made my mind up beforehand that, if I got a clean-cut chance, I wouldn't snatch at it, and when Peter Davenport put me through with only the keeper to beat, thankfully I remembered that. I saw Packie Bonner commit himself and flicked the ball over the other side. He did throw out a desperate hand to get a touch, but I knew he hadn't done enough to make the save and I raced away to celebrate.'

Lineker's performance had drawn a real line in the sand, with his boss delighted to see a glimpse of the clinical finishing his emerging striker could add to England's frontline.

'I was impressed with his [Lineker's] pace, I admire the patience he showed for a year getting his first full England game and I'm very pleased with his general attitude,' said Robson. 'He played with great spirit, proved he can hold the ball well and took his goal exceptionally well.'

There was still work to be done for Lineker to bolt down a regular England place, but a first international goal in his maiden start wasn't bad going. And with little over one year to go before the Mexico World Cup and rumours of a big move in the offing that summer, it was the perfect time for Lineker to put himself in the shop window.

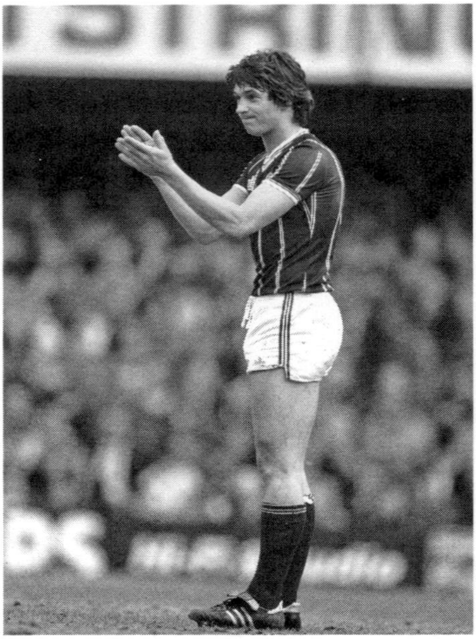

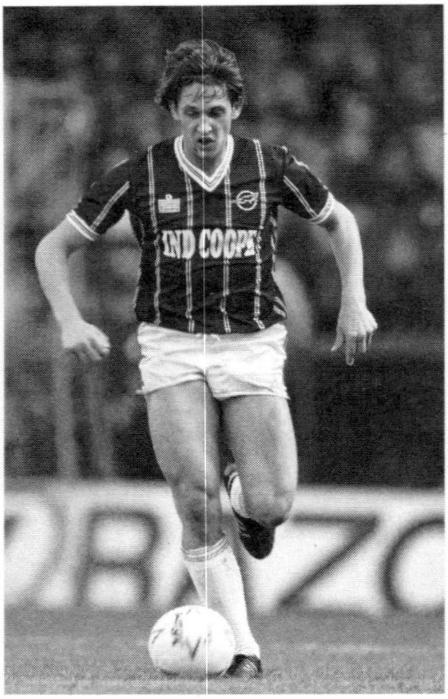
IND COOPE

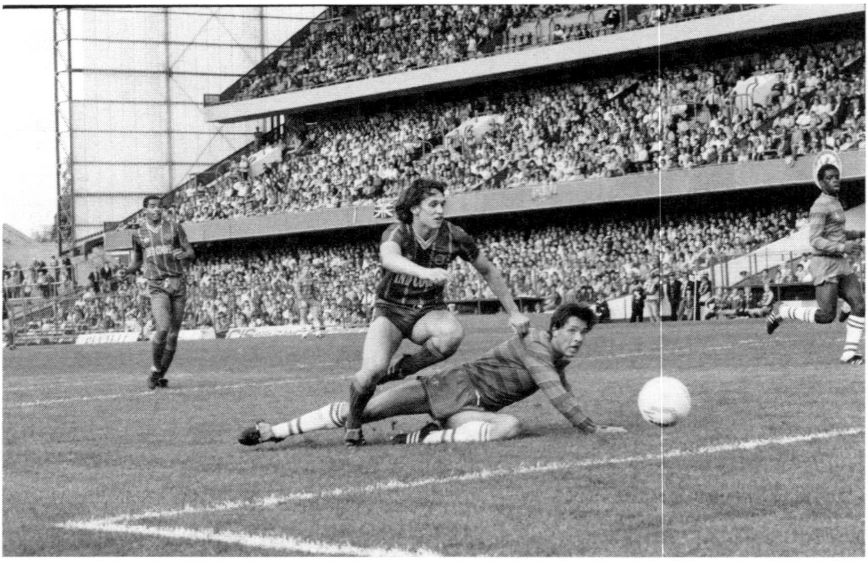

6

MOVING ON

Leicester City, 1984–1985

'This sort of opportunity doesn't come along very often and I had to take it [...] my world turned upside down in an instant.'

Gary Lineker was up in court. Well, kind of.

The England striker hadn't become embroiled in some sort of criminal case, though. Instead, he was the subject of a tribunal at the FA's headquarters in Lancaster Gate, London. After eight years playing for hometown club Leicester City, Lineker was on the move and was in attendance to find out how much English champions Everton would be paying for his signature.

The 24-year-old's contract at Filbert Street had come to an end and, after a lot of soul searching, he decided his future belonged on Merseyside. The Foxes were due some compensation and as were the rules at the time, if the clubs couldn't agree themselves, that meant summoning both sides and the player to a court-like proceeding to settle on a fee.

This wouldn't be a deal scribbled on the back of a fag packet and sealed with a handshake. There would be official statements given by both sides explaining why they felt Lineker should cost a certain amount, providing enough evidence for a committee to decide on a final sum. The Lancaster Gate offices provided a grand setting, with the five-storied, white-bricked building looking resplendent as a venue for a meeting bordering on the litigious.

The large wooden doors, perfectly shaped pillars and balcony overlooking the street below provided an almost regal feel as the key protagonists from both clubs filed into the offices. Along with Lineker, in attendance were Leicester City's chairman Terry Shipman, manager Gordon Milne, and their Toffees equivalents, chairman Philip Carter and boss Howard Kendall.

While the two clubs had clearly defined roles in the proceedings, Lineker was in an awkward position. On one side was his beloved hometown club, reportedly in debt and hoping to raise a good wedge of cash with the sale of their local star, whereas on the other were his new side, aiming to get the best deal possible in their quest to establish themselves as the major force in English football.

In hindsight, it was a preposterous situation and the wranglings make for comic reading by modern-day standards.

'The tribunal in itself was a joke,' Milne remembers. 'I knew Howard Kendall, he'd played for my dad at Preston in the cup final, but they [Everton] offered something daft. We put the price up, the bloody tribunal said we wanted a million and set the fee at £800,000 and said, "If he moves again in the next two years, it's another £200,000." Howard was chuffed to bits because he thought he'd snatched him, which he had.'

The two clubs' starting positions had been predictably disparate. Milne had stood up first, bursting with superlatives about Lineker's quality and potential, suggesting a fee north of £1 million; then it was Kendall's turn, and he'd played down what he thought of the striker and valued him at £500,000. It was all a pantomime considering the Everton manager was desperate to add Lineker's goals to his team.

'Kendall said, "He hasn't done anything yet. I don't want to pay all this money. He's threatened a bit, but he's not really got a track record,"' says Milne. 'Lineker was only a young lad, so how could he? We said there's potential, but Howard said, "Ah, there's potential, but you never know." Howard came away and he was chuffed to bits – we wanted a million, which in those days had never been heard of.

'At that time, Everton had a great midfield, good players, so I'm just thinking that Lineker would score 100 goals for them. I said something to Howard about that, and said, "Christ Almighty, you've got a bloody bargain."'

For Lineker, he'd had to sit through the tribunal and listen to his new boss playing down his talents and pouring doubt on his ability to hit the standards required to lead Everton to glory.

'In the end, I'm standing there thinking, "What have I done here? I'm signing and I'm not going to get a game,"' Lineker told the *Eddie Hearn: No Passion, No Point* podcast in 2020.

'So we walk out of the tribunal, go out the front door, walk down the street and Howard Kendall puts his arm around me and says, "Don't believe any of that, you're going to be my man, you're going to be in the team. I just needed to do that to get the price down a little bit."'

Kendall then ushered Lineker into a nearby Sainsbury's, bought several bottles of champagne and popped them open as they took the train back to Merseyside, where he took his new striker to Kendall's favourite Chinese restaurant to celebrate.

Lineker's Leicester exit had been on the cards for a while. Winning the Second Division Golden Boot in 1982/3 had put him on the map and within months of promotion, stories of rumoured interest from other clubs had been whispered about.

Even as the Foxes struggled to initially get to grips with their new level in early 1983/4, reporters had been asking about the striker's possible availability. There'd been talk of Lineker's future England manager Graham Taylor making overtures from Watford, as he looked to find a replacement for Luther Blissett, who had made a move to AC Milan a few months earlier.

Leicester were reported to have considered cashing in on their coveted frontman, with Taylor's Hornets said to have made a

£200,000 bid – a notion Milne dismissed at the time. Lineker, on the other hand, made it clear he wanted to serve out the last two years of his contract and that 'everything else was up to the manager'.

That interest only intensified as Lineker found his feet in the top tier, with 22 league goals and an England call-up proving to any potential suitors that he was more than simply a lightning-quick forward who could tear up the second tier. Previous criticism from his early years about his ability to receive the ball with his back to goal and turn had started to be addressed as well, as Lineker aimed to add more to his game.

There had been more stories about his departure in the summer of 1984, but once more rumours of interest from Tottenham, who were looking to replace Steve Archibald, were dismissed by Milne as fanciful speculation. Leicester wanted Lineker to stay, but with him entering the last year of his contract at the beginning of 1984/5, that idea may have been fanciful in itself, with the only hope being that his hometown loyalty may prove decisive in persuading him to remain at the club.

Lineker's form was doing nothing to silence the gossip, as he continued to score goals with great frequency, keeping him among the frontrunners for the First Division Golden Boot. Leicester were reportedly in need of selling a player but opted to let Kevin MacDonald leave for Liverpool in the November instead of seriously entertaining the prospect of losing Lineker's goals.

'My recollection is that when Leicester sold me, Gordon [Milne] was told he had to sell either Gary or myself,' MacDonald says. 'I don't know if it was to balance the books or it was just the way Leicester was, but he said to me, "Kevin, as much as I'd like to keep you, Gary is going to score the goals that are going to keep us in the First Division."'

Despite the Foxes making a better start to the previous season, they were still nervously edging towards the prospect of First Division safety once more. While Milne's position seemed emphatic when it came to picking between Lineker and

MacDonald, the transfer links kept on coming. And the duo kept on batting them away.

'Gary knows where he stands with me and the club,' Milne said to the *Leicester Mercury* on 17 December, amid another story about Lineker moving to Spurs. 'He's one of the hottest properties, if not the hottest, in football at the moment, and I hope he gets hotter. I said to him last week that it was good for him to be associated with every leading club in the country. When someone wants to find the goalscorer to help them in a bid for honours, they want the best and we've got the best.'

A few days later, it was Lineker's turn to use his *Mercury* column to silence the reports. 'As far as I'm concerned, all the talk of me moving clubs is simply that, talk,' he wrote. 'I've said all along I'm in no hurry to make a decision about my future. I'm contracted to the end of the season with Leicester City and I've always been happy here.'

Liverpool were the next to be linked in February, and with Leicester being pulled back into the relegation mire due to a winless run in 1985 that spanned to a victory against Aston Villa in March, there was a fear the attention was taking its toll. While there wasn't a fervent press pack baying for stories in quite the same way as is the case with the modern game, talk of Lineker's departure and the resulting 'Should Gary stay?' campaign in the *Leicester Mercury* was an unappreciated distraction. But Lineker remained unmoved.

'I appreciate the thoughts of the fans,' he replied in April. 'I was a terrace supporter in the days when the club used to sell their best players, so I can understand their feelings. It's nice they want me to stay, but all I can say is, it's a decision I will have to make on my own when the time comes.'

Milne confirms that version of events. 'He never once knocked on my door and said, "Is there any truth in this or that? I'm a bit fed up, I want to move" – nothing like that at all. If we had been doing better and doing well, with maybe a couple of new players or big signings coming in – at that particular time – his mind wouldn't have been anywhere else.'

That would soon change, though. Lineker had promised to consider Leicester's offer when the time came, but as the season reached its climax, it was clear that he was keen to hear out his other options too. He had bettered his previous season's goal tally to share the Golden Boot with Chelsea's Kerry Dixon on 24 goals and it was clear he could expect a lot of interest from elsewhere. Leicester may have had his heart, but Lineker knew a move to one of the big clubs would provide him with the best chance of silverware, playing in Europe and winning more England caps.

He was in no rush to make a decision and still hadn't as late as the final home match of the 1984/5 season. The fixture against Sunderland could conceivably have been Lineker's last for Leicester at Filbert Street, but instead of opting for a big send-off, he was keen to leave the door open, claiming he was 'yet to hear of any offers from anywhere else', despite being two weeks away from the end of his contract.

The uncertainty led to a night that hung in purgatory. The home fans who lined Filbert Street's low-slung terraces wanted to show their appreciation, but still clung to the faint hope Lineker would be back at the start of the following season. They were trapped, like a hopeless lover knowing in their heart that their romance won't last but unwilling to acknowledge it for fear of extinguishing any glimmer of a final reprieve.

Lineker had scored many of his century of Leicester goals in the tightly pulled nets at Filbert Street over the years and, if the Monday night clash with Sunderland was to be his last appearance in Foxes blue, he wasn't about to pass up the opportunity to add more to his tally.

It only took 14 minutes for him to get on the scoresheet. He looked to have been forced to an impossible angle on the left, but managed to fire a shot almost along the goal line that somehow went through Mackems goalkeeper Chris Turner and into the net. Lineker had the bit between his teeth and bagged a second less than 10 minutes later, heading in a Smith knock-down to ensure the partnership notched up yet another strike to add to their combined tally.

'If he does go, then this was a performance he would be proud to be remembered by,' wrote the *Leicester Mercury*'s Bill Anderson in his match report. 'His characteristic tenacity, pace and steadily developed skill were there in abundance.'

If there was one blot on Lineker's copybook, it was that he didn't crown an otherwise perfect night with yet another Leicester hat-trick. With the clock ticking down, Steve Lynex was upended in the Sunderland box to win a penalty – and while the winger himself was the side's normal penalty taker, he handed his teammate the match ball to give him the chance to get his treble. Sadly, it wasn't to be, as Turner made an impressive save to keep out a powerful low effort.

'I didn't really want to take it, to be honest, but when Steve handed me the ball, I could hardly refuse,' said Lineker to the *Mercury* after the match. 'I hit the shot well enough, but the keeper made what I thought was a very good save. I'll not be taking another one, though, I've made my mind up on that.'

It was a penalty miss that wouldn't tarnish his reputation, as he and his teammates were cheered off at the final whistle. Lineker's personal immortalisation was complete and he only enhanced it further by winning the Midlands Football Writers' Player of the Year award a few nights later. If that was to be the end of his time at Leicester, he could hardly go on a better note.

As the curtain came down on Leicester's season with a 4–0 defeat to Luton, the situation began to become clearer, with the *Leicester Mercury* reporting Lineker's 'come and get me' plea to England's biggest clubs. Although the striker's words weren't quite as clear cut as that.

'I won't go just anywhere,' Lineker said in his interview. 'City have been tremendous to me in the eight years I've been here and it will take one of the recognised giants of the game to get me to leave.

'It's not really about money. City have made me a very lucrative offer, which shows me they want me to stay as part of their ambitions to chase success, and it's a nice feeling to be wanted. In the light of City's offer, I wouldn't be all that better off with a move, but I want to be involved at the highest level, and that means playing for a team battling for the First Division championship, cup finals and a place in Europe.

'You can't help being envious of, say, Everton, going for so many honours all through the season. That's the sort of standard I want to be part of at this stage in my career.'

Lineker's mention of the Toffees would prove prescient, but their interest didn't transpire until late June. It was reported that both Aston Villa and Sheffield Wednesday had made offers earlier in the summer but, true to his word, the hometown hero turned them down because they weren't sufficiently bigger clubs than Leicester.

There had also been fleeting interest from Manchester United, but after Red Devils striker Frank Stapleton turned down a £500,000 move to French champions Marseille, they no longer needed a replacement.

'The only time I really had to talk to him [Lineker] was when Everton were coming on the scene and it was looking as though it was going to happen,' says Milne. 'It happened in a gentle way with no confrontation or "I don't want to go" or "I want more money". It just happened to be like that, it was a matter of fact.

'He wasn't reluctant to leave, because he could see this was the right time to move, but he wasn't causing any trouble for me or the club. It kind of happened gently and went to the tribunal and that was it.'

And that was it. The opportunity to join the reigning Football League champions and Cup Winners' Cup holders was too much of a carrot to dangle in front of Lineker. He'd remain playing in blue for the next season, but after scoring 103 goals in 216 appearances, it would no longer be for Leicester.

'This sort of opportunity doesn't come along very often and I had to take it,' Lineker told the *Leicester Mercury* after announcing the deal. 'It came just as I felt no one was going to come for me and I would be staying at Filbert Street, so my world turned upside down in an instant.

'I always said it would take a really big club to tempt me away from Leicester and I hope the fans don't blame City in any way because they tried all they could to keep me. They made me a tremendous offer and it was nice to feel they wanted me to stay. I had always been happy at Filbert Street, but I just wanted to join one of the big glamour clubs and try my luck there.'

It was the end of an era. Although Lineker wouldn't be away from Filbert Street for long.

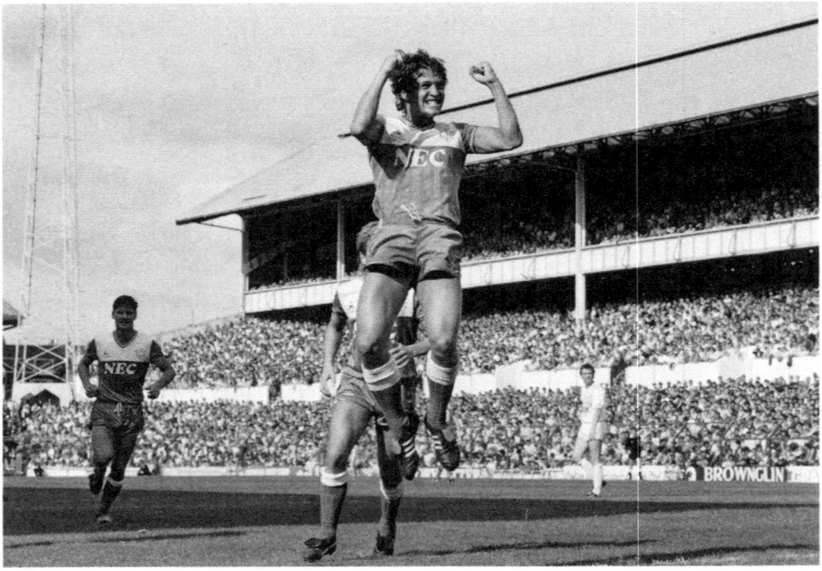
NEC
NEC
BROWNGLIN

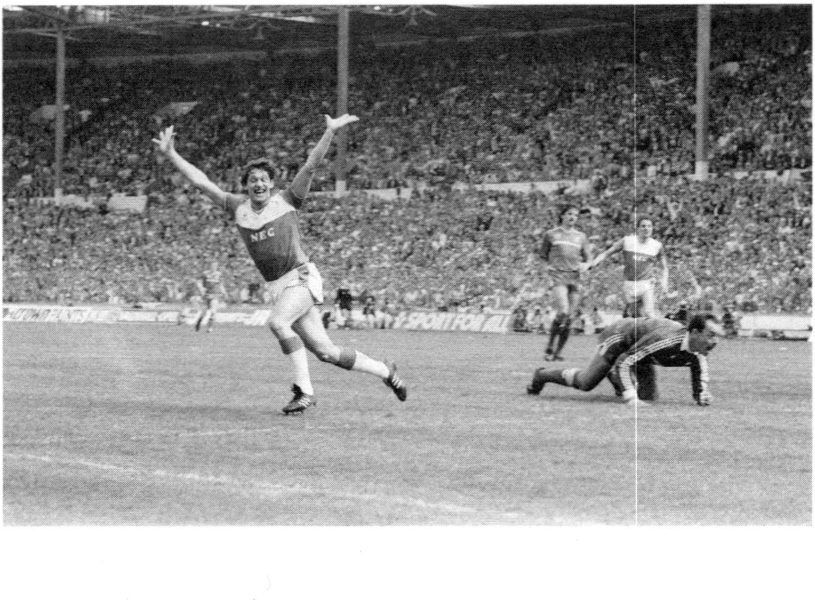
NEC

7

GOODISON GOALS

Everton, 1985–1986

'If you were looking from the outside, you'd probably think "Why are we buying Gary Lineker?"'

It was the opening day of the 1985/6 season and Gary Lineker's name was on the teamsheet for the first match at Filbert Street. The England striker had left Leicester for Everton that summer, but it seemed there was no keeping him away from his hometown club.

The First Division fixture list had paired the Toffees and the Foxes together for the first game, meaning Lineker would be facing off with his boyhood team at their home ground on his very first league outing for his new side. There could be no starker reminder of what he'd left behind before he'd even got used to the new reality.

From the low-roofed corrugated stands at ground level to the familiar gaggle of faces standing in their usual spots around the terraces, nothing had changed at all as the new campaign got under way. Yet for Lineker, the occasion was as alien as it possibly could be. All the sights and sounds he'd grown accustomed to around Filbert Street since his first visit as a youngster still swaddled his senses like a warm blanket. And yet he'd arrived on a team bus to walk into the away dressing room, to pull on a shirt that no longer had the comforting visage of a fox emblazoned on its chest. The task was now to puncture the spirits of the same fans who'd always hung on his goals to inflate their dreams.

Lineker knew the potential clash was on the horizon before his move to Goodison Park had even been finalised, but it would make it no less strange. 'Playing my first league game with my new club at Filbert Street is a very interesting coincidence,' he told the *Leicester Mercury* on the completion of his move several weeks earlier. 'I don't know how the fans will treat me now after supporting me so well for all those years.'

Thankfully Lineker didn't receive a hostile reception. Without his goals in the past three seasons, Leicester may not have been starting their third successive season in the top flight, and he'd left with the club's blessing. For the fans, who didn't get a chance to give their former striker an official send-off at the end of the previous season, it was an opportunity to say thank you and bid him farewell.

Lineker's former teammates had a point to prove. With their 24-goal star striker one of a few notable departures that summer, Leicester had been predicted to struggle, and a visit from the reigning champions was a great opportunity for the players to prove they still had the ability to compete on their own.

The debutant had no chance to be sentimental, though. And with his first touch, he teed up Paul Bracewell to the left of the box, but the midfielder wellied his shot narrowly wide of the target. Lineker was clearly keen to make an impression on his new employers, getting sight of Leicester's goal on a few occasions himself, but finding goalkeeper Ian Andrews and defender Russell Osman there to deny him.

When Derek Mountfield's volley eventually gave Everton the lead, it looked like it was going to be a happy return to Filbert Street for Lineker. But the momentum changed on half time with Bobby Smith levelling. The whistle blew for the break with the sides level at 1–1, but the action wasn't over for Lineker, who mistakenly walked into the home dressing room, before remembering himself.

If the Everton man had forgotten he was no longer wearing Leicester's number 8 shirt, he couldn't fail to realise after the interval.

His replacement Mark Bright, who had spent the previous season as Lineker's understudy, was now ready to take centre stage and struck two excellent second-half strikes to tip the game in favour of the Foxes. A 3–1 loss away at his former club was not how Everton's new striker would have envisaged his first league match going.

Lineker had arrived at Goodison Park to much pomp and ceremony. After the transfer was finally agreed at tribunal, all the talk had been about what he might achieve at Everton with the support of a midfield that been instrumental in landing an unexpected title triumph the season before.

But after drawing a blank against Leicester, having done the same in the Community Shield victory against Manchester United a week earlier, Lineker then failed to score against West Brom and Coventry in the next two matches. Four matches into the campaign with his new club, some Toffees fans were already questioning their star signing.

'He was getting loads of chances and missing them at the start of the season; it wasn't like he wasn't getting a sniff,' recalls Everton supporter Graham Ennis, who was 19 at the time of Lineker's arrival.

The signing had been a coup for the club, but some supporters had started sending letters into the local newspapers expressing their dissatisfaction at the former Leicester man's slow-scoring start. Lineker even received boos from a small portion of his own fans when his name was read out before his first home matches as a Blue.

The new forward had been at the club for a matter of weeks, yet already some were debating if he had the ability and mentality to make the step up to a side that expected success. *Liverpool Daily Post* reporter Ian Ross wrote in his match report after Everton's 1-0 win against Spurs in August that Lineker had 'struggled to come to terms with his new celebrity status since a move from Leicester City'; while Lawrie McMenemy – despite backing the forward to be a good signing for Everton in his *Liverpool Echo* column – conceded 'a number of people find it strange that Lineker' had been signed given what had been achieved at Goodison Park previously.

With the talent that Everton had at their disposal and with Adrian Heath waiting in the wings, it was crucial that Lineker didn't let the doubt fester.

'It didn't click with the team [straight away] because Kendall changed the way we played for Lineker,' Ennis continues. 'Our game had been to put a ball up to Graeme Sharp, who was an expert at laying the ball off for other people, but we turned into a team that hit teams on the break, putting the ball over the top for Lineker to run on to.

'I was at Springfield Park for a pre-season friendly against Wigan and Lineker scored a hat-trick then, so it wasn't that he wasn't scoring, it was people mocking it a little bit, but they weren't really concerned about it. He'd missed chances in all of those early games.'

An added pressure was that Lineker had been brought in as a replacement for cult hero Andy Gray. The Scottish forward was a big character in the side and had won the hearts of Everton supporters by playing a key role in turning the team from relegation battlers to FA Cup, Cup Winners' Cup and First Division winners in the space of two years. At the age of 30 and with a chequered injury record, Gray's best years were behind him, but his strength of character and no-nonsense attitude still made him very popular.

'Andy Gray was a wonderful player and more of a battler than Gary,' says former *Times* and *Sunday Telegraph* journalist Patrick Barclay. 'To characterise Gray as just a battler would be damning him with faint praise because he was much more than that and but for injury, I think he would have been capable of being there with the [Alan] Shearers and Linekers.

'Don't forget, Andy Gray won Player of the Year and Young Player of the Year in his first season in England [in 1976/7], that's how classy he was. I can understand why the Everton fans wanted Andy Gray; he could fight the opposing back four, run through and finish well.'

Despite his popularity, the numbers suggested that Everton manager Howard Kendall's decision to make the change was sound. They had two different playing styles, but in the previous three seasons, Lineker had scored 72 league goals – albeit with one campaign in the second tier — and Gray had netted 26. The Englishman was also five years younger and had a much better recent fitness record, having played 115 times across those campaigns compared to Gray's 86.

What had stung was the ruthless nature of Gray's departure. The 1.8m (5ft 11in)-tall frontman had been moving into a new house in Southport when Kendall arrived unannounced and informed Gray that he wasn't part of his first-team plans for the coming season, and that a move back to former club Aston Villa had been arranged. He'd need a new home closer to Birmingham.

'Andy called me and said, "Listen, can you meet me?" so I did in a pub in Southport,' recalls strike partner Graeme Sharp. 'He said Kendall had just visited him on the day he was moving into his new house and told his wife, "Stop unpacking." Howard Kendall said he was getting Gary Lineker and Andy could stay if he really wanted, but he wasn't going to play many games because he wanted to play me and Gary up front.

'It was a difficult situation for Gary to come into, not just because it was a new club, but because he was replacing somebody who was a fans' favourite in Andy Gray. The season before, we'd won the league. I'd struck up a good partnership with Andy, and Adrian Heath was also there and I'd struck up a good partnership with him. If you were looking from the outside, you'd probably think, "Why are we buying Gary Lineker?" Yeah he had a good goalscoring record at Leicester, but you'd wonder why the manager was doing it.

'It was a big move for Gary, but I don't think the fans were overly enamoured with it to start with and he had to fight to try to get them on side.'

Ennis remembers feeling ambivalent at the time. 'Lineker was the bright, young thing, so the fact Everton spent an initial £800,000 on him was a positive thing,' he says. 'But I remember being upset that Andy Gray was going, but not to the point of doubting Kendall. Only two or three years prior to that, people were saying Kendall should be sacked and we should get rid of the board, then it suddenly all turned around. So for us to buy one of the best up-and-coming strikers in the country was never going to be a bad thing.'

Lineker's arrival signalled a change of style for an Everton side that had steamrolled their way to the championship in 1984/5, scoring 88 goals on the way to picking up 90 points from 42 matches. The Toffees had achieved that feat by playing an expansive style of play for the time, getting the ball forward to Sharp, who expertly held it up and brought others into play. They'd shared the goals around, with Sharp bagging 30 in all competitions, and Trevor Steven, Derek Mountfield and Kevin Sheedy all netting more than 13 each too.

With Lineker on board, Everton would now be set up with him in mind as the principal goalscorer. Kendall wrote in his autobiography that his new striker was 'unlike anyone I had at Everton at the time' and therefore would need to be accommodated for accordingly.

'Players determine style,' Kendall said in the 1987 biography, *Lineker: Golden Boot*. 'Before Gary came, we shared the goals more. Our build-up was slower and we put more players into the penalty box. With Heath or Sharp, we played it more to feet, whereas with Gary we became a bit more direct, using his pace to knock balls beyond the back four. When you've got Sheedy on the ball, he sees the opportunities to use the direct ball for Gary to make runs into the channel between the centre-half and full-back.'

Perhaps it was only natural that Lineker and Everton would take some time to really hit it off. As the striker and his new teammates experienced those early growing pains, he also needed to get used to life away from Leicester – not just the club, but also a world living away from his family home.

It would have been difficult for any player to adjust so quickly, but with Lineker's burgeoning reputation, the upheaval of his arrival and the fact he was joining the English champions, there was a lot for the 24-year-old to contend with.

'When Gary came, it was a completely different ball game because he was a big name and he came for a lot of money, so there were a lot of expectations around him,' says Everton legend Neville

Southall. 'But the type of person he is, it didn't bother him at all. He's got the ideal mental attitude for football: he's pretty laid-back, nothing much bothers him – he just gets on with it and does what he's got to do.

'If you're going to come into a successful club, you've got to bring something different, you've also got to prove your worth, and it takes time. When players first come into the club, people say, "Let's have a look at you and see what you've got in your locker." Sometimes you have to prove yourself and he did that.

'People were used to a certain style – we got the ball down and we crossed it, there were diving headers, contact, there was a lot more aggression– so it was a change because people up to that point had never seen someone like Gary in our team before. We hadn't got someone who was naturally quick and was an out-and-out goalscorer, so for him to come in was a change of style, a change of personality, a change of the way we did things. It was difficult for him to come in, but because of his temperament it was water off a duck's back.'

Lineker got off the mark in his fifth match in an Everton shirt, stooping to head home a Gary Stevens cross to give the Blues a 1–0 victory away at Spurs at the end of August. The goal may not have been in front of many of his new supporters back on Merseyside, but seeing his name on the scoresheet would go some way towards allaying those early concerns. It was certainly enough to get *Liverpool Echo* reporter Ken Rogers excited. He wrote: 'If the quality of this effort is a hint of things to come, then the fans will be more than happy.'

Rogers' words were proved accurate as Lineker showed the Goodison Park faithful what he could do in the next game, bagging a hat-trick in a 4–1 win over Birmingham. The trio of goals were true poacher's efforts: the first an emphatic close-range finish after Gary Stevens' shot came back off the post; the second a glancing header from a Stevens free-kick; and the third converting a Peter Reid cross from the right.

If there had been any lingering doubt about Lineker's goalscoring abilities, he scored two more – this time in a 5–1 win at Sheffield

Wednesday – just four days later. Now, the England striker was sitting pretty at the top of the First Division goalscoring charts once more.

Just like at Leicester, one of the key reasons for Lineker's form was the strength of a good strike partnership. Where Alan Smith had been his perfect foil in the East Midlands, he quickly struck up a similar understanding with Sharp, segueing well with the midfield support act that backed them up. It was clear Lineker would be benefiting from even better service at Everton than he had at Filbert Street and that his already-impressive goalscoring numbers were set to skyrocket even further.

'Everybody knew his record at Leicester and his relationship with Smudger [Smith] up front and it was very good what he had at Everton with myself,' explains Sharp. 'Gary brought his Leicester form to Everton, but he scored more goals – no disrespect to Leicester, but we had great guys like Kevin Sheedy and Trevor Steven, who were a dream for centre-forwards. They could go past people; they could get the ball into the box.

'Gary scored lots of different types of goals: he scored headers as well as using the blistering pace. Gary was an accomplished footballer and was a very good finisher, and one on one, he was very good. At that time, Ian Rush was the great goalscorer, but Gary was up there with him, absolutely.

'With Gary in the team, he was very intelligent and I knew if I flicked it on, he'd be on the shoulder of the last defender and get it in. I don't know if the back four and the midfield looked for that more because he had that pace, but we certainly never did a lot of work on the training ground; it was a case of playing off the cuff, playing what you see, and Gary knew nine times out of 10 I was going to get the flick on.

'His movement was exceptional and that's one thing the team never had before Gary. I wouldn't say Gary was the most comfortable with the ball at his feet and holding it up, but he had unbelievable pace and he could run all day, with diagonal runs in behind people, so we took advantage of that. For me, my job hadn't really changed, but it was just a case that I knew if I flicked things on or around the corner, Gary would be in there. We had a great partnership.'

As at Leicester, Lineker was a midfielder's dream. Whereas in their title-winning season, Everton predominantly played with two forwards in Sharp and Gray, who liked to work with their backs to goal and bring runners in around them, the Merseysiders' new frontman posed the opposition with a different challenge.

'What Gary did do was he gave us that option when we used his strengths of running on to stuff with his pace and power,' says central midfielder Paul Bracewell. 'It added a new dimension to us, so as a midfield player, you had the offer to play it into feet, but if you've got somebody running in behind like Gary used to do at times, he'd stretch the defence and give us more time. We didn't see him coming in as a change of style; we saw him as giving us another dimension, which was a great option.'

Lineker had a quiet assurance about himself that filled his new teammates with confidence. After his goalscoring splurge in late summer, he seemed to be finding his feet in his new surroundings, further doing his relationship with his new fans no harm by netting against old enemies Liverpool – albeit in a 3–2 defeat in September.

The goal against the Reds may not have resulted in any points, but it showed what Lineker offered in even the biggest matches, hanging back at the far post as a flowing passing move developed, before bursting into life to ghost away from his marker and slide the ball home from a few yards out. It was a show of predatory instinct that the sea of blue supporters in the vast Gwladys Street End could only appreciate.

It was to be his last league strike for another seven weeks, which coincided with Everton's disjointed run of three wins in nine matches. But he was still keeping his overall tally ticking over with goals in both legs of a League Cup win against Bournemouth and a goal apiece against Manchester United and Norwich in the Football League Super Cup, which had been created as a makeweight for a lack of European competition due to UEFA's ban on English sides following the Heysel Stadium disaster a few months earlier.

The tragedy that happened when a wall fell in the Brussels ground, crushing 39 Juventus fans during the Italian side's 1985 European Cup final with Liverpool, had a huge impact on the English game. Not only did the incident serve as a sobering moment in the battle against hooliganism that blighted 1980s football in the country, but it also stunted the development of the domestic club game with the ensuing five-year European ban imposed on all English sides.

Everton fans felt particularly aggrieved with the punishment. As league champions, they were blocked from entering that season's European Cup, a competition they felt they'd have done well in, having won the Cup Winners' Cup in the previous campaign. There was a sense of frustration and anger around Goodison Park, which may have accounted in part for their side's inconsistency throughout the autumn.

As many players will attest, getting on the wrong side of the Goodison crowd isn't for the faint-hearted. With its tall, multi-tiered stands looming over the pitch, the fans stood like walls above the players, with every groan, jibe and harangue reverberating from terrace to terrace to create a fierce atmosphere. Conversely, when things were going well, the famous Goodison Roar created an electricity that prickled like very few other grounds in the country. Get the fans onside and the benefits were huge.

As the nights gradually drew darker, Everton finally started to hit their straps. And so did Lineker. A 6–1 romp against Arsenal in early November was the catalyst for a run of 13 league wins from a possible 16, in which he scored 17 goals – including a second hat-trick of the season, this time against Manchester City.

The marksman also scored another goal against Liverpool, this time getting the second to seal a 2–0 win at Anfield, inflicting the Reds' first home defeat in 11 months and only their third loss at home to Everton in 16 years. Lineker's goal was a thing of striking perfection, beating the offside trap with a well-timed run and clipping a finish past goalkeeper Bruce Grobbelaar into the net.

Ironically for Lineker, the only blight on Everton's record during that run was another defeat to Leicester, this time losing 2–1 at Goodison Park, with the forward failing to score against his old teammates once again. Regardless of that, by early March, it looked for all the world as though Everton were set to retain their title, spearheaded by their new talisman.

'Nobody can teach what he's got: you've either got it or you haven't,' Southall says. 'Yeah, he got cleverer with experience, but that thing inside him is from birth. If you've got a talent and you work hard, then the thing you've got to do is learn to make the most of it. He was cleverer than a lot of people think. He wasn't just one over the top; he did a lot more than that. When you're blessed with a talent, it's about how you harness and use that, and I think that's a skill in itself.'

For Lineker, that meant replicating his training schedule from Leicester, Southall recalls. 'His normal week was, on Monday he had a bath, Tuesday he had a walk around, Wednesday he had off, Thursday he may train, Friday he had a bath, and Saturday he usually scored a hat-trick,' the goalkeeper says, laughing.

'Gary wasn't the only player who had [leeway not to train],' explains Bracewell. 'One of Howard Kendall's massive strengths was man management and, in those days, the likes of Reidy and Andy Gray were managed and the most important thing was to get them on the field. I'm sure some of those players played with things [injuries] some of today's players wouldn't have done and they've got bigger squads now to allow for rotation. But there was no rotation in our time and it was all about managing the players.'

Perhaps tiredness played a role in what came next. With 12 games remaining of the league season, Everton were three points clear of second-placed Manchester United at the top and eight points ahead of Liverpool. But one win in the next four brought them back into the pack, with Kendall lamenting a 2–1 defeat at Luton on the Hatters' artificial pitch as a key blow to his side's chances.

At the same time, Liverpool were coming up on the rails, amid a run of 11 wins from 12 unbeaten matches, which meant Everton couldn't afford any more slip-ups. Three successive victories against Arsenal, Watford and Ipswich steadied the ship, but injuries were mounting. Southall was ruled out for the season after dislocating his ankle and suffering ligament damage while playing for Wales against the Republic of Ireland, then the Toffees stuttered to a 0–0 draw with Nottingham Forest – a result added to by Peter Reid leaving the ground on crutches.

There were two more absentees by the time Everton arrived at struggling Oxford for their final away match of the season, this time in the form of Lineker's lucky boots. Ordinarily, the striker would regularly change his boots throughout the season, but due to his hot streak of form, he'd been playing in the same ones for almost the entire campaign. By the time they'd reached April, they were battered and worn, but they'd continued to do the business in front of goal.

So, when the kit was unpacked at the Manor Ground and it was discovered that the boots – which have since been donated to the Adidas Museum in Munich – had been left in Liverpool, Lineker was forced to borrow a pair from a teammate instead. Not only was the confidence inspired by wearing his 'lucky boots' in tatters, but he'd be wearing boots that were half a size too big.

'It's not like now when there are kit men,' remembers Sharp. 'These were kids and apprentices [packing the kit] so things got forgotten and these things happened. Gary was one of those guys who liked to have the same boots, so when they weren't there, it could have affected him.'

It was a night of high drama in Oxford, with the hosts fighting for their lives at the other end of the table. The Us may have been in the same division, but there was an air of a cup tie to the evening, with the home side looking to bloody the noses of their more illustrious rivals after not winning on their own patch for more than four months. If Lineker was feeling uncomfortable without his boots, the Manor Ground surroundings would do nothing to assuage him.

A heavily worn, bobbly pitch, paired with a rowdy home following who intimidated many a side during Oxford's march to the First Division created a tetchy atmosphere – disparate old-school stands creating a lower-league-like feel that would have almost seemed open-air compared to Goodison Park's tall structures. Any weakness would be put under the microscope.

A trio of uncharacteristic Lineker misses suggest that the visitors were feeling the pressure. Sheedy was the provider on each occasion, but his normally reliable teammate couldn't find the finish he needed to break the deadlock. On two occasions, Lineker manoeuvred himself ahead of his marker to get on the end of crosses, only to skew them past the crossbar and post instead of hitting the target. His worst miss was arguably his first, as he scampered away from the chasing defenders, only to see goalkeeper Alan Judge turn a close-range effort around the post in a position that Lineker had so readily scored from throughout the campaign.

Another scoreless draw was bad news for Everton's title challenge, but a 1–0 defeat was worse. So, when Les Phillips struck a low effort into the corner of the net with only 90 seconds remaining, the Blues' hopes of retaining their championship were hanging by a thread.

Liverpool's win against Leicester on the same night meant they now held the advantage. If they won their final two matches, they would snatch the title away from their Merseyside rivals, whereas all Everton could do was dispatch Southampton and West Ham and hope for favours elsewhere. A 6–1 win with Lineker scoring a hat-trick against the former, followed by a 3–1 triumph over the latter, helped by two more Lineker strikes, meant the Toffees kept up their end of the deal, but the Reds had already done enough to clinch the title.

Lineker has since spoken in several interviews about how, despite scoring 30 goals in the First Division that season, his misses at Oxford were the difference between Everton winning and not winning the league that season. Southall, however, explains that it's too simplistic to think like that.

'Sometimes it just takes a little bit,' he says. 'A ball going across the area and not quite getting there, maybe a ball that hits the post, the ball bouncing out when you're trying to force things, sometimes it's luck. If you knew why everything happened, we'd all be millionaires, but sometimes it just doesn't happen for you.

'Sometimes there's no rhyme or reason, but over a season, the best teams win the league because they're consistent. Maybe we weren't quite as consistent as we needed to be, but we were very close. It's nothing major, it's just fine margins when you get to that point. Sometimes I'm a great believer that it's just not your time; no matter how hard you try, it's just not your time. It's over a season and you can't just put it down to one game.'

The team had to dust themselves down and put that disappointment behind them because the season wasn't over yet: there was the small matter of an FA Cup Final the following week. They'd be meeting old adversaries Liverpool at Wembley, with their Merseyside rivals gunning for a cherished league-and-cup double.

In the week before the final, Lineker's fine season in front of goal was acknowledged when he was named Football Writers' Player of the Year – an award he'd put with his Professional Footballers' Association Player of the Year gong. His 30 league goals meant he was the clear winner of the First Division's Golden Boot – an accolade he had won the previous season too, albeit in a share with Chelsea's Kerry Dixon – while nine goals in other competitions left him one away from a 40-goal campaign. In just 56 appearances, it was a ratio that put him in the same realm as such prolific luminaries as Francis Lee, Bob Latchford and Ian Rush.

Lineker would therefore arrive at Wembley buoyed by the accolade and having scored five goals in his last two appearances. If Everton were to get their hands on silverware, their star striker was surely going to be key.

'When he is injury free, you see something special. He is a totally different player,' said Kendall in an interview that appeared in the *Northamptonshire Evening Telegraph* a few days before the final in May. 'Mentally, he hasn't felt right in certain games because of injuries, but he has been absolutely superb in the last couple of games.'

Lineker looked sharp as the final got underway at a sunny Wembley, stretching the Liverpool defence with his direct running from the off. He showed a sign of what was to come early on, as he narrowly missed out on a long Sheedy pass that was cleared by Grobbelaar. The Zimbabwean goalkeeper had dealt with the danger the first time but couldn't keep Lineker out again a few minutes later – the forward streaking clear of Alan Hansen to latch on to Reid's pass, only to see Grobbelaar parry away his first effort, before following up from close range. Everton were 1–0 up thanks to Lineker's 40th goal of the season.

The final had been billed by some as Lineker versus Rush, with the two great goalscorers spearheading their sides' quest for glory. But while the Englishman had struck first, his Welsh counterpart was about to have his say. Rush, who had been strongly linked with a move to Juventus that summer, wanted to leave the Reds with a parting gift, running out of a pack of players to get on the end of Jan Mølby's sublime pass, round Toffees goalkeeper Bobby Mimms and rolling the ball into an empty net.

Ominously, Liverpool had never lost a game Rush had scored in at that stage and so it proved again. As Lineker and Everton were increasingly silenced going forward, their neighbours grew in confidence, with Mølby playing provider again to tee up Craig Johnston for 2–1, before Rush struck again with seven minutes remaining to seal the win. Everton had come so close and missed out on silverware once more.

If narrowly losing out on the league and FA Cup to their Merseyside rivals weren't enough, the Toffees squad had to suffer the ultimate ignominy of taking part in an open-top bus parade alongside the Reds players days later. Liverpool City Council, wanting to mark the city's dominance that season, had booked two buses for the event, and despite not having anything to shout about themselves, Everton were obliged to attend.

Lineker may have hoovered up the individual awards and hit new heights with his goalscoring, but his side had ultimately ended the season trophyless. It would prove to be Lineker's only season playing on the blue half of Merseyside, sandwiched between two title-winning seasons, and created a dichotomy that still exists among fans today. Was he a success or a failure? For several Everton supporters, it's the latter.

'We threw it away in what we call the "Lineker season,"' says fan Ennis. 'Broadly, I think the 85/86 season is seen as a failure because we lost the double to Liverpool. Had we won the league or Lineker scored the goal that won the cup, he would have been looked on very differently. For us then, it was a failure, so any achievement that Lineker got that season was part of it. That's probably very unfair on him, but the season isn't fondly remembered.'

Not everyone agrees with that assessment. 'You couldn't say he went to Everton and failed, could you?' deadpans Southall. 'He scored tonnes of goals.'

However Lineker's season-long dalliance at Goodison Park is remembered by the people who watched him most at the time, there's no doubting the striker's star had risen considerably from a professional standpoint. He'd gone from being the main man at a club in the bottom half of the league to an established goal-getter at the very top. Any doubts about his ability to hold his own at the elite level had gone.

'It's bizarre to think Everton won the title the year before and the year after he was there, yet he rattled in the goals,' journalist Barclay surmises. 'I think by the time he went to Everton, bear in mind they were one of the top teams – arguably the top team at the time – that removes any doubt as to his status.'

Lineker's stock was rising, but it was yet to reach its true peak.

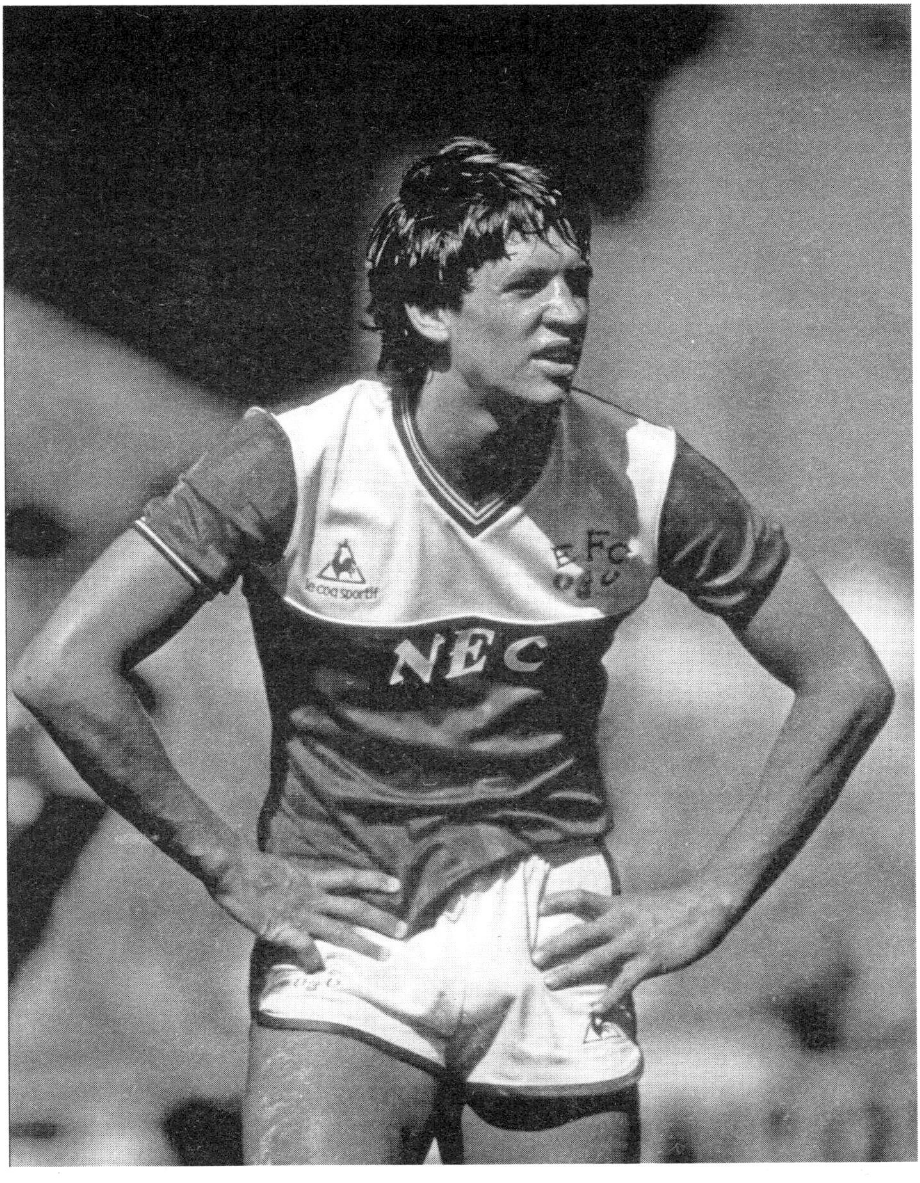
le coq sportif
NEC

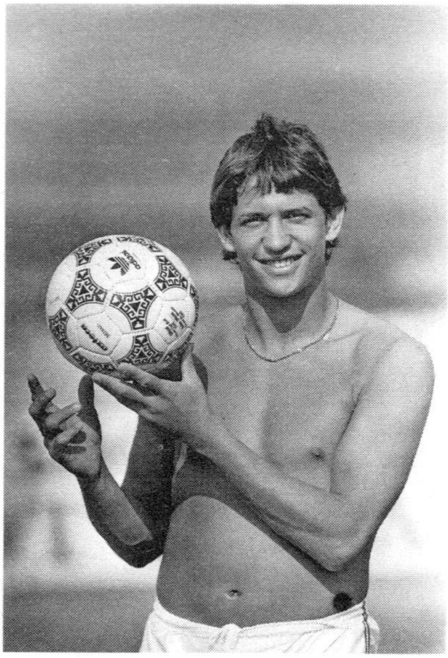

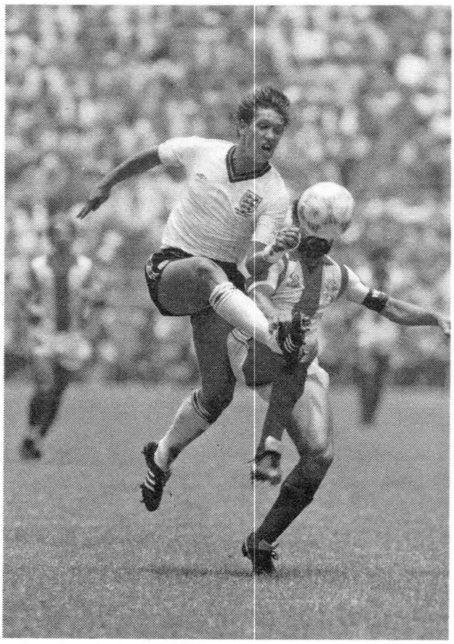

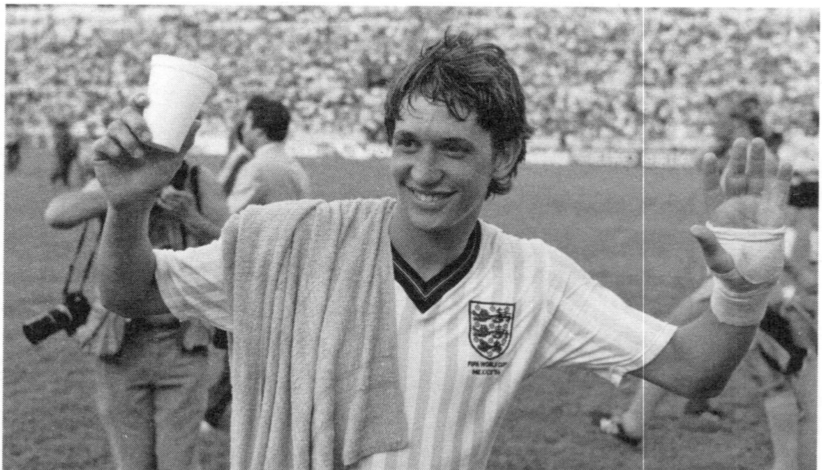

8

ONE GAME IN MEXICO

England, 1986

*'We all saw him as the superstar that he was.
We all recognised what a great player he was.'*

Diego Maradona held up his hand to the referee to temporarily stop him, then approached Gary Lineker. The Argentine playmaker lifted his hand apologetically before crossing the few yards that lay between him and his English adversary.

Nearly 115,000 people were packed into the Azteca Stadium in Mexico City – with millions more watching on television sets around the world – but they'd have to wait as El Diez paused proceedings to greet Lineker. Forget the official timeline, this was a schedule being set by the world's greatest player.

There had been seconds to go before the World Cup 1986 quarter-final between Argentina and England kicked off, although Maradona felt the stoppage was necessary. He wanted to pass on his appreciation first. The diminutive genius jogged up to Lineker, thrust his palm into his and gave him a brief embrace, before returning to his position for the kick-off.

It wouldn't be the most notable action Maradona would make with his hands during the contest, but it was a sign of the mutual admiration between the two players. Not to mention the status that Lineker had now reached.

'I'll never forget, just before England–Argentina at the Azteca Stadium kicked off, Maradona broke ranks just as the referee put his whistle in his mouth,' recalls journalist Patrick Barclay, who was working for the *Today* newspaper at the tournament.

'Maradona ran over to where Lineker was about to kick off and shook hands with him and then ran back to his part of the circle. There was respect after Lineker's hat-trick against Poland, from the greatest player in the world for the greatest goalscorer. He was a contemporary of one of the greatest players who ever lived and that incident in the centre circle showed he had the utter respect of Maradona.'

For that to happen in that instant was significant. This wasn't a handshake in the tunnel or a slap on the back and a few words in private long before the action took place; Maradona was showing his appreciation in front of the world, with the cameras rolling. What was a small gesture had huge significance.

It was one of the biggest indications of how that summer in 1986 was changing Lineker's life. Those sweltering weeks in the Mexican heat were a real breakthrough moment in his career. While his domestic goalscoring exploits had reached new levels in the English club game following his move to Everton the year before, he was yet to truly show to the global football fraternity what he could do on the biggest stage. Yet under the scorching Central American sun, Lineker had transformed from being England's most-likely goal threat to the world's deadliest striker.

The 25-year-old left the 1986 World Cup with a new level of notoriety, along with six tournament goals, the Golden Boot and the adulation of some of football's great and good. Not least that of Maradona.

Of course, for all the personal accolades Lineker had received, the competition hadn't been the success he and England had hoped for. The Three Lions were now 20 years out from having won their last major trophy and had been sent packing by La Albiceleste under controversial circumstances, thwarted in part by Maradona's Hand of God goal when the 1.65m (5ft 5in)-tall playmaker outreached goalkeeper Peter Shilton to punch Argentina into the lead in a tightly matched quarter-final.

But among all the anger and frustration, it was hard to ignore that England had uncovered a new worldwide superstar who was capable of holding his own with the best players on the planet.

It's difficult to believe that a year previously, Lineker was still on the periphery of Bobby Robson's England plans. A goal on his full debut in the friendly win against the Republic of Ireland in March 1985 may have suggested that the First Division's top scorer would get his chance to prove his worth again when the World Cup qualifiers with Romania and Finland came around two months later.

But instead of retaining his place in the side, Lineker found himself on the bench in Bucharest – getting only five minutes as a late replacement for Paul Mariner – and then didn't see any game time at all in Helsinki.

Two underwhelming draws in which England only scored once had left Robson's side keeping one eye over their shoulder in the hunt for a place at Mexico '86, but there was still no starting spot for Lineker in the friendly against Scotland to round off the month. He was forced to make do with a substitute's appearance once more, being introduced in the 79th minute as England failed to turn around a 1–0 deficit against the Auld Enemy.

There was still a feeling that it wasn't so much Lineker's ability to sniff out a goalscoring chance that needed to be proved for him to warrant more of a role for England, but more everything else that went on around it.

'At that time, Sir Bobby [Robson] was one of them who wanted everybody contributing to the team performance,' explains defender Terry Fenwick, who made his England breakthrough at a similar time to Lineker. 'Gary wasn't necessarily like that. What he would put in would be a goal, but you might not see him for 15- or 20-minute spells of a game in between, he'd just go missing. In the game at the time, it was so important that everybody contributed, everybody worked their stuff, everybody worked together to get that win.

'We had some great players in Bryan Robson, Ray Wilkins and Chris Waddle – they were fantastic players – but they also worked their balls off when we didn't have the ball. That wasn't necessarily Gary Lineker and I think a lot of people found that difficult at times, and I think Bobby Robson did too.

'I think that's why it took longer for him to establish himself than the others, but he was better than the rest and he scored more goals than the rest. I just don't think people always appreciated his gameplan, how he was going to get his goals, how he would manipulate the opposition over 90 minutes – how he'd calm them, cool them, before he scored his goal and killed them. But that was Gary.'

The positive news was that Lineker was now back to being a regular in the squad and was named in the party for the Azteca 2000 tournament that summer. Held in Mexico, the round-robin competition was devised as a test event for the World Cup the following summer and was a great opportunity for England to familiarise themselves with the conditions they'd face when the real event took place.

It was therefore key for Robson to take with him as many players as possible whom he expected to make his World Cup squad in a year's time. Lineker's inclusion was a clear sign of intent and with a prospective move away from Leicester still to be decided, a welcome fillip for his long-term England future.

First up on the tour was a match against Italy, a game that resulted in another defeat – England this time losing 2–1 – and another brief appearance from the bench for the final 11 minutes for Lineker. There was more frustration as the Three Lions then lost 1–0 to hosts Mexico, with no sign of the striker on the pitch.

That was now five matches without a win for Robson's men. So, it was no surprise when changes finally came for the next game against West Germany, with a new-look attack of Lineker and Chelsea's Kerry Dixon, the First Division's joint top goalscorers from the previous season. The duo had scored 24 goals each and, from a goalscoring perspective, were the two most in-form forwards in the squad.

It appeared to be a match made in heaven, Dixon bagging a brace in a 3–0 win. They were paired together again a few days later for the final match of the tour against the USA, with Dixon and Lineker both scoring twice in a 5–0 win. Lineker's first was particularly noteworthy, with the striker christening it in a press conference as 'one of my best goals' after taking a lofted pass from Hoddle down on his chest with his back to goal, before spinning and striking a volley across his body and into the net.

With goals apiece, albeit against lesser opposition, perhaps England had landed on their new strike partnership.

'I didn't discuss anything with Gary [about the partnership],' says Dixon. 'We all knew the positions and it could have been anyone because you never knew what Bobby Robson was thinking, you just had to do well in the team when you went in. He just got on with it and you've got to do what you've got to do to get selected.

'There was no point players talking about partnerships and who worked well or should you do this or whatever because you never knew if you'd definitely be in the partnership and it could change on a regular basis.'

And so it proved. Despite their exploits together in Mexico, Dixon and Lineker only started together once more again, a 0–0 draw with Northern Ireland in November 1985.

'The partnership was quite good and I always thought it could have worked, but obviously people had other ideas and they didn't see it. Bobby Robson had obviously gone out and was looking at ways for it all to work, the entire team and the pattern,' adds Dixon.

'Gary was definitely a threat and, in many cases, we were both a threat, we both had pace and we were always an option for the likes of Glenn Hoddle with passes over the top. The variation was if I came to get the ball deeper so Lineker could get the ball over the top.'

While Dixon's starting opportunities failed to hold, the Mexico tour was the catalyst for Lineker getting more chances in the starting XI. Combined with his form since joining Everton after returning from the Americas, he was fast becoming a guaranteed England starter.

A hat-trick against Turkey in October, which included two headers, helped confirm World Cup qualification, but the goals didn't continue to flow in the same way as they had been at Everton. In fact, by the time he arrived in Mexico, Lineker hadn't scored in four England games, all of which he'd started in. By Lineker's club standards, that was a veritable drought.

Major tournaments can often be a different kettle of fish and that definitely applied to Mexico '86. A combination of the searing heat and high altitudes would make the competition a physical test as much as a football one, with the European nations at a particular disadvantage in such conditions.

England headed to North America pre-tournament for an altitude training camp, taking in two matches in preparation. The first saw Robson's men beat hosts Mexico 3–0 in Los Angeles' Memorial Coliseum and, although Lineker didn't play a part, he was starting a week later for the final warm-up match against Canada.

Lineker was paired with Hateley up front, with it widely anticipated that they were Robson's preferred strike partnership for the tournament. England were unspectacular in securing a 1–0 win courtesy of a Hateley goal shortly after the hour mark, with the manager saying to the press that playing badly would give them a chance to 'get it out of our system'.

More concerning was an incident involving Lineker, who went down heavily on his left wrist during the game following a tussle for the ball with defender Randy Samuel. The challenge was hard and fair, but the ground was rock solid and the striker landed awkwardly on his hand, raising fears he'd fractured his wrist. Lineker was in a lot of pain and was quickly whisked off to hospital, with worries abounding that a break would rule him out of the tournament.

Thankfully, an X-ray showed he only had a minor fracture and while he'd need special permission from FIFA to play with a lightweight plastic guard, Lineker was passed fit – recovering in time to take part in England's first training session as their Saltillo training base.

'I don't play with my hands so, if I can get some support on the wrist, there's no reason why I shouldn't work with the other players,' a nonchalant Lineker told the press pack upon his return.

The session appeared to be a success and Robson was satisfied he'd have his 40-goal striker available for the tournament opener with Portugal. 'Lineker looks to me to be 85 per cent certain of being able to put himself up for selection on Tuesday,' he said. 'He took a few falls in training and it was good to see him able to join in.'

And so it proved, with Lineker named alongside Hateley for England's first group game in Monterrey. Unfortunately, it wouldn't be a recipe for victory, with the Three Lions passing up on several decent opportunities during a 1–0 defeat inflicted on them by Carlos Manuel's 75th-minute goal after he ghosted away from three defenders at the back post to score.

Lineker may have made it through the whole 90 minutes with his wrist unscathed, but he was out of luck in front of goal. Either side of half time, he got on the end of two through balls, only to lose his footing on both occasions as he stretched to get the ball under control. Lineker's best chance came on the hour mark when he took down a long ball forward by Terry Butcher and slipped an effort beneath Portugal goalkeeper Manuel Bento, only for defender António Oliveira to slide in to clear the danger.

It had been a frustrating afternoon and one that would be repeated three days later as Lineker and England drew another blank, this time in a 0–0 draw with Morocco. The Atlas Lions starved Robson's men of any room, leaving Lineker short on service, with his only real sight of goal coming in the first half when he got in on the left side of the box, only to be run out of space by an onrushing defender and the goalkeeper.

Frustration was building and it only got worse before the break. First, captain Bryan Robson was forced to come off after agitating a historic shoulder injury, with his midfield partner Ray Wilkins following only moments later after receiving a second yellow card for throwing the ball at the referee in an act of dissent.

Ten-man England toiled in the heat but couldn't make a breakthrough – leaving the field to boos with their World Cup hopes hanging by a thread. On paper, their final group game against Poland would be their trickiest assignment yet and they needed to win to progress.

If Robson and Wilkins' unavailability grabbed most of the headlines before that match, it was England's toothless displays that looked most damaging to their chances. Changes were necessary and Bobby Robson had to find a new combination to get the best out of his side.

Lineker had now gone six games without a goal for England. Stretching further back, his record of six goals in 15 international caps was hardly setting the world alight – especially considering three of those had come against Turkey and another two in a match with the USA. He may have been scoring goals for fun domestically, but there were starting to be a few questions about whether he had the ability to step up against the elite nations when it really mattered.

England had a host of forwards who appeared to fit the same profile but couldn't be relied on to score with regularity internationally. After such an abject start for the team in 1986 and with Lineker only showing flashes of promise in front of goal, those concerns were being raised about the Everton man too. Did he have what it takes to lead the line for his country and, if so, how could Robson coax the form that had seen him score so many goals for the Toffees in an England shirt?

The critics were out in force back home and in Mexico. *The People* reported that a significant proportion of England fans who'd travelled to Monterrey for the Morocco draw gathered around the team coach baying for blood, shouting 'Robson resign' and 'We want our money back.'

There was plenty of debate about how the manager would react in what could be his final throw of the dice if England failed to beat the Poles. Nobody was safe, especially with the side drawing blanks up top.

Lineker was one of the names raised as a potential victim of Robson's axe, with the *Manchester Evening News*'s report of the Morocco draw lamenting that 'Mark Hateley and Gary Lineker haven't exactly set the World Cup on fire up front' and debate over who should give way to allow room for more technical players, Barnes and Beardsley, to come into the side.

Most damning of all were comments from England World Cup-winning manager Sir Alf Ramsey, who specifically named Lineker in a *Daily Mirror* interview as one of a quartet of players he'd leave on the bench. Ramsey's belief was that removing Lineker and Hateley from the starting XI 'would offer England a variation in their attacking ideas' and mean England 'wouldn't have to keep knocking in long balls'.

Losing his place under such circumstances would significantly dent Lineker's long-term international ambitions. He later admitted he thought he might be the one to make way to freshen up the frontline, but instead it was only Hateley who was replaced.

'I have to say when Mark Hateley was getting left out, I got the vibe it was between me or Peter Beardsley to get the nod,' Dixon recalls. 'I thought Gary was a permanent fixture and it was a battle between the rest of us. The big man–little man situation looked like the one, but in the end Peter got the nod. He was a great player, as was Hateley, but we all had different attributes and it was what worked.'

As Dixon references, Beardsley's selection alongside Lineker was a break to the normal style of the time. Robson seemed to favour pairing Lineker's pace and goalscoring instincts with a bigger forward, yet, at 1.73m (5ft 8in) tall, Beardsley was 5cm (2in) shorter than his new partner. It was a change of approach, but one Robson felt was needed to make England less predictable going forward.

'The issue Bobby Robson had at the time was, "Where are we getting the goals from?"' says Fenwick. 'With Chris Waddle playing in the wide positions, Beardsley coming in instead of Hateley created more openings and we were sharper up front because of that. Those two alone, Waddle and Beardsley, were perfect for Gary

Lineker because they would see that little pass, they'd see that ball in the box and they'd deliver to exactly where he wanted, whereas Hateley was a bit more brash.

'Beardsley would work his socks off, he was great on the ball and the delivery on that final pass, he just knew where Gary would be. They could almost play blindfolded and knew exactly where the other one was.'

The Lineker–Beardsley combination wasn't completely untested. The pair had started together in England's 1–0 win away in the USSR in the March before the World Cup and while neither of them had scored, they did combine for the game's only goal, Beardsley winning the ball with a slide tackle wide on the right before putting in a low cross that Lineker dummied for Waddle to steer home just inside the box. The link-up had clearly made an impression on Robson.

The Three Lions boss tried to keep his selection under wraps until an hour before kick-off so as not to show his hand to Polish counterpart Antoni Piechniczek, but it was widely reported beforehand that Robson would make the change. And it proved to be the right one, with Lineker bagging a 28-minute hat-trick to transform England's previous struggles.

The first goal, on eight minutes, was an instant example of how Lineker and Beardsley could combine to great effect, playing a one-two to launch a counter-attack that put the Poles on the back foot. While Lineker cantered forward with the ball, Beardsley's intelligent running drew two defenders into the box with him, allowing room for Trevor Steven and Gary Stevens to get in down the right and pick out England's number 10 with a low cross that he slid home from six yards out.

The fluency of the move was a sign of things to come, with Lineker adding a second goal six minutes later. This time, Beardsley played a first-time pass down the left side to set Steve Hodge into space down the flank, with the midfielder playing a sumptuous cross that Lineker expertly finished into the net. 'They're tearing Poland apart,' yelled commentator Martin Tyler in delight, and it was hard to disagree.

Where in the previous two matches Lineker had been feeding off scraps, he was now gorging on the service he was getting. And he completed his hat-trick soon afterwards, benefiting from Poland goalkeeper Józef Młynarczyk failing to claim a corner to take the ball down and fire into the roof of the net from close range.

As Lineker reached to the heavens in celebration and fell into the embrace of Hodge, England's travelling fans launched into a conga around the stands. The shackles had come off and England were on their way to the last-16 in impressive style – and their new front two had played a significant role.

'If you look at how many times Beardsley put that ball into the space for Gary to get on the end of, it was incredible what a great partnership that was,' Fenwick continues. 'We didn't do drills like you see today all over football, but I think from that very first game they played together, they just clicked and it was brilliant.

'Every time you saw Beardsley on the ball, you knew the next ball he was looking for was Lineker in behind. It was one player who had all the skills in Beardsley and another [in Lineker] who had the speed and was so decisive in front of goal, it was the perfect partnership. From that first one or two games, Bobby made his mind up that this was his pair and everyone who saw it knew it was coming.'

Lineker had become the first England player to score a hat-trick at a World Cup since Geoff Hurst notched one in the final in 1966, although Robson wasn't about to let his striker bask in the glory for too long.

'There was no attempt to close things down in the second half,' the under-fire boss said in a press conference afterwards. 'Lineker's three goals were magnificent. I told him at half time that no one had ever scored five goals in a World Cup match and urged him to go out there and get two more.'

Momentum had suddenly shifted, with odds on England returning from Mexico with the trophy being slashed from 16–1 to 6–1 with some bookmakers. Their next assignment was a knockout match with Paraguay, who remained unbeaten after coming second in a group alongside hosts Mexico and Belgium.

By this stage, the players were more used to the searing Mexican heat they were playing in, although they'd now have to contend with an Azteca Stadium pitch covered in long grass and divots. The Poland victory had relieved some of the pressure that had been building on the side, but defeat to Paraguay would also be viewed as a failure and it was important to shut out the external noise. While everyone had understandably been talking about Lineker's goalscoring prowess in the run-up to the game, situations like these also brought out another side to him that benefited the team.

'It was red hot in our first games, but then we went into Mexico City, which was 10,000 feet above sea level – it was quite remarkable,' Fenwick remembers. 'It was so difficult physically, I lost nearly half a stone in fluids in the first game, it was amazing. That's when you needed Gary, who was such a calming influence. He'd just say, "Ah don't worry about it," that was pretty much it, and he'd just move on – and that was great for everybody else as well.

'We all saw him as the superstar that he was. We all recognised what a great player he was, a goalscorer and all that, but he also just took the sting out of everything and wouldn't let you go too overboard either.'

A brace in a 3–0 victory over Paraguay did nothing to stop the fervour building back at home, though. The goals not only propelled England to a quarter-final showdown with Argentina, but also saw Lineker become the tournament's top scorer with five overall, with the poacher moving into his groove.

Both of Lineker's goals came from within the six-yard box, highlighting his ability to pounce at any given moment. His first showed off all his best attributes, starting the move by running the channels, before popping up on the opposite side of the box to narrowly miss getting on the end of Glenn Hoddle's low cross, only to react quickest when Hodge managed to cut the ball back into the centre. His second saw him finish off another good England move from close range after a Gary Stevens cross.

On another day, Lineker could have been celebrating another hat-trick, seeing a snap shot brilliantly turned over by Paraguayan keeper Roberto Fernández while it was 1–0. He also watched on enviously, while he received treatment for a blow he received to his throat from a defender's elbow, as Beardsley picked up the 'Lineker position' from a corner to convert Fernández's parry into the net for 2–0.

'Gary Lineker can't half take chances, but little Peter Beardsley played his part – the whole team was superb,' beamed Robson in his TV interview at full time. 'We were very solid in defence and they tried to intimidate us, but we kept our discipline, kept our nerve and kept our cool and the lads have really done very well.'

Lineker was typically humble in the praise he received at full time, as he further showed himself to be one of the deadliest finishers in world football. 'It's all down to the lads and the two chances I had were basically simple goals really,' he said. 'I suppose I had to be there, but the balls in were superb, just like the last match. It's a great honour to be ahead of some of the names that are in the competition, I just hope I can stay and we can get to the final and even bring the cup home.'

To do that, England would have to get past Argentina in the last-eight first. La Albiceleste had been looking ominous in their progress, combining the pragmatism of their head coach Carlos Bilardo with the ingenuity of Maradona to cut a dangerous force. El Diez was undoubtedly the star, and there was plenty of talk about how Robson planned to keep him quiet.

However, when the England boss was quizzed ahead of the game about the relative talents of his and Argentina's talisman, he was surprisingly combative, saying, 'Diego Maradona is a wonderful, gifted played with great dribbling ability, but will he score more than Gary?' Perhaps it was these words that encouraged Maradona to have his pre-match embrace with Lineker.

What happened next was one of the most famous displays in football history. Maradona, at his impudent best, took on the role as England's tormentor-in-chief, constantly attempting to unlock their defence. The Three Lions managed to crowd him out in the first half, but then came the kicker as the Argentinian turned the game by scoring twice in four minutes at the start of the second period – punching in the first for his famous Hand of God goal, before scoring the so-called Goal of the Century with a mazy dribble that left England's players bewildered.

The introduction of Waddle and John Barnes managed to turn the tide, with Lineker halving the deficit with 10 minutes remaining by heading in a left-wing cross from the Watford winger. It was that combination again that nearly found the equaliser, Lineker stretching with every sinew to get on the end of Barnes's ball in the 88th minute as the entire world gasped.

The ball appeared to be destined to hit his head and end up in the net. Yet as he got half a pace ahead of the two defenders in electric blue, Lineker felt the ball brush across his forehead without making proper contact as he clattered into the post. There was a split second when the realisation would have dawned on him that the noise filling the Azteca was of astonishment rather than celebration.

Everything else had turned to goals for Lineker in Mexico, but instead of making contact with the ball, he'd collided with the post – contact that caused an injury that may have ended his tournament even if he had levelled things for England.

'I still can't believe how his last effort didn't go in, but it didn't and it went just past the post,' remembers BBC commentator Barry Davies. 'I think England would have gone on to win that game if he'd scored at that stage, I sensed there was a possible comeback on. I'm sure Gary would agree with my observation "Why didn't the ball go in?"'

England were out, with all of the post-match talk being about Maradona's handball to open the scoring. But while the injustice of the situation appeared to consume his teammates, Lineker's sense of calm and perspective presented in a different way.

'There's a lot to be admired about Lineker's sense of proportion, his composure, his intelligence,' journalist Patrick Barclay says. 'After that quarter-final when England were knocked out, I remember going back to the hotel and Terry Butcher and all the others were saying they'd liked to have wrung Maradona's neck or worse. And I asked Gary asked about it and he just forced a smile and said, "I wish we'd scored it." That was his sense of proportion.'

'Gary wasn't going to let that [Maradona's Hand of God goal] affect him,' Fenwick affirms. 'The rest of us all showed a lot more passion, but Gary was very "Get on with the job." He was always the one who was "Come on, it's on to the next, let's forget it." That was Gary.

'Links would take it on the chin and move on to the next step much quicker. In his mind, he was "It's done, it's gone, it's happened, we can't do anything about it, let's move on." We couldn't move on as quickly as Gary had coped with the situation himself.'

While the furore around Maradona had dominated immediately after the match, Lineker's goal had taken him to new levels too. It was his sixth of the tournament and enough for him to finish one strike ahead of Maradona, Spain's Emilio Butragueño and Careca of Brazil to clinch the Golden Boot. The accolade earned him comparisons with some of the world's greatest ever goalscorers, not least West Germany legend Gerd Müller, from one of the striker's former teammates.

'I saw Lineker only touch the ball eight or nine times – and he scored six goals,' Paul Breitner was quoted as saying in several newspapers. 'That is a fantastic rate in a World Cup. If I was a coach or a manager, I would pay millions to sign him for my club. He only scores goals. You can forget about him for 89 minutes, but then he does his job – he has the killer in him and that makes him one of the most valuable men in the world.'

Lineker was now a world star and everybody wanted a piece of him. His face became an almost permanent fixture of TV screens, he appeared on primetime talk show *Wogan* alongside Peter Shilton, and he was invited to play for the Rest of the World All Stars in a UNICEF fundraiser held in the USA.

There was no doubting Lineker was box office. And where there's attention, there's usually one of Europe's biggest football clubs sniffing around.

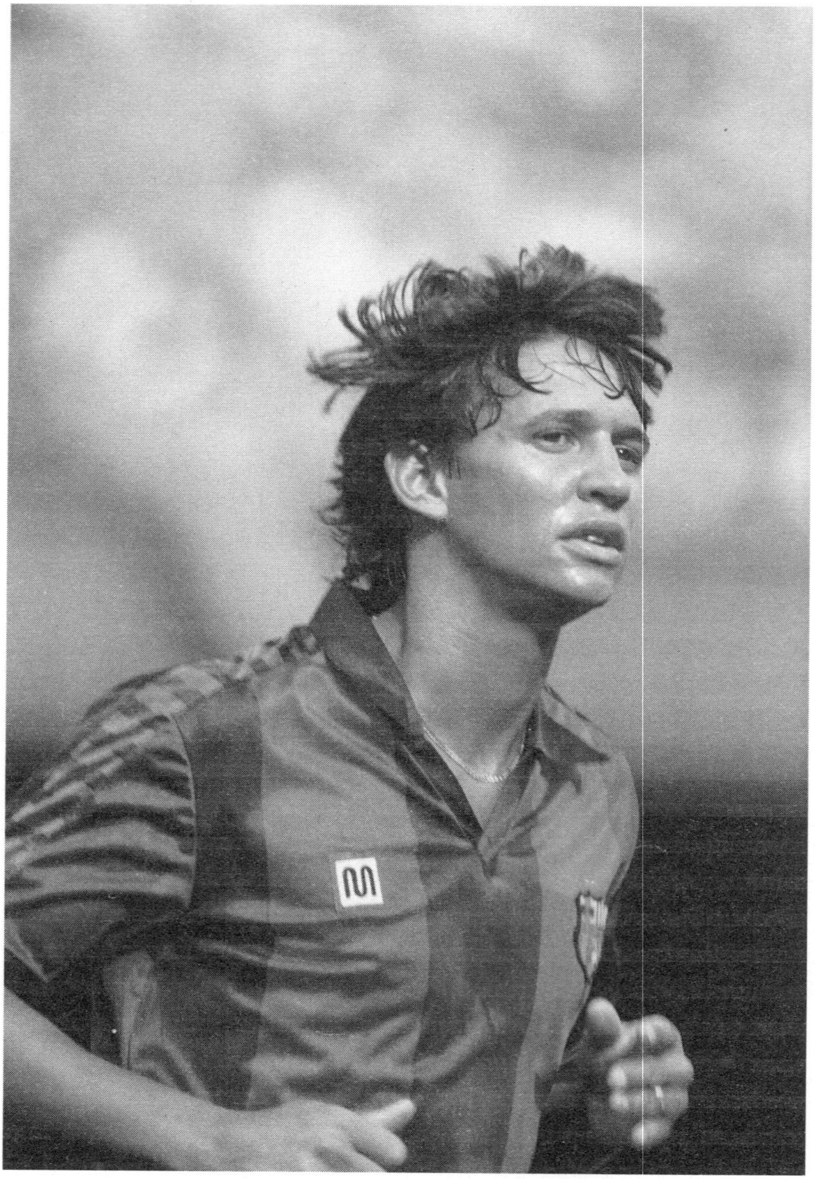

9

A NOU ADVENTURE

Barcelona, 1986–1988

'His finishing is clinical. He gets in there where it matters, but I've become impressed by his whole game. His movement, everything about his game was very good.'

'I think you're all out of order,' Lawrie McMenemy scolded in his broad north-east accent. 'He's signed a contract; you should be asking Howard Kendall.'

The three other men on camera looked sheepishly around the television studio. 'I never brought it up, he asked me the question,' Barcelona boss Terry Venables volleyed back in defence, while Gary Lineker stared down at the desk in front of him.

Ever the coolest man in the room, presenter Des Lynam continued with his line of questioning. 'Do you mind who you play for next season?' he quizzed the Everton forward sitting next to him.

'Well, I shall be playing for the team I want to be playing for next season,' Lineker responded with a smirk on his face, before shooting a glance towards Venables.

It was the clearest sign yet of the England striker's intentions for the season ahead. The 25-year-old had been invited on the BBC panel for the 1986 World Cup Final with the hope he might be crowned winner of the tournament's Golden Boot live on air. And after watching Argentina beat West Germany 3–2 without Diego Maradona getting on the scoresheet, it was a moment captured perfectly in front of the watching millions. What the Beeb weren't banking on was the most infamous moment in one of the decade's biggest transfer sagas playing out for the masses.

Murmurings of Barcelona's interest in signing Gary Lineker had first emerged before Mexico '86 had even begun. As his goals tally continued to rise throughout a prolific season for Everton, Lineker's name was continually mentioned as the answer to the Blaugrana's quest for a world-class marksman to lead the line for them.

It was no real surprise. With English clubs still banned from playing in European competition due to the Heysel Stadium tragedy, there was a talent drain of the First Division's top players, as they looked beyond their shores for a way to win the continent's most coveted silverware. Lineker was in no rush to jump ship again after less than 12 months at Everton, but as Barcelona's interest intensified following his goal-laden World Cup, the transfer suddenly become a probability.

While Venables was the man in the studio to field Lynam's questions, he hadn't always been the manager associated with being the architect of the move. 'El Tel', as he was called by the nation's tabloids, had been Barca head coach since 1984, but appeared to be on his way out towards the end of his second campaign in charge, with Everton's Kendall said to have signed a provisional agreement to take charge for the 1986/7 season. Perhaps it was no wonder Lineker was expected to follow him.

'There was talk at the time that Kendall was going to Barcelona,' recalls Everton fan Graham Ennis. 'And there was an idea – a mischievous one – or just a downright fabrication that Kendall agreed to sell Lineker to feather his own future nest. I don't think that's true; I think Everton just saw it as amazing business.'

Kendall's move never came to fruition as the rumours died down, whereas the noises about Lineker only appeared to get louder. It was reported that Barcelona first made contact about the striker's availability following the 2–0 victory over Watford in mid-April, although the Catalonians appeared to blow hot and cold as they considered their options.

Kendall had considered keeping the interest to himself so as not to distract Lineker from the end-of-season run-in but felt duty-bound to let him know that a club with such appeal was sniffing around. By the time of the World Cup, talk of the move had quietened down – or at least until after the tournament had started.

Popular football folklore suggests it was Lineker's hat-trick for England against Poland at Mexico '86 that reignited the Spanish side's interest, yet that's not quite how it happened. Barcelona had been in touch with Lineker's long-time agent Jon Holmes before the Three Lions' final group match, with a face-to-face meeting scheduled to discuss a prospective transfer shortly after the game. There's no doubt Lineker's treble in the meantime greased the gears, but a move was in the offing already.

With their man still out in the Americas, a summit meeting was held at the home of Lineker's fiancée, Michelle Cockayne, to decide on the best next move. The informal discussion between Holmes, Gary's brother Wayne, Michelle and her father Roger came to the conclusion that he should not take the offer to the forward until after England had exited the tournament. This decision made fertile ground for transfer gossip to spread.

'We knew what the newspapers every Sunday were telling us about what was going on,' says Lineker's Everton strike partner Graeme Sharp. 'We knew that if you're doing well, you're going to get interest from elsewhere – and when Barcelona come knocking, whether it's for Howard Kendall or Gary Lineker, they're going to have their heads turned by that. Gary was bright, he was one of those guys who wouldn't have a problem with moving abroad, he was going to enjoy the experience.'

Despite Lineker's 40 goals in the previous season, Everton were open to selling him. There was a school of thought that Kendall believed the Toffees weren't as good a side with Lineker in it, with an over-reliance on the striker's goals rather than a more even spread across the team as they'd previously had. But the reality was that Lineker had arrived on Merseyside from Leicester for £800,000, rising to £1 million if he was sold within his first two seasons there, and Barcelona were willing to pay £2.8 million only a year later.

Negotiations for the move began at The Connaught hotel in London. Among those in attendance were Barcelona president José Núñez, vice president Joan Gaspart and Venables; where Everton were represented by Kendall, Everton chairman Philip Carter and secretary Jim Greenwood. It now only seemed like a matter of time before the move would happen, with the BBC studio incident immediately after the World Cup Final only adding to the feeling of inevitability.

A combination of the way the move came about, Lineker's perceived attitude towards Everton, and the side's success either side of his time at Goodison Park means his legacy as a Blues player is mixed.

'There are a couple of things that always left a bit of a bad taste [among Everton fans],' says Ennis. 'There was the whole Kendall–Barcelona rumours … but nobody fought to keep Lineker. There was also a feeling that he went to Mexico as an Everton player and never really came home as one. He was suddenly a national hero and he wasn't ours any more.

'It was like he was just passing through to the extent where some people even say that he forgot he played for Everton, but I don't think that's true.'

Lineker's move to Barcelona was confirmed on 1 July and he arrived at the club alongside another British import, Mark Hughes, whose move to Spain from Manchester United had been announced several months earlier. The new-look attack had been designed by Venables to provide the extra element his side had lacked in the previous campaign.

The British press loved the idea of a homegrown strike force, led by an Englishman, showing the Spanish league how it's done. And while there was some disappointment that English football was losing one of its biggest stars to play in a different country, there was an appreciation that the lure of Barcelona and European football was too much to turn down. The only question that remained unanswered was whether Lineker could transfer his form in England to the more technical Spanish league.

Just as Lineker had experienced the agony of going close to achieving one of the greatest seasons in Everton's history but ultimately been left disappointed, so had Barcelona in the previous campaign. Los Culés had managed to win the League Cup in 1985/6, but it was a mere footnote to coming second to old rivals Real Madrid in La Liga, losing the Copa del Rey final to Real Zaragoza, and, most painfully, being defeated on penalties by Steaua Bucharest in a turgid European Cup final.

Barcelona's top goalscorer was German Bernd Schuster, but with only 12 goals in all competitions. It was clear that Lineker's introduction was expected to remedy the issue of needing a more regular source of goals. There was pressure on Lineker to succeed immediately in Catalonia, but that's how it should be when a 40-goal-a-season striker arrives to earn a reported $1.75 million across his six-year deal with the club.

'This is the start of a great challenge and one I'm looking forward to,' Lineker told the *Leicester Mercury*. 'I'm just happy to be with a club as important as Barcelona.'

If the move from Leicester to Merseyside the previous summer had taken some adjusting to, getting used to the Spanish culture would be something else entirely. As with the switch to Everton, Lineker would have now-wife Michelle to accompany him, with both committing to help each other learn Spanish as quickly as possible. They'd made the decision to move together, discussing the pros and cons before each independently writing down 'yes' or 'no' on pieces of paper and then revealing them to each other to see if they agreed to the transfer. When both showed 'yes' to each other, the move was on.

The young lovebirds had tied the knot at a ceremony at St Mary Magdalen Church in Knighton on the outskirts of Leicester only weeks earlier. Despite only 100 people being invited to the wedding, fans flocked to see the happy couple outside the church and while well-meaning, it stopped them from having their pictures taken outside. They would now have to settle into married life in a new country.

It was a different world to the one they were used to. Lineker's new regime was made up of two hours' training in the morning, before a trip to the beach and a late lunch. After arriving home at five, it was time for a siesta before dinner in the late evening. Gary, in particular, noted the difference in drinking culture. Whereas in England at the time, team drinking sessions were the norm and even encouraged by managers for team bonding, the roles were reversed at Barcelona. Alcohol at most non-social team lunches would have been a recipe for disaster back home, yet the Barca team would be greeted with wine on the tables – even on matchdays – because the club's doctors thought it was a better alternative to sugary soft drinks. There wasn't the same desire from the players to get drunk, to such an extent that some players would even sneak in soft drinks because they didn't want the wine.

'He took the move to Barcelona in his stride,' Venables said in his autobiography, *Born to Manage*. 'There are players who blend easily into a new life, coping with a new culture and being determined to learn the language and integrate. It means they can concentrate on their football without being constantly homesick and wondering where they can find a restaurant that serves a full English breakfast with tomato sauce.'

The Spanish playing style was different too. It wasn't as direct as the British game at the time, with a more patient build-up and a greater number of sideways passes. The first time Lineker chased back after a full-back, he was met with quizzical looks about what he was doing. Lineker's job was to score – after all, the local papers had dubbed him the 'Prince of Goals' upon his arrival at Barcelona.

To do that, he'd need to strike up a good understanding with new partner Hughes. The pair knew one another from having played against each other in England but had no personal relationship prior to meeting in Barcelona. Time together both on and off the pitch would be crucial to hitting it off quickly, and they both adjusted to their new surroundings and tried to make a good impression.

'We've been good friends and there is no question of us trying to outdo each other,' Hughes told the *Sunday Mirror* while on a pre-season tour in Mallorca in August. 'We work as a team for the team and there is no competition between us. If he were to score more goals, it wouldn't matter. It's good for the team and that's the important thing. We would still be friends. I don't feel any pressure to outdo him and I'm sure he feels the same way.'

Lineker's pre-season preparations were interrupted by a broken rib and sore tonsils, but he was fit and raring to go by the time the competitive action kicked off at home to Racing Santander at the end of August. And it took only two minutes for him to score his first Barca goal, before netting a second on 25 minutes.

It was the perfect introduction to the Camp Nou crowd and a great way for Lineker to familiarise himself with his new surroundings. A walk around the stadium and across the pitch upon joining the club couldn't match the sights and sounds of matchday in Barcelona. Los Culés were the city's pride and joy, with the Catalonians adoring their superstars with a special passion that didn't exist back home in England.

When tens of thousands of fans were packed into the stadium's steep stands, it provided a formidable atmosphere – a wall of people that appeared to roll endlessly up into the horizon from the open-roofed stands at either end of the ground.

Two goals on his debut had certainly endeared Lineker to the masses, as the Barca natives purred over their new purchase. The image was the ideal picture postcard to send home to show how he could do the business in Spain as well as England. Not too many defenders were replying with 'wish you were here'.

News back home of his brace was overshadowed by a club-versus-country dispute over Lineker's availability for England's friendly with Sweden 10 days after the match against Santander. Barcelona had a match with Cádiz scheduled on the same night as the game, with Venables telling Three Lions boss Bobby Robson that 'Barcelona comes first' and refusing to grant the striker permission to travel – leaving Robson to lament that he couldn't 'expect any favours from Barcelona'.

Venables' decision was vindicated when Lineker scored the first of the night against Cádiz with a close-range finish, while Hughes, who was unavailable to play for Wales that night due to suspension, scored the second. It was only the third league game of the season, but it sent the Blaugrana to the top of La Liga.

It would be the high point of the Lineker–Hughes partnership. The duo got on famously off the pitch, with Gary and Michelle spending lots of time with Hughes and his girlfriend, but they were struggling to make waves in Spain in the quite the way that had been hoped. Hughes' brash playing style jarred with the Spanish game, with his approach deemed to be overly physical, soon marking him out to referees and picking up a series of cautions.

Lineker, despite his early goalscoring form, was also taking some time to adapt initially – although due to Hughes' struggles, he escaped some of the media scrutiny the Welshman faced. Lineker's overall record of five goals in his first 11 games wasn't too bad, but some of the daily sports papers were far from complimentary, with *Marca* saying after an unconvincing 1–0 win over Sporting Lisbon in the UEFA Cup in October that 'Hughes and Lineker did not exist, not for one moment.'

Barcelona's issues weren't restricted to just their expensively assembled new strike force. They failed to register back-to-back league wins until the 15th time of asking and while they'd embark on long unbeaten runs, they were drawing far too many games, including an eye-watering six 0–0s in the regular season and two more in the end-of-season championship group.

Venables considered part of the problem to be a hangover from having narrowly missed out on winning the European Cup the previous season. A public show trial between Schuster and the club in a dispute about being kept away from the first team due to a high-profile spat with Venables and club president Josep Lluís Núñez on the back of the European Cup final was also an unnecessary distraction.

Lineker suffered more disappointment at the tail end of 1986, as he narrowly missed out on that year's Ballon d'Or, coming second to Dynamo Kiev's Igor Belanov after the Soviet striker took a huge share of the Eastern European vote. Lineker was also runner-up in the BBC Sports Personality of the Year, losing out to Formula One driver Nigel Mansell.

As ever, Lineker was keen to brush off any disappointment as quickly as possible and focus on what was coming next – although Venables remembered one occasion when the striker's upbeat attitude didn't go down as well as intended.

'There was one particularly poor match that ended with the team desperate and upset,' Venables recalled in his autobiography. 'By contrast, Gary bounced into the dressing room all smiles, looked around and shouted "Come on, cheer up – it's not the end of the world." I rounded on him [and said], "It might not be the end of the world for you Gary, but it is for them. Why don't you shut it?"'

More work was needed on Barcelona's training ground, which at that point was a tiny sand-covered ground sitting in the shadow of the Camp Nou rather than a large training complex that many other clubs had. Lineker would also regularly go for lunch with Venables as the two became close, with player and manager discussing football and movement as a striker among other subjects. They worked together to get the most out of Lineker in Barcelona's style and discussed areas where they felt improvements could be made.

Lineker's big night came at the end of January. Now nicknamed 'Gary Gol' by the Barcelona fans, the England man lived up to the moniker by scoring a hat-trick to give his side a priceless victory over Real Madrid in his first experience of El Clásico at Camp Nou.

The two great rivals epitomised the culture clash between the two cities: Real Madrid representing Spanish nationalism with its 'royal' moniker, while Barcelona being the team of the Catalonian independents. When the two collide, there have always been fireworks, with anyone leaving their mark in slaying the other eternally revered.

Going into the lion's den at the Bernabéu Stadium in October, Lineker had sampled what the Madridistas had to offer in a 1–1 draw, but it couldn't match the overflow of emotion he would feel at Camp Nou. The noise that night was on a different level to anything Lineker had experienced before, with the four banks of supporters around the ground creating a stentorian boom that must have travelled some way across the city.

The decibels were set to go even higher, thanks to Lineker. Within only five minutes, the Leicester lad had blown up El Clásico, bagging twice within the opening stages of the contest – sliding in to convert a low cross from within the six-yard box for his first, then knocking a rebound into an empty net after Lobo Carrasco's mazy run and shot opened up the Real defence. The home fans were going crazy, with their joyous cries reverberating beneath the covered stands alongside the pitch before escaping out into the Barcelona sky behind the goals.

Lineker's crowning moment came shortly after the break when an up and under from goalkeeper Andoni Zubizarreta set the lightning-quick striker racing through on goal. As he instinctively lifted the ball over Real's goalkeeper Paco Buyo and floated towards the goal, the realisation hit Lineker: he was about to score a hat-trick on the biggest stage Spanish football could offer.

There was no time for him to bask in his achievement, as Los Blancos staged a fightback in the last half an hour to leave Lineker worried his treble would be for nothing. But despite Real pulling two goals back, Barca held on to win 3–2 and open up a three-point lead at the top of the table. Cue pandemonium in the stands as the home supporters showed their appreciation for their new goalscoring hero.

The treble earned Lineker the title 'The Matador of Madrid' from his adoring public, but not the match ball, as is customary for hat-trick scorers in England. Instead, when he went to collect his prize at the end of the match, he was met by vacant looks from the referee before he realised the tradition wasn't the same in Spain.

'His finishing is clinical,' Venables said to the *Daily Mirror* afterwards. 'He gets in there where it matters, but I've become impressed by his whole game. His movement, everything about his game was very good.'

While a Clásico hat-trick was a great way to soften any criticism of Lineker, things still weren't quite flowing for Barca. They couldn't shake their inconsistency and endured a nightmare run from late February to mid-March when they won only once, including a 4–0 home defeat to Sporting de Gijón.

Their European hopes also came to an end during that time, with their UEFA Cup campaign ended in the quarter-finals by Dundee United – the Tangerines winning both legs of the contest, including a 2–1 victory at Camp Nou. Losing to the Scottish outfit was a damaging blow to Venables, who took a lot of criticism for the defeat, as did Lineker, who missed a simple chance in the first leg at Tannadice Park and put in a muted display in the return match.

The Dundee United defeat tolled the death knell for Hughes too. Debate about the Welshman's place in the team had rumbled on throughout the season and, by March, talk that Scottish forward Steve Archibald was going to win back his place as Barcelona's second overseas player from the Welshman was deafening.

Naturally, the press were keen to get Lineker's take on the situation. 'Any other questions?' Lineker retorted. 'I'm a friend of both Mark and Archie. I prefer what happens on the field to do the talking.'

Archibald did score two goals in three games after returning to the side but was unable to stop Real Madrid overturning Barcelona's lead to win La Liga by three points, leaving the Blaugrana trophyless by the end of the campaign. Lineker ended the season as the club's top scorer with 21 goals in all competitions and only finished behind Real's Mexican frontman Hugo Sánchez in the league goalscoring charts.

While it had been a disappointing season for the club, Lineker's record in front of goal was encouraging. He was now more settled in the city and after living for the first five months of his time in a box room at a hotel, he and Michelle now owned a four-bedroom luxury house complete with palm trees, swimming pool and tennis courts. They felt more at home and regularly dined out on the city's freshly caught fish.

Now with their own space, the sociable couple were regularly hosting visitors to the city, even welcoming BBC cameras to join them to film documentary *It's Lineker for Barcelona* about his first season on the continent.

'We call our place the Hotel Barcelona,' he told the *Daily Mirror* on 20 June. 'There is nearly always somebody staying with us. The beach is just 15 minutes away, so people jump at the chance of coming to stay with us.'

Hughes was moved out on loan to Bayern Munich during the summer, but Venables remained in charge as the 1987/8 season rolled round. Lineker had been linked with a move to Inter Milan, among other clubs, while several other managers were reportedly being lined up to replace him, but the status quo remained when the new season kicked off in August.

A victory over Las Palmas got things underway, but then an unthinkable run of three successive defeats led to the change that had been mooted for a while, with Venables being ousted and replaced by Luis Aragonés in the dugout. Bidding farewell to his fellow Englishman was a blow to Lineker, but he realised it was almost inevitable once the tide started to turn on him.

'Nothing surprises me about football in Spain,' Lineker told reporter Tony Smith as reported by the *Western Daily Press* and other newspapers in September. 'It is silly to judge anyone after so few games, but football is very intense here so I wasn't really surprised when the rumours started. I'm very disappointed the way it has gone, but for me personally, it's a matter of settling down and starting to score goals.

'The trouble is that when you're losing, the team confidence goes. You can only get that back by starting to win. The incredible pressure doesn't help though.'

A quirk of the managerial merry-go-round meant Aragonés' first game in charge was against one of Lineker's old bosses, former Everton manager Howard Kendall, who was now in charge of Athletic Bilbao. The appointment didn't spell an immediate end to the bad run of form, though, with the Basques running out 1–0 winners.

If Lineker had found his reunion with Kendall didn't go quite to plan, he found his former Everton teammates a lot more hospitable when he trained with them during the pause in the Spanish season for Christmas. Well, kind of.

'When he went to Barcelona and they had their winter break, he came back to Everton to train,' remembers teammate Paul Bracewell. 'But he was always last pick in the five-a-side matches, even though he was a Barcelona player. He was always last pick; the lads hadn't forgotten what he was like in training!'

Thankfully that wasn't replicated at the Camp Nou, as Aragonés continued to select Lineker as his main forward, although the Spaniard had failed to have a sustained impact on Barcelona's fortunes. Following the Bilbao defeat, they lost again – this time at home to Atletico Madrid – to make it five losses in a row, before Aragonés did finally get a bounce out of Barca with six wins from the next seven league games.

But as soon as December came around, the bad form returned. Four wins from 17 from mid-December to the end of March left them marooned mid-table and only a rally towards the season finale saw them recover to finish sixth in La Liga – but this still represented Barcelona's joint-worst campaign since the 1940s.

Their UEFA Cup excursions had been equally as patchy, as they failed to win a single game away from home – losing on trips to Portuguese side Belenenses and Albania's Flamurtari Vlorë but progressing on aggregate. Bayer Leverkusen finally put pay to Los Culés, winning 1–0 over two legs in the quarter-finals.

All that was left to salvage Barcelona's season was the Copa del Rey. Despite the inconsistency that had blighted their campaign, Barca had navigated a relatively comfortable path to the final, including a 4–1 aggregate victory over city rivals Espanyol in the last-16. Second-tier CD Castellón were dispatched in the quarter-finals to tee up a meeting with Osasuna, who were having a good season in La Liga.

A 0–0 draw at the El Sadar Stadium meant the Blaugrana would make it to the final if they could win at home, and they duly obliged – winning 3–0, with Lineker grabbing two of the goals. A brilliant first-half header that opened the scoring was described as a 'dream goal', with fans in the Camp Nou standing to salute and waving handkerchiefs in appreciation of its quality.

It was a double delight for the Englishman, who had been dropped along with Schuster for the goalless first leg, with Aragonés saying at the press conference, 'other players seemed more appropriate for this match'. The message was clear: Lineker was still Barcelona's top scorer and remained their greatest goalscoring threat.

So there was no question that he should start the final against Real Sociedad, who were managed by former Liverpool striker John Toshack. Lineker repaid that faith, playing a key role as Barcelona triumphed 1–0 – twice going close with headers under close attention from Real's defenders, before setting up the winner for captain José Alexanko. The victory had personal significance for Lineker because it was the first trophy win of his career.

Copa del Rey success also guaranteed the Catalonians a place in the next season's Cup Winners' Cup, maintaining their record of having appeared in every year of European competition. It wouldn't save Aragonés his job, though, with the Spaniard bidding farewell before the end of the season.

Barcelona legend Johan Cruyff was set to take over in the summer. The Dutchman had worked wonders at Ajax, leading a young team to Cup Winners' Cup glory in 1987 and two KNVB Cup successes. His team achieved it with a swagger that confirmed Cruyff's place as a football visionary, and Barcelona wanted to get in on the action.

Cruyff's arrival spelled a new chapter in Barcelona's history but would prove to be the closing of another for Lineker.

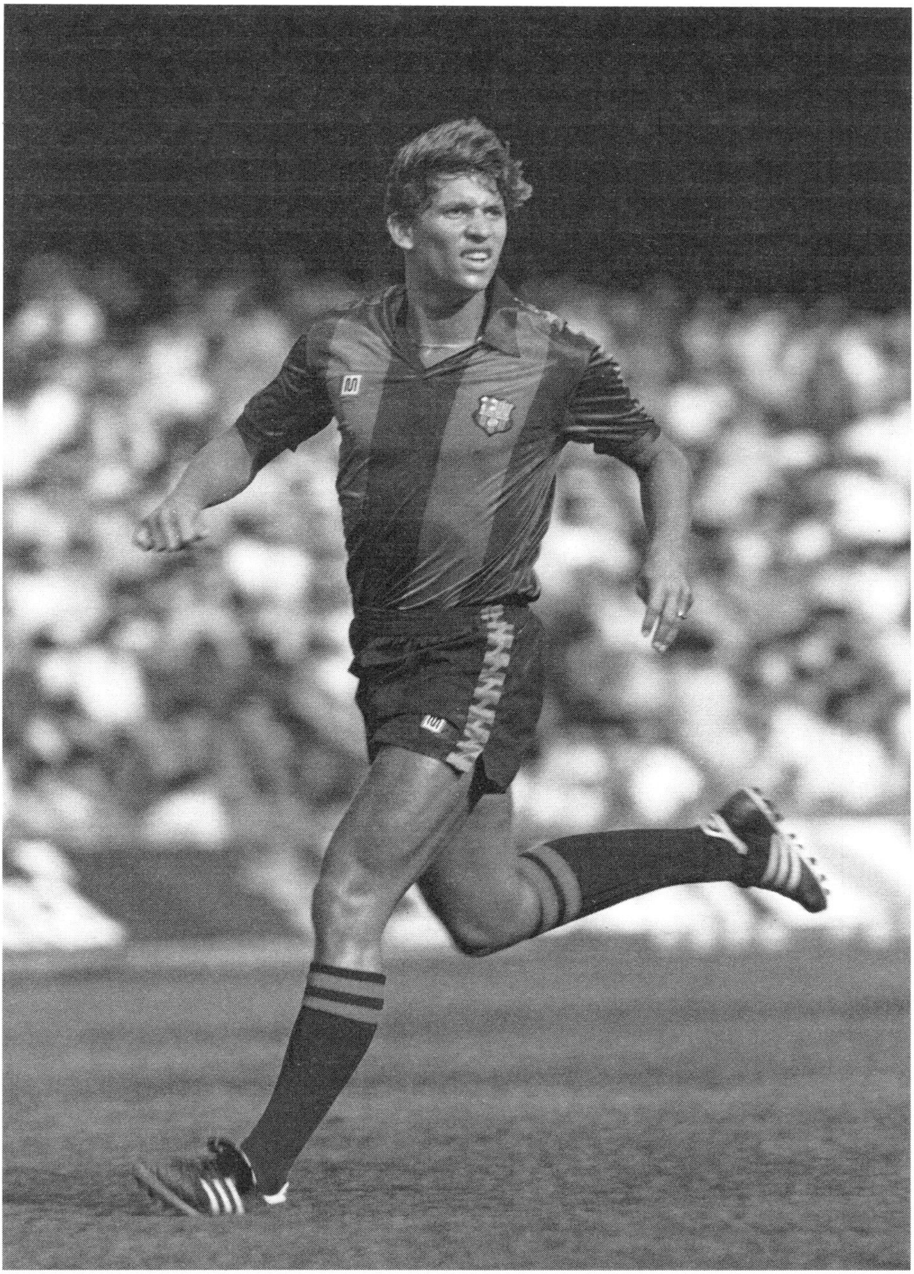

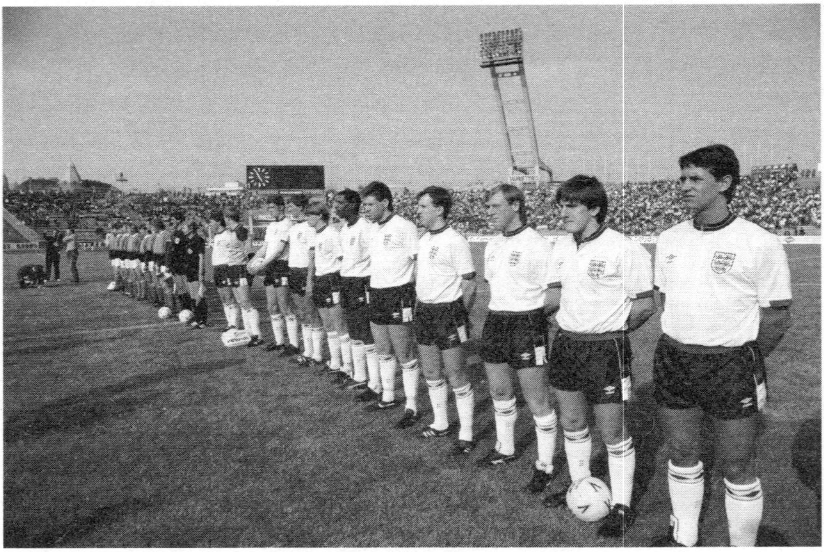

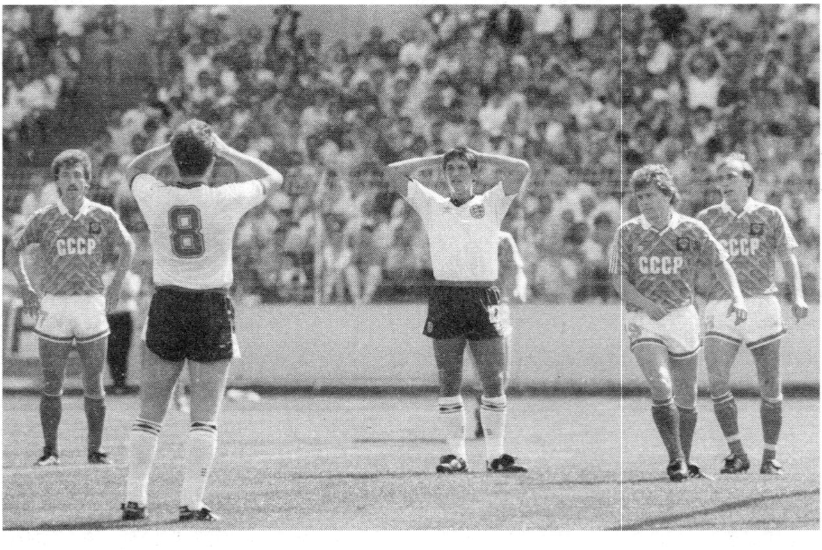
8
CCCP
CCCP
CCCP

10

EURO FAILURE

England, 1988

'... after the game I sat down and just couldn't get up.'

Gary Lineker hurled his copy of the newspaper article towards Bobby Robson. England's star striker was livid with his manager. It had been a testing couple of weeks for the Three Lions at Euro '88 and the tension boiled over as the team prepared to leave the tournament.

Robson sat on the bus, waiting for everyone else to join him as the group readied themselves to go home. The players and staff were sloping on board, glad to depart their nightmare in West Germany, but anticipating the backlash they'd get at home. They'd already got a flavour of what would greet them, having been faxed a selection of what was being said in the press – and Lineker had been irked by what he'd seen. So as the forward walked down the aisle in the centre of the coach, he paused next to where Robson was sitting and made his feelings known.

'You're out of order,' Lineker declared, gesturing at Robson's column in that day's paper before tossing it to the grey-haired 55-year-old. In it, the England boss had ripped into his side, claiming they'd let him down in the final match of a disastrous Euro '88 tournament – and Lineker felt like it was a personal attack.

'I think there were some players that just didn't want to play because we were already out at that stage,' Robson had written in the *Daily Mail* about the dead-rubber encounter against the Soviet Union that the Three Lions lost 3–1. The coach was clearly feeling the pressure and his words had been taken to suggest his charges could have given more in the final game to avoid further ignominy.

It was too much of a coincidence for Lineker not to believe Robson had been thinking of him. Only days earlier, England's star striker had asked his boss if he could not play in the match due to an illness that turned out to be hepatitis. But assuming the Barcelona man was simply trying to pull a fast one to get out of playing, Robson and his assistant Don Howe named Lineker in the starting XI anyway before giving him a rollicking at half time for his lethargic display. By the time Lineker was withdrawn in the second half, England were on their way to another defeat.

The loss to the Soviets left England with zero points from their three group matches and with tensions running high, Lineker confronted Robson about his comments on the team bus. It was the only occasion when the duo had a proper falling-out in the years they worked together for England and highlighted what a desperate time they'd had throughout the competition.

Although the manager refused to rise to the bait, it was a sorry end to a sorry tournament – England's worst ever finals performance. What made it worse was it was a result that nobody had seen coming before the action got underway.

'We're close to being a real force, we now have the genuine goalscorer we've always wanted,' said captain Bryan Robson confidently. 'If there isn't much between two teams, someone like Lineker can make all the difference. [Gerd] Müller did it for West Germany, [Michel] Platini for France, and if we had such a goalscorer in Spain [in 1982], we would have been very, very close to winning the World Cup.'

EURO FAILURE

It was the sort of endorsement that makes the hairs stand up on the back of English football fans' arms. England looked to have the final piece of the jigsaw they'd always craved as they entered the two-year cycle leading up the 1988 European Championships in West Germany. They'd always had creativity and grit among their ranks, but the breakthrough of Lineker as a world-class goal poacher was the secret ingredient they'd been missing.

The striker's six goals at the 1986 World Cup hadn't just sent his career into a new stratosphere, they had given his international teammates the boost they needed to truly believe they could do something special. With Lineker in the side, they always had a chance.

Although England were without Lineker for their first match post-Mexico due to the friendly with Sweden clashing with Barcelona's league match with Cádiz on the same night, his influence was still felt. The Three Lions drew a blank in Stockholm, going down 1–0 with a meek display that mustered very few goalscoring chances.

When Lineker was available, it was a different story. A month after the Sweden match, he was back for the Euros qualifier with Northern Ireland and scored twice in a 3–0 win, showing the predatory instincts that can tip a game in his team's favour. After a tight first half an hour, Lineker opened the scoring when a corner dropped to him on the edge of the six-yard box and he swept it home in a flash.

That's how it stayed until the final quarter of an hour when, with the Northern Irish tiring, Chris Waddle added a second before Lineker wrapped up the points with a left-footed chip from just inside the penalty area that dipped perfectly over goalkeeper Phil Hughes. The goal was particularly significant because Lineker had been played through by Peter Beardsley, his accomplice in Mexico, and was a further sign of their partnership blossoming.

'Provided we both keep doing it, there's no reason for our partnership to change,' Lineker told the BBC after the match. 'Perhaps it was a little unlikely when we were first put together because England traditionally put a big man up with a little man. But Peter's a terrific little player, we decided to give it a go in Russia during a pre-World Cup friendly and we struck up an understanding right away.'

Even better was still to come for Lineker a few months later, as England travelled to Madrid for a friendly with Spain in February. By now settled at Barcelona, playing against the country where he was plying his trade was always going to have big personal significance, but doing it in front of the Madridistas at the Bernabéu carried some extra needle.

The grey terraces that surrounded the pitch may only have been sparsely filled, but there was still no mistaking the hostile home support that blanketed the stadium. If any visiting side wouldn't have been welcomed to Madrid, Lineker was certainly *persona non grata* among the hosts. Only 18 days earlier, he'd netted a hat-trick for Barca against Real at Camp Nou; now he was in their own back yard to do more damage.

La Roja had lost only one of their last 17 matches before the contest, so it was set to be a stern test of England's credentials – even more so when Real Madrid striker Emiliano Butragueño put the hosts 1–0 up after 14 minutes. But this was Lineker's night and he wasn't about to be upstaged by a Los Blancos player.

The Barca striker levelled things up less than 10 minutes later, heading in to finish off a move between Robson, Beardsley and Glenn Hoddle, which ended with the latter chipping a hanging cross in for Lineker to score. As the striker wheeled away in celebration, shrill whistles from the Madrid crowd filled the airwaves to drown out the English cheers from the travelling fans.

The second followed only minutes later, as he pounced on a knockdown from a Viv Anderson shot to put England ahead. Lineker was enjoying the extra space he was being afforded by Spain manager Miguel Muñoz's decision to play two sweepers, Ricardo Gallego and Juan Carlos Arteche, instead of a more orthodox stopper, and was a constant thorn in their sides. La Liga's best defences had been struggling to keep the Barcelona hotshot quiet and now so was the Spanish national team's back-line.

After the break, it was time for the Lineker–Beardsley axis to come to the fore once more. First, the duo traded passes on the edge of the area to set the Liverpool man free and while his shot was initially saved, Lineker positioned himself underneath the rebound to nod in for his hat-trick. They then combined again on the edge of the area to play Lineker through to guide a first-time effort into the corner of the net for his fourth of the evening.

While Spain did get a consolation late on, there was no detracting from Lineker as the main talking point of the night. 'He was sick he didn't get six,' smirked Bobby Robson to the press pack after the final whistle. Lineker, on the other hand, humbly said he 'was just the man that finished off all the lovely, lovely football we played'.

There was love-in all round, although Lineker was keen to put one story to bed. Before the game, there had been a lot of talk in the press crying for Robson to pair the Barcelona striker up front with either Tottenham's Clive Allen or Mark Hateley instead of Beardsley, but Lineker wasn't having any of it.

'I don't pick the team, neither do his critics,' he was quoted as saying across a host of newspapers the next day. 'But I will say this: I love playing with Peter Beardsley, he is my ideal partner. He plays in the area that is not my strength, just outside the penalty box. I play where he isn't strongest, in the six-yard box.'

While Lineker had endeared himself to his England teammates, the same couldn't be said of his colleagues from Barcelona, in particular goalkeeper Andoni Zubizarreta, who had to pick the ball out of his net four times.

'Zubi was on the receiving end of one of Gary's more memorable goalscoring nights,' recalled Terry Venables in his autobiography, *Born to Manage*. 'Gary recalled that when he came face-to-face with Zubi in the dressing room area after the match, they looked at each other, Zubi shook his head and said "Fuckin' ell Gary." Zubi must have picked up some Anglo-Saxon phrases in the short few months since he had joined us.'

It was the first time in Lineker's senior career that he'd scored four times and the significance of achieving that feat in Spain wasn't lost on the English press as they dubbed the red-hot goalscorer the 'Matador of Madrid' and declared that Spain had been 'Linekered'. There were few, if any, more in-form strikers in world football.

The Spanish goal glut meant Lineker's record now stood at 12 goals in his last six internationals and that rate of scoring wasn't about to stop. He'd bagged five more before 1987 was out, including a hat-trick against Turkey – the second time he'd scored a treble against the Anatolians in two matches with them.

As calendars turned to 1988, optimism that England would have a good Euros was growing. A 2–2 draw in a friendly with a talented Netherlands side was further proof they could mix it with the continent's best, along the way to the Three Lions extending an impressive run to only one defeat in 16 matches as the tournament approached.

If England were going to triumph in West Germany, there was no time for them to play themselves into the competition after being drawn with the Republic of Ireland, the Netherlands and the Soviet Union in a formidable-looking group. Robson's men were capable but couldn't afford any slip-ups.

England's opening match pitted them against the Irish and, with injuries stacking up on the eve of the game, there were a few nerves among the camp. Of particular concern was the lack of senior centre-halves for a game that was sure to be bruising as they faced Ireland's no-nonsense, direct style of play. With Terry Butcher already ruled out of the tournament due to a broken leg, a hamstring injury for Mark Wright, and Dave Watson's thigh strain, Tony Adams was left as possibly the only fully fit defender in the squad. Lineker was also a doubt with a knee injury but was given the all-clear a couple of days before – a relief given how reliant England were on his and Bryan Robson's goals, with 47 between them.

It didn't do them much good, though, as the Republic of Ireland ran out 1–0 winners. The decisive goal came within six minutes, Wright and Gary Stevens colliding on the edge of the box to allow Tony Galvin to put a cross into the centre where Kenny Samson miskicked his clearance. England were at odds at the back, with John Aldridge's knock-down falling for Ray Houghton to direct a header into the net.

With Ireland now having something to defend, they sat in and challenged the favourites to break them down. And it wasn't until past the half-hour mark that they mustered a shot on target. In fact, it wasn't until Glenn Hoddle's introduction after an hour that England hit their stride, but when they did, they were dominant.

The best chances fell to Lineker, but he found goalkeeper Packie Bonner in inspired form. The Irish shot-stopper had sprinkled holy soil on his boots before the match and it certainly told, as he pulled off save after save to keep the lead intact – saving a left-footed Lineker strike with his legs early in the second half, then denying him from close range at the near post with minutes remaining.

On paper at least, Ireland were the weakest side in the group and with two heavyweights left to play, England were now on the back foot almost immediately.

'It's not irretrievable,' Robson told the media afterwards. 'We were in a similar position [at the '86 World Cup] two years ago when we lost our first match against Portugal. We didn't expect that and we didn't expect to lose to Eire. Now we know we possibly have to get four points from the last two games if we are to remain in the championships.'

Lineker hadn't felt at his sharpest during the Ireland game and was still feeling jaded when the clash with the Netherlands came around a few days later, but the striker brushed it off as a bug. The Dutch were brimming with talent and all of the talk before the match was how England would have to keep Milan forward Ruud Gullit quiet if they were to have any chance of success. But they were far from a one-man team, with the likes of Ronald Koeman and Frank Rijkaard providing smooth assurance all over the pitch.

They had also suffered a surprise defeat in their opening match, losing 1–0 to the Soviet Union, so were in a similarly precarious position to England. It was a clash worthy of the latter stages of a tournament and was a de facto knockout in itself because the loser would be eliminated.

The two sides had played out a 2–2 draw in a friendly at Wembley a few months earlier and Lineker felt that would give him and his teammates the edge when it really mattered.

'We learned more from them than they learned from us at Wembley,' Lineker said in an article published in the *Shields Daily Gazette*. 'They played really well but we were below par.

We had Peter Beardsley and Dave Watson injured, and didn't play as well as we know we can. I'm sure we can improve on that performance.'

After seven minutes, England nearly had their breakthrough when a superbly weighted pass from Bryan Robson put Koeman on the turn, with the defender heading the ball beyond his own goalkeeper and leaving Lineker with an unguarded net to aim for. But by the time he'd reached the ball, the angle was tight and his effort bounced back off the post and was cleared to safety.

The same post was rattling again later in the half when Hoddle saw his free-kick smash back off the upright, but England were later left to rue those fine margins when Marco van Basten struck right on half time – the forward twisting and turning past Adams before planting a left-footed shot into the net.

The Three Lions were level eight minutes after the break, though. Lineker played a one-two on the edge of the box with Robson, setting the England captain through to poke the ball over goalkeeper Hans van Breukelen and into the net.

As the game wore on, the Netherlands took charge and Van Basten struck twice in four minutes to take the game away from England. The first arrowed past Peter Shilton from just inside the area, whereas the second was a close-range volley after Wim Kieft flicked on a corner.

While one striker celebrated a hat-trick at one end, it was a different story for England's top marksman after the final whistle had blown.

'In the second game against the Netherlands, I felt lethargic again, then after the game I sat down and just couldn't get up,' Lineker told *FourFourTwo* several years later.

Lineker wasn't the only one. England's second defeat consigned them to an early exit from the tournament and no matter how they got on against the Soviet Union a few days later, they'd be returning home early.

Manager Bobby Robson was adamant his side wouldn't be checking out early and wanted to leave West Germany with a victory under their belts. Lineker was open about his own struggles to be part of that and says he 'could barely lift' his legs in the training session a day before the game.

'I'm feeling a bit fluey,' Lineker told reporters. 'It could just be tiredness or exhaustion because it's been very hot out here and it's come at the end of a very long season.'

He let Robson know, but his request to sit out the game fell on deaf ears. Lineker would start, and remained on the pitch for 69 minutes, despite being able to make very little impact on proceedings. The pressure was mounting on the England boss and in a desperate attempt to get a reaction from his players, he laid into them – giving Lineker in particular a piece of his mind at what he felt was a performance with more to give.

'I know [England assistant] Don Howe and Bobby Robson thought I was just trying to get out of the game – they all but said as much,' Lineker said in the *FourFourTwo* interview. 'I played against the Soviet Union and came off after about an hour. I'd never played in a game where I was so certain I shouldn't be on the pitch. I was in a dreadful state.'

Lineker's clash with Robson unfolded on the team bus the next day. The striker had been struggling to get himself out of bed, lacked the energy to do even the simplest of tasks and had lost more than a stone of weight – privately, at a time when misinformation was rife about the illness, Lineker even feared he'd contracted AIDs. The final straw was seeing Robson question his commitment to England in the newspapers.

Any animosity that developed on the back of the Three Lions' disastrous Euros soon dissipated as Lineker's condition worsened to such a point that he was admitted to hospital upon his return to England. He'd remain there for the next two weeks after being diagnosed with hepatitis. A few days later, Robson visited his stricken forward to apologise for doubting that there was anything wrong with him.

It was the end to a sorry summer for England. But only the start of the issues for Lineker.

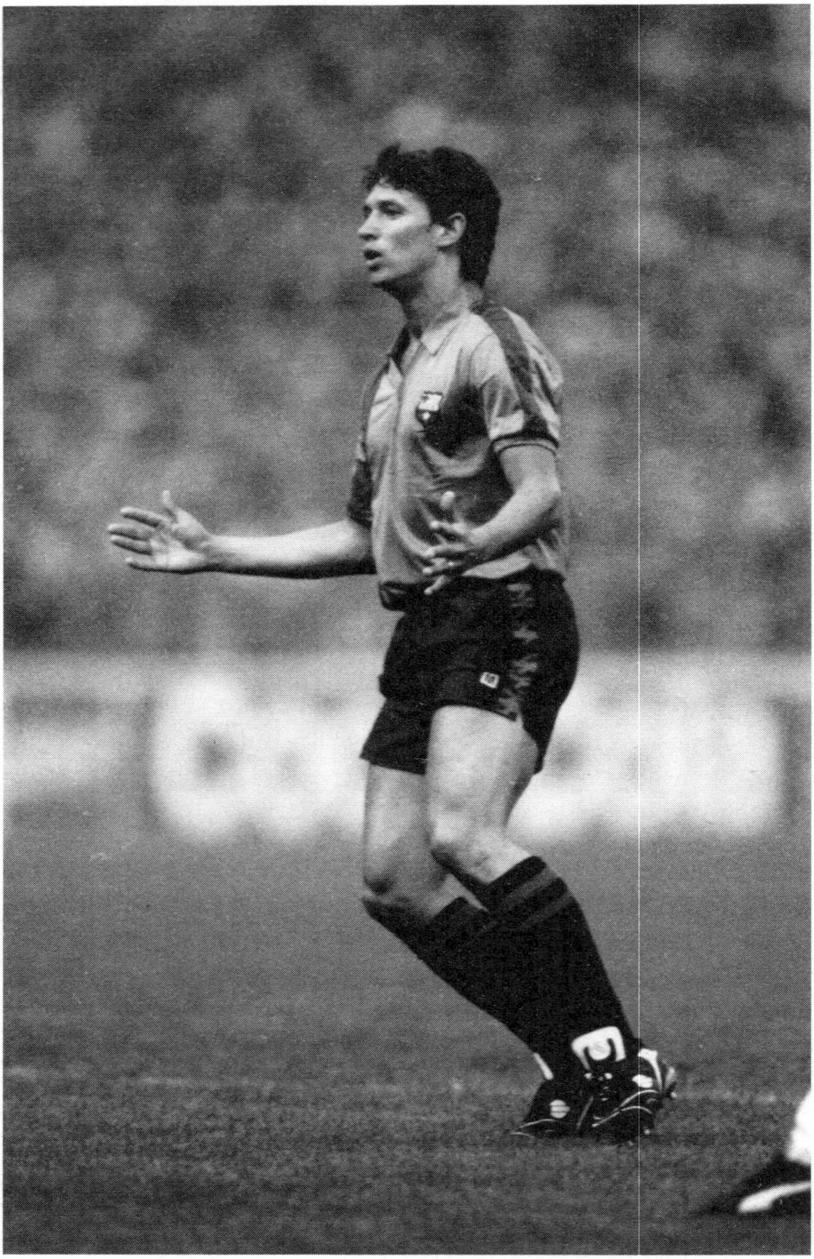

11

CATALONIAN CULL

Barcelona, 1988–1989

*'Cruyff has made it plain he will be looking for
new players and Gary's place could be under threat.'*

Johan Cruyff pointed at the formation he'd just drawn on the blackboard, much to the bemusement of his squad. The Dutchman had sketched out his vision of how Barcelona would play now he was in charge, but there was nothing too familiar about it.

Turning to face his new charges, they stared back. Taking in the diagram that lay in front of them, they sat expectantly, waiting for Cruyff to explain, shooting micro-glances around the room to check on each other's reaction. They'd expected innovation, a gradual morphing into a brave ideology devised by one of the founding brains behind the Netherlands' Total Football revolution. But the tactical plan that lay in front of them was even bolder than they'd initially imagined.

The 3–4–3 he'd illustrated was at odds with how most teams lined up at the time, defensive security being sacrificed for a more attack-minded team that overloaded the midfield. Cruyff had been brought in to shake things up at Camp Nou and based on his opening gambit, he wasn't wasting any time in doing it.

Huddled on pews in close proximity to each other, looking up at Cruyff's ideas, some of the players later admitted to wondering where or how they fitted into Barcelona's new world order. Or at least they recognised that the anticipated change they'd feel compared to the previous season's malaise would be even more significant than they'd imagined.

Despite winning the Copa del Rey, 1987/8 had been a disaster by Barca's standards. A joint-lowest league finish for more than four decades had only been achieved thanks to a late run of one defeat in eight matches, although it wouldn't be allowed to paper over the cracks. Nobody was safe in the era Cruyff had in his mind.

Not only would 'The Flying Dutchman' have to remould an underperforming squad to play in his more technically demanding style of play, but he'd have to get hold of the dressing room mutiny that emerged during the previous season. This wasn't a case of an underperforming team in conflict with each other, more a club being torn apart from top to bottom.

'President Josep Lluís Núñez has deceived us as people and humiliated us as professionals,' said skipper Alexanko in a press conference arranged by the players. 'In conclusion, although this request is usually the preserve of the club's members, the squad suggest the immediate resignation of the president.'

The revolt had been triggered by an investigation called into each player's contract by the Spanish treasury, due to a tax discrepancy within their agreements. Núñez was of the belief that any deficit should be settled by the players, which naturally caused huge discord among the squad. The Hesperia Mutiny had undoubtedly changed the face of Barcelona at the time and Cruyff had to pick through the wreckage.

What followed was a mass clear-out, with 12 players being shown the exit by the end of June and £10 million spent to replace them. Among the departures had been most of Los Culés's foreign quota, with Bernd Schuster defecting to Real Madrid, Scottish forward Steve Archibald released, and Mark Hughes being sold back to Manchester United after a season out on loan at Bayern Munich.

Only one of the overseas players remained: Gary Lineker. But while that might have appeared to be a big tick in the box for the England star, the reality was decidedly different.

'There is a feeling in Barcelona that Lineker may not figure in the new coach's plans next season,' a club source was quoted as saying in the *Liverpool Daily Post* on 25 June. 'Johan Cruyff has made it plain he will be looking for new players and Gary's place could be under threat.'

Naturally, the rumour mill had been churning all summer. Only a few months earlier, Barcelona had rejected interest in Lineker from Italian giants Inter, but now it seemed that if anyone was willing to pay the price tag – said to be around £3.5 million – slapped on his head, then he was available to a good home. A number of clubs were rumoured to be taking a look, although a return to England was ruled out early on and swap deals seemed a more likely fix because of how much a standalone transfer fee would cost.

One story doing the rounds in the close season was of a deal that would see Lineker swap places with his England teammate Glenn Hoddle at Monaco. Even if the move wasn't a goer, an article published in the *Leicester Mercury* about the possible transfer reportedly showed the scale of the task Lineker had on his hands to convince Cruyff he could fit into his new-fangled system.

'I have signed two Spanish strikers, [José Mari] Bakero and [Julio] Salinas,' the newspaper reported Cruyff to have said. 'And I don't think the Spanish game really suits Gary Lineker. I have spoken to him about his deal and he's not against it. He understands he could be on the bench next season in Barcelona.'

At Barcelona, the Englishman's game had developed to be more than simply a lightning dash of opportunism and clinical finish as some suggested. In his two seasons in Spain, Lineker had improved his hold-up play and had scored 41 times against stingier defences than he'd faced in England, learning how to get the better of teams that chose to sit back and absorb pressure, particularly at Camp Nou.

Yet it was still felt that Lineker's new manager had eyes for somebody else. Another name that was regularly touted for a possible swap for the former Leicester man was Marco van Basten, whom Cruyff had managed at Ajax. Not only was the Dutchman's compatriot flavour of the month after starring for the Netherlands as they won Euro '88, but it was an open secret the Blaugrana boss favoured a forward with the touch and vision of Van Basten rather than the pace of Lineker.

Cruyff's admiration for Van Basten was well-known, but to have any hope of pulling off the move, he'd need Lineker's stock to remain at its peak too. Any inference that Lineker was surplus to requirements wouldn't do.

'There has been a lot of speculation about Lineker and Van Basten, perhaps too much,' Cruyff told the *Daily Mirror*. 'I have no plans or intention of letting Gary leave Barcelona, although obviously I cannot say what would be the decision if we got a big bid from Italy. It would not be my decision. Why should we not want to keep him at Barcelona?'

Any hopes Lineker had of making good on that praise would have to wait, though. The bout of hepatitis A that had impacted him so badly at Euro '88 wasn't going to be shaken off easily and meant his entire pre-season would be wiped out. What could have been priceless time familiarising himself with Cruyff's vision and ingratiating himself to the new manager was lost while he recovered.

While Barcelona sent club doctors over to London to visit Lineker in hospital and check on his condition, there were stories that their striker hadn't received any direct contact from Cruyff. It wasn't the start the relationship needed, with any hopes of it sparking having to wait until Lineker was back in Spain on the training ground.

'At the moment I'm really bored,' Lineker told the *Leicester Mercury* upon an appearance at the opening of a new drugs advice centre in Leicester on 8 July. 'All I can do is watch TV and read, and it's very frustrating. I can't even play cricket; I'm just reduced to watching it. Training is out as well. I just haven't got the energy to do anything.

'I won't be able to do anything until the blood tests prove I've got rid of the virus. I could be laid up for six weeks or more, which is obviously going to put my training programme back.'

Lineker had lost a stone in weight and, paired with the fatigue, still had the yellow hue hepatitis sufferers carry for a while after leaving hospital. The season would start without him being among Cruyff's first-team squad, but at least he was still on Barcelona's books, unlike so many of his former teammates.

When Lineker was finally given the all-clear to return, he was sent off for a 10-day intensive training camp in the Pyrenees before being integrated into the group. By this time, Barca had made a good start to the new campaign, taking seven points from a possible nine in La Liga and winning the first leg of the Cup Winners' Cup first round tie away at Iceland's Fram.

So it was no surprise that Lineker's comeback was from the bench, coming on at half time in a 1–1 draw with Osasuna, before doing the same against Real Madrid in the second leg of the Supercopa de España. A start then followed in a 4–0 league triumph over Sporting de Gijón and although Lineker completed the full 90 minutes, Cruyff had played him on the right wing of his forward three – a position he hadn't been deployed in since his early days with Leicester.

The forward was out on the right again a few days later as he scored his first goal of the season in the second leg of a routine win over Fram before being withdrawn at half time. Lineker was then not in the squad for the next game against Real Sociedad and was an unused substitute the week after against Real Betis. It would be a pattern he would have to get used to.

What was clear was that if Lineker was to force himself into Cruyff's plans on a more regular basis, his best bet appeared to be out wide rather than through the middle. Even if it wasn't getting the best out of him.

A report carried by several of England's national newspapers at the end of October seemed to make Lineker's position clear. After being taken off during the 3–2 defeat to Real Madrid, comments attributed to Cruyff said the striker 'plays too egotistically' to fit in with his playing style and that 'he is not my first choice any more'. While the quotes were later found to be incorrect and retracted by the media outlets that ran them, the fact they were so widely accepted as true gave the impression of where Lineker's situation was thought to be.

'Lineker is a good player and I have total confidence in him,' Cruyff said in a statement responding to the false reports of his criticism in England. 'I am certain he will soon be back among the goals. He is still fighting off the effects of hepatitis, that's why I have rested him occasionally – like earlier this month when he was faced with three games in eight days.

'This is just being prudent and following normal medical advice. He had a very good game in a recent league match and was not as sharp in the next. That's to be expected in the aftermath of such an illness. Of course he figures in my plans. A goal or two will boost his confidence.'

A first league goal of the season away at Oviedo in mid-November appeared to do just that as he followed that up with a brace at home to Real Murcia a week later. But for all of Cruyff's insistence that he was behind Lineker, stories about him being touted about for a move away from Catalonia wouldn't dissipate. Every week, it seemed as though a new club was being mentioned as a possible destination.

Most damaging to the relationship was the revelation from Manchester United manager Alex Ferguson that Cruyff had been doing the leg work himself in an attempt to offload the striker. 'Cruyff phoned me and I'm considering all aspects of the situation,' the Scotsman said. 'I will be getting back to Barcelona.'

If Lineker felt like he was short of friends in Cruyff's camp, he certainly wasn't elsewhere. England manager Bobby Robson wasn't shy about telling the world the Dutchman was playing the striker out of position by putting him wide on the right, while the Barcelona fans still showed their appreciation for Gary Gol from the stands.

Cruyff simply batted off the attention Lineker's situation was attracting. After all, while his decisions weren't popular with those who had the England international's best interests at heart, Barcelona were doing well under their new manager, winning regularly and flying high towards the top of the league. It was in its infancy, but Cruyff's vision was already starting to take shape.

'Johan's idea about football was that he transformed the authentic centre-forward into a Total Football centre-forward, which Johan had been himself with the Dutch team at the 1974 World Cup,' says Jaap de Groot, Cruyff's ghost-writer and long-term friend.

'Gary was a specialist. You could see it later with the use of Salinas, who was not as good as Gary but a similar player, that he was used as a pinch hitter. Johan thought the centre-forward should be multi-functional like him and that's why he eventually used Michael Laudrup and players like that there as the team developed.

'Johan saw Gary as a specialist and more of a pinch hitter than part of the dream team he had in his mind, especially when he wanted more multi-functional players in the attacking positions. He wasn't the centre-forward in the gameplan he had and you can see that later on when the dream team came together as a modern version of Total Football and how the attackers all moved together.'

When Lineker did get a rare chance to play through the middle, he usually performed. But it seemed like a thankless task to change Cruyff's mind, with the tactician freely moving Lineker across the frontline as he saw fit – starting him as the focal point of the attack one week, before moving him to right the week after and even to the left on a couple of occasions.

The 28-year-old was determined to make it work. He kept his head down and, like a hopeful lover trying to win his unreceptive sweetheart's approval, stoically continued with his mission to change Cruyff's mind. The party line was consistent: Lineker was happy in Barcelona and wanted to win back his place as the team's main striker as long as he wasn't asked to leave.

'To stay here at Barcelona, I've got to win the confidence of the manager. He is the most important figure at any club,' Lineker said to the *Daily Mirror* on 29 November. 'If he stakes his confidence in me, it will make a big difference. But that confidence must be stressed.

'I've reached the stage where I can only live one day at a time here. I will only do what I consider best for myself and if that has to be elsewhere, then so be it. As for returning to England, the whole thing hinges on who can afford me and if Barcelona decide to let me go. Equally, I'm more than happy to stay at Barcelona. We're challenging for the championship and I'd love to be part of it.'

Cruyff's response? To question Lineker's goalscoring record. Treat 'em mean, keep 'em keen.

'Gary Lineker was top goalscorer in the 1986 World Cup – that was three years ago and I was worried he wasn't doing the job for us,' said Cruyff in a press conference after Lineker had shown a glimpse of goalscoring form. 'He has scored three goals in the last two games and if he can carry on scoring goals for us, I'll be a lot happier.'

With hindsight, Lineker admits he was wise to Cruyff's antics. In an interview with *FourFourTwo* in 2015, the former England striker revealed he wasn't so naive as to think Cruyff was for turning, but refused to take the bait. It was a great example of Lineker's temperament that through frustration and goading, he remained calm and never put a foot out of line when it would have been easy to.

'It was quite clear from an early stage that Cruyff wanted his own foreign players,' Lineker told *FourFourTwo*. 'That's understandable, but instead of coming over to me and saying, "I want my own people, maybe we can get you a move that works for everyone," he messed me about. While he clearly should have played me up front because his system was made for a striker like me, he stuck me out on the right wing.

'He did it to piss me off in the hope I'd go squealing to the press, but I wasn't that daft. I understood what he was doing. I knew his game, so I did the professional thing and got on with it.'

De Groot disagrees that Cruyff was deliberately disrespecting Lineker by playing him on the wing, though. While the Dutch journalist concedes things didn't perhaps play out in the best possible way between the two parties, he has a strong belief that putting the forward out wide was nothing more than a different philosophy at play.

'The only things you can debate are the human aspects, but that's football – you sometimes have to take severe decisions and that's what happened with Gary,' explains De Groot. 'Johan always wanted to have fast wingers, and in Spanish football, they had two tough defenders and there was more space on the wing, so Gary could be more effective on the wing with his speed because there was more space out there.

'With the wing situation, it proves that Johan was thinking about how he would have Gary play and was looking for a role for Gary. It was not like he dropped him as a footballer, there was a kind of respect for his quality, his authority and he really tried to say, "OK, if it doesn't work in the centre-forward position, give it a try on the wing" to get him on the team. That's a way to look at it – that he was trying to get the best out of Gary in relation to the team.'

The pattern continued as the season progressed. Lineker was in and out of the team, predominantly playing wide on the right, and saw his goalscoring ratio plummet. He'd pop up with the odd goal here or there, but the number and quality of goalscoring opportunities he was getting had dipped to such a point that he was struggling to get to double figures for goals for the first time since he was a fresh-faced 20-year-old at Leicester.

That didn't mean he wasn't playing a role in Barcelona's quest for glory, and he weighed in with the only goal of a tense two-legged Cup Winners' Cup quarter-final with Danish side Aarhus. This highlighted the value a world-class finisher could still have in the tightest of games and Lineker was keen to make that point post-match.

'I won't score as many goals in this system I'm asked to play with Barcelona,' Lineker said to the *Daily Mirror*. 'I'm not given the freedom of the penalty box to go where I want to go. It is my strength to be in the right place at the right time to score. But I have to run to the near post every time to take the two marking defenders with me. It's a different system to the one I'm used to and I'm playing to different instructions.'

If there were signs of Lineker's frustrations after the Aarhus game, it was about to bubble over even more. Despite making several important contributions as winter turned to spring, he found himself on the bench for the crucial top-of-the-table clash with Real Madrid at Camp Nou after being dropped in favour of new signing Romerito, who had only landed in Spain from Paraguay days earlier.

Lineker dutifully sat on the bench, but as the game yawned on at 0–0, the need to make an attacking change to break the deadlock became apparent. The Barcelona fans sensed it too and they gradually grew louder in their chants for Lineker to come on, but Cruyff remained unmoved. Instead, when he decided to take off forward Txiki Begiristain, he replaced him with midfielder Amor.

Towards the end of the match, with the crowd baying for Lineker to be introduced and Cruyff seemingly ignoring their cries, the benched striker finally snapped, shouting, 'You don't have the balls to bring me on now' in his manager's direction. Cruyff didn't move an inch.

'I was at Johan's house that night and even his wife said to him, "Hey, what are you doing? Gary is a star and you insulted him by doing this,"' recalls de Groot. 'Johan just kept quiet; I remember that. He just said, "It was not a game to do it."

'But he didn't say anything to his wife because she reacted like a human. Maybe there was something in it that everybody was shouting for Gary and the [Cruyff's] ego came up a bit, but I can't prove that because he never responded to the criticism after that game, he just kept his mouth shut.'

Lineker called the Real Madrid snub 'humiliating and embarrassing', especially as England manager Bobby Robson had travelled over to Spain to watch his star play, only to see him sit on the bench. It felt like a watershed moment for the Three Lions striker, who had finally lost his patience. The fall-out was likely to be significant, but Lineker was back to his self-deprecating best by the time the next week rolled around.

'It was very funny because I met Gary the Monday after the Madrid game and I got a lovely quote from him,' de Groot says.

'He had a small car, I think it was a Seat, and after training we walked to his car because I had an interview with him. He said "OK, we do the interview at the Princess Sofia hotel" and as we walked in I saw on Gary's front seat was a bunch of roses. I said, "Gary, look what Johan Cruyff left you," and he said, "Yeah, Johan Cruyff is always like that on Monday mornings."'

Lineker's sense of humour may still have been intact, but the Real Madrid incident appeared to be the final straw. It didn't take long for the British newspapers to be full of rumours that a move was now imminent, with several reports claiming that former manager Terry Venables visited Barcelona to sound out a move to his current team, Tottenham.

If Venables was keen, he'd have to join the queue of admirers. As well as Spurs, there was interest from several other English clubs and the likes of Genoa, Fiorentina, PSV and Bayern Munich on the continent. It was reported that Lineker favoured staying in mainland Europe, although publicly he stuck to the line he'd taken all season – he wanted to stay at Barcelona. And so the merry-go-round continued to turn.

The coveted star did his reputation no harm by scoring in both legs as Blaugrana beat CSKA Sofia 6–3 on aggregate in the Cup Winners' Cup semi-final, and he was starting from the right wing again for the final with Sampdoria a few weeks later.

Positioned out on the flank, Lineker played a key role against I Blucerchiati, terrorising left full-back Fausto Pari with his pace. He'd already beaten Pari on a couple of occasions before spinning away in the fourth minute to deliver a high cross towards the back post that Roberto headed back towards goal for Salinas to convert from close range. It was a crucial moment, as Sampdoria were forced to pile forward in the hunt for an equaliser, leaving space for substitute Luis López Rekarte to add a second late on. It was Lineker's second major trophy for Barcelona and widely expected to be his last.

He continued to play regularly from the wing for the rest of the season but didn't score in the famous blue and red strip again as Barca came in five points behind champions Real Madrid to finish second in La Liga. Lineker was playing a role, but not having the goalscoring impact that had made him one of the most-feared marksmen in the game before he moved to Camp Nou.

Something had to give, so it was no surprise the impasse was finally broken in the final weeks of the season. As May was drawing to a close, it was reported that Cruyff had officially submitted a list of players to Barcelona's hierarchy that he wanted to let go in the summer.

'I'm very surprised to hear this news – no one has told me officially what has happened,' Lineker told his old friends at the *Leicester Mercury*.

Barcelona were reportedly reluctant to confirm the news for fear of driving the price down by letting interested sides know Lineker was available, with the striker having a meeting with deputy chairman Joan Gaspart to corroborate the stories after returning from playing for England against Denmark.

It was the news everyone expected, so much so that Lineker received a call from Nottingham Forest boss Brian Clough while on England duty asking if he'd be interested in moving to the City Ground for the following season. Lineker didn't take long to turn down the offer, telling Clough that he couldn't betray his Leicester roots to play for their East Midlands rivals and that he wanted to play for a 'big club', much to the Forest manager's chagrin.

Barcelona put a price of more than £2 million on Lineker's head, to which the striker quipped, 'If I were a club chairman, I wouldn't pay that much for Gary Lineker.' But apparently there were plenty who would.

Lineker and his agent Jon Holmes soon set about having discussions with potential suitors, sparking what almost became an auction as they hosted representatives from Fiorentina, Genoa and Monaco at a Barcelona hotel. Fiorentina had originally seemed to be in the box seat, although the recent departures of manager Sven-Göran Eriksson and forward Roberto Baggio put Lineker off.

Despite the interest, the talk of a move to Tottenham wouldn't go away and as June wore on, the stories grew louder. Venables eventually brokered a deal with his old club, but not before

Manchester United nearly stole in with an 11th-hour bid after it seemed Spurs couldn't find the money needed to complete the deal. The saga had rumbled on for more than a year, but as Lineker was unveiled at White Hart Lane, his time in Barcelona had finally come to an end – leaving behind a host of adoring fans, who held up 'Gary don't go' banners during his final outings for the club.

'Everybody assumed that I would stay abroad and I thought the time was right to come back to England, so I got in touch with Spurs,' Lineker said to the press upon the deal being confirmed. 'Basically, I decided that if I came back [to England], I wanted to come back to Spurs. I wanted to come back to a big club and Tottenham are one of those.'

As ever, Cruyff's final message damned Lineker with faint praise as he said, 'I'm convinced he will triumph at his new club because English football is made for him,' no doubt in reference to his belief that the striker wasn't suited to the Spanish game.

The season had ended in as barbed a fashion as it had begun.

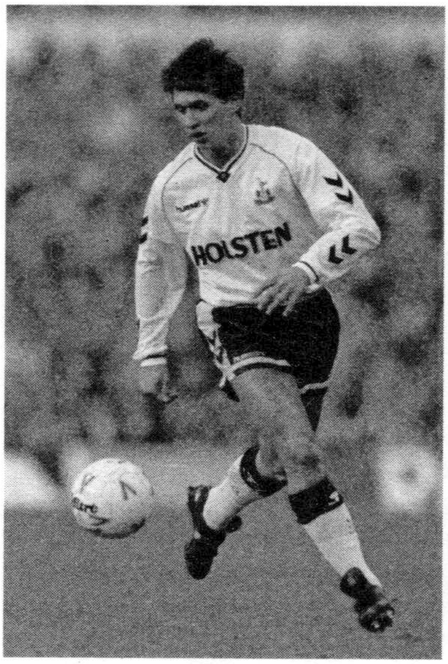
HOLSTEN

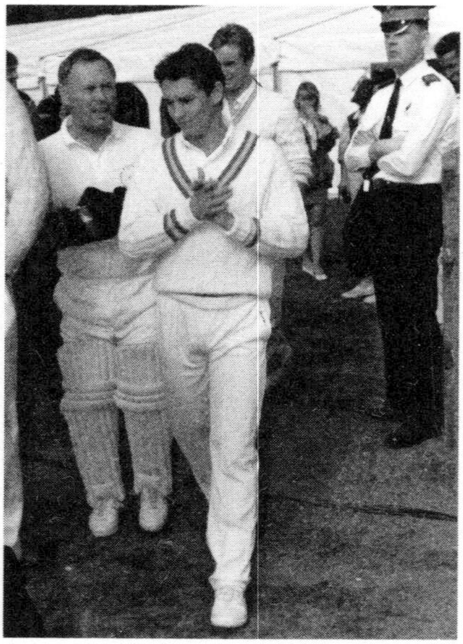

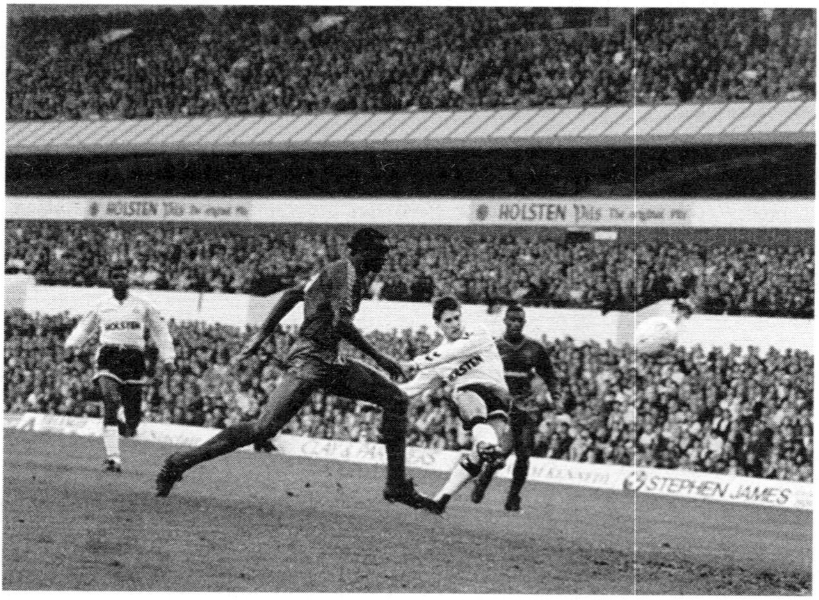
HOLSTEN
HOLSTEN
STEPHEN JAMES

12

A RETURN HOME

Tottenham, 1989–1990

'If you know where to move, you can score 20 goals a season easily in this division, it's a piece of cake.'

Joining Spurs was the perfect move for Gary Lineker. Not only would he be returning to England, but he'd be getting a reunion with his former Barcelona manager Terry Venables at White Hart Lane and joining up with international teammate Chris Waddle, with whom he'd cultivated a deadly relationship for the Three Lions. The potential was huge.

After the tumultuous past 12 months he'd spent out in Spain, Lineker could finally look forward to getting back to what he loved best – playing regularly through the middle and scoring goals. And Spurs seemed like a great place to be, with an exciting young side that also included the emerging Paul Gascoigne, yet to play for England but destined for the big time.

Venables appeared to be building something special with Tottenham and after steadying the ship to finish 13th following his appointment during 1987/8, the next campaign saw the Lilywhites come in a creditable sixth place, winning 15 and drawing 12 of their 38 league games. Among them were draws with Liverpool and

Manchester United, as they started showing they could compete with the top sides.

The arrival of Lineker, a two-time First Division Golden Boot winner, international superstar and forward who was prolific wherever he'd been, was a coup, adding an extra sprinkle of world-class talent to a side that was already starting to excite.

Venables wanted to add a top striker to his side for the 1988/9 season and had watched on with interest as he saw Lineker frequently played out on the wing for his old club Barcelona by manager Johan Cruyff, a move the Spurs boss felt 'neutered one of the world's top strikers'. There was a deal to be done and the £1.1 million Tottenham paid for a 29-year-old in his prime appeared to be money well spent.

'Even before Gary had kicked a ball for us, I knew we had signed the bargain of the season,' Venables wrote in his 2014 autobiography, *Born to Manage*. There weren't many around the club at the time who would disagree.

'Gary came to Spurs a year after me and Paul Gascoigne did,' says Lineker's Tottenham strike partner Paul Stewart. 'To be honest with you, when there was word of him coming, I think everyone was elated because Terry Venables had been at Barcelona with him and obviously Gary's career was laid out in front of everyone – what he'd done at Everton, what he'd then done at Barcelona and England. For him to be coming to Spurs, everyone was elated because a player of his quality was only going to enhance the team.'

This was no move of sentiment for Lineker, though. He also had big ambitions for what could be achieved at Spurs and was in pursuit of the winners' medals that had so narrowly eluded him during his goal-laden season with Everton. There had been silverware at Barcelona, but the potential of winning something on home soil had a special appeal.

'Terry has been at Spurs now for over a year and I think the club are on the brink of something big,' said Lineker upon his unveiling in an interview published in the *Liverpool Daily Post*. 'It is nice to join a club like that, rather than a big club who maybe have been at the top for a while. I'm very excited about coming here.

A RETURN HOME

'Obviously I've played with Chris Waddle quite a few times for England. Things worked very well between us in the World Cup against Poland. I haven't played so often with Gazza, but I know he is a high-quality player with a great future. I'm looking forward to playing with them both.'

There was a lot of excitement about what a supply line like that could provide for Lineker and was clearly one of the major factors in his decision to move to Tottenham. In their games together with England, Waddle and Lineker looked to have a great understanding, the winger terrorising full-backs and delivering a string of chances for the striker to get on the end of.

Only, the prospect of a Waddle–Lineker partnership for Spurs remained just that: a prospect. Only weeks after Lineker had signed on the dotted line in North London, Waddle left Spurs. French side Marseille had shown an interest in buying the Geordie winger and while the move wasn't one that Venables was keen on, chairman Irving Scholar said the offer was too good to turn down and the money would be used to reduce some of Tottenham's overdraft.

Marseille's initial offer of £2 million eventually rose to £5 million and also included striker Paul Walsh, and while Walsh's move later collapsed, Waddle still moved for a British record fee of £4.5 million. There was no doubting that the transfer was good business for Spurs, who unbeknown to Lineker at the time were facing some serious financial pressures, but it robbed the White Hart Lane faithful of a partnership that could have been special.

'Chris [Waddle] went off to Marseille, which was disappointing because had we had him in that side, we could only have gone on to even better things,' laments Stewart. 'I was fortunate to play with Chris in the season when he came second in the PFA Player of the Year and he was phenomenal.

'If you can imagine someone like Waddle and Lineker linking up, Chris playing wide and the amount of chances he'd have created, Gary would have scored more goals – I have no doubt about that. It was a shame really that they couldn't link up and play together. I know they did for England, but it would have been nice to be part of it at club level too.'

Lineker shared that disappointment, but he was still confident of achieving success with Spurs. On a personal level, it was a return to the First Division for the first time in four seasons and he was relishing the chance to get stuck into the defences, against whom he'd scored 40 goals in all competitions while with Everton in 1985/6.

The British style of play promised to provide Lineker with more chances too. While he'd got a good goalscoring record from his time at Barcelona, he'd commented previously that he'd sometimes been frustrated by the Spanish approach of building up a more gradual, slower attack. He may not have said it publicly at the time, but Lineker smelled goals back in England.

'I'll never forget when he came back from Barcelona to Spurs and I'd just won the Golden Boot,' recalls Lineker's former Leicester partner in crime, Alan Smith. 'He said, "Oh Smudge, if you know where to move, you can score 20 goals a season easily in this division, it's a piece of cake," and it seemed quite simple to him. And I said, "I don't find it a piece of cake, Gaz, to be honest." But he was very clued-up, he was very canny in terms of where he needed to be at what time in the box and he had that burst of acceleration where he could get ahead of his man.'

This was the first time in Lineker's career that he wasn't making a discernible step up to the club he was moving to, so his status as the newbie in the dressing room was different. He was now a senior player and arrived with a profile that most others in the squad were in awe of. With an already established reputation, many of the younger players were looking up to Lineker to be a leader.

'We had a relatively young team when Gary came around,' says midfield Vinny Samways, who was 21 when Lineker joined. 'We obviously had some senior professionals in Gary Mabbutt, Mitchell Thomas and Terry Fenwick, but Gary had a big profile coming from Barcelona. He gave advice to the youngsters because we had a few coming through the youth ranks, but he was never a shouter or a baller.

'When he spoke, people listened because you have to respect and listen to your seniors. He was a very good influence for the youngsters coming through, especially the attacking players, who could see the way he conducted himself, the little things he did that made him into a top player.

'Any player with that kind of background and CV, of course you're going to respect them as soon as they come into the dressing room. They have to conduct themselves in the right way because it doesn't matter who you are, you have to do it, which he did.'

The relationship between Venables and Lineker cemented that impression. The two bounced ideas off each other in the same way they had done during their time in Barcelona and would often be seen together around the training ground. Venables was ahead of his time in many of his methods and tactics but had the same sense of cool and calm as his new striker – a trait also reflected in captain Gary Mabbutt.

That created fertile ground for a collegiate environment to grow, with a Players' Committee already in place long before Lineker's arrival to aid the improvement of the side. Although the forward elected not to join the committee, there was no doubt his words were holding sway and impacted the decisions that were made.

'He was looked upon as a senior player and there was no doubt Terry Venables consulted him from time to time on different aspects of how we should and shouldn't play,' says Stewart. 'They certainly had that relationship when I was at Spurs, it was open and they would talk to each other.

'Venners [Venables] helped that situation because he was very good at talking and speaking to individuals, and I think both their personalities were quite similar in terms of what they'd done in the game, and they'd never get too riled about anything. You'd never see Gary throwing boots about in the dressing room or effing and blinding, and Terry was the same and didn't shout a lot like a lot of others at the time. They were very calm and collected; even when you were up against it, there was no panic.'

Lineker developed a strong relationship with fellow England international Fenwick, who was another key member of the Players' Committee at the time, and the two found each other to be good sounding boards.

'I lived in South Hampstead around the corner from Gary and got to know him very well,' Fenwick explains. 'It's a difficult one because he was just a lovely fella, almost to the degree that he was a bit boring. He was straight down the middle, he was always looking to do the right thing, a nice guy.

'I lived round the corner from him, so he would often pick me up for training and vice versa. He was a great guy to sit down and talk things through with because you got a very honest answer and sometimes he'd bring things to the table that you hadn't considered. He was always thinking ahead of himself and that was the measure of the man: he recognised all of the positives from everybody else. He very much stayed in the background; he was there if you wanted to have a chat with him, but he wasn't one to ruffle anybody's feathers.

'I was one of the guys at the time who was on the Players' Committee and Gary was one who didn't want to have anything to do with it, but he'd often quietly share his thoughts and was always very positive about how we moved forward as a club at the time.'

Lineker bagged a few goals during pre-season trips to Ireland and Norway to get his Spurs career off to a decent start, but that form didn't translate immediately when the competitive action got underway. Tottenham got the season off to a winning start with a 2–1 victory at home to Luton, but then failed to win any of the next five – picking up only two points in a run that included a 4–1 drubbing by rivals Chelsea at White Hart Lane.

Lineker's first official strike in Tottenham white didn't arrive until 23 September when he scored the second of Spurs' two goals in a 2–2 draw with Norwich. It was an underwhelming start for both player and team, and there was some unrest that for all the positivity that surrounded the side before the season had begun, they were closer to the wrong end of the table than the top.

The goal against the Canaries at least provided some light relief in that Lineker was off the mark. It had come about after Gascoigne had knocked down a corner to defender Pat Van Den Hauwe, who offered up a chipped cross for Lineker to head home from eight yards out.

Lineker had come close to breaking his duck earlier in the match, with his strike bouncing back off the post to Gascoigne to convert the rebound to make it 1–0. Another encouraging sign was that the move had come about after Lineker's new strike partner Stewart had flicked on a long goal-kick. There were signs that things were coming to life for the England frontman and his relationship with Stewart was starting to take shape.

'I was fortunate that I was selected to play up front with him,' says Stewart. 'He was so easy to play with because you knew that given one chance, he was going to score it – there was never any doubt that he was going to score. For me, what I noticed was that quality, and that he was so self-confident and had so much self-belief, he never thought he was going to miss. When you're playing up front with a striker like that, it only enhances your game because if you can do your job and play him in, he's going to find the back of the net more often than not.

'If he did miss, it never weighed on his shoulders and that's a quality in all great strikers in that it never affects them and they just think they'll bang the next one in. That's what I saw most in Gary.

'It [our partnership] was all set up. I have to admit that when Venners was there, we went into training and it was always interesting and we did a lot of attack against defence. As a footballer, you sort of work out what your strengths are and when you're playing alongside somebody like Gary, you work out what will work best between the both of you. I knew that for all the best will in the world, Gary wasn't going to run the channels and most of that was left to me, which I had no problem with.

'I think with quality players like that, you don't really have to work stuff out too much. You know that given the chance, he'll put them in the back of the net, so you're trying to provide those opportunities for them to do so. The more you create, you're confident they'll score.'

By now, Lineker's reputation for not enjoying training was well-known, no less than by Venables after their time together in Barcelona. As an established star, he now had no qualms with being even more blatant about his dislike for sessions he felt had no value and had an agreement with Venables to take a bag of balls, an outfielder and a goalkeeper away from the main group to practise his finishing instead.

Team shape was one of those activities Lineker liked least, as were team shooting sessions, which the entire squad would do together, therefore meaning each player would have roughly one shot every 10 minutes. They were two of many quirks that now characterised Lineker's training regime, which included refusing to shoot in the warm-up before matches so as not to 'waste any goals' when they didn't matter.

'There were quite a few players who would stay behind after training and practise finishing as a club, but Gary never did,' says Stewart in what's now a familiar story. 'People find that strange that he didn't stay to practise crossing and shooting, but it was that belief that he had in himself in what he could do.

'A lot of us worked on our game to try and improve it, but Gary wasn't one of those players – as soon as the manager said that training was over, Links would be off, showered and gone from the training ground. That was something that stuck out – he was so clinical and didn't need to practise.

'Gary was one of those players who didn't have to work hard in training or on his game because everything came so natural to him. When you look at the best goalscorers in the world, it's a natural thing that they're born with and Gary was one of those. Sometimes it's frustrating when you're a player and you look at others like Gary who doesn't have to work for it. But when they're your partner, you can't really ask for a lot more than if you give them chances, they'll probably score. That gives you confidence when you're playing alongside him.'

It was a recipe that had always worked for Lineker and it was soon casting its magic again. After getting off the mark against Norwich, the goals started to flow, with six goals in the next four matches, including a hat-trick against QPR. The winner came in the 87th minute and ended Spurs' winless run, with his treble showing his full array of finishing – the first finishing off a through ball from Gascoigne, the second a clinical turn and shot from the edge of the box, and the third converting a Nayim cross to win the game late on.

In fact, Lineker goals became like lucky charms for Venables' side. Every time he scored in a league match between the end of September and Boxing Day, Tottenham took maximum points. Amid that run was a goal against former side Everton in December that inspired a 2–1 win, and the only goal in 1–0 victory at Manchester United a week later. Ironically, these were two of the sides that had approached Lineker about joining them in the summer before he picked Spurs.

The goal at Old Trafford was particularly rare in that Lineker scored from outside the penalty area. The England striker picked up the ball 20 yards out and hit a curling effort into the net, with the significance not lost on the goalscorer.

'It's always been one of my ambitions to put one in the top corner from outside the area,' Lineker told the *Irish Independent*. 'I have never done it before, except for in a testimonial.'

A brace in the 3–2 defeat at home to Nottingham Forest on 30 December meant he ended the calendar year with 13 league goals and one in the League Cup. They weren't quite the numbers he'd posted at Everton last time he was in the First Division, but they left him in the mix to be the league's top scorer yet again. Spurs had also recovered from their shaky start to look more like the side they were expected to be.

Lineker may well have been in contention to win his third Golden Boot in his past three First Division seasons, but there was no sign of it going to his head. He remained the same Gary Lineker he'd always been: self-deprecating, quick-witted and happy in his own skin.

'You can still be humble and have that air of greatness around you,' insists Stewart. 'I think that's maybe what sets him apart: he doesn't have to wander around like he's high and mighty to give off that aura of brilliance. You knew that Gary had that and you knew that if you gave him one chance when we were up against it, he'd be the individual you wanted the ball to fall to if there was a goalscoring opportunity. He carried that well without flaunting it.'

A sign of how grounded Lineker remained is reflected by his continued relationship with Aylestone Park, his junior football club. He took on an honorary position and never forgot his roots, even inviting former manager Bob Stretton into his home while at Tottenham in order to guest star in a promotional film.

'Because I was a policeman, we were doing a crime prevention video and everybody knows my connection to Aylestone and they asked, "Would you get Lineker involved?", so I said I'd get in touch and try,' remembers Stretton.

'We ended up going to his house in London. It was one of these spacious houses and the basement downstairs was where the kitchen was and it opened out on to the lawn. We walked in and there in his lounge is this grand piano. I said, "I didn't know you played the piano," and he said, "I don't, but when you live in a house like this you've got to have one."

'He asked if we wanted a cup of tea, so he shouts down, "Michelle, make us eight cups of tea will you?" They came up, all different cups, some of them chipped – I don't know if that was a reflection of who he was entertaining or his normal lifestyle, but that's the sort of person he is. That typified him; he hasn't got any major airs and graces – he has his Rolex watch because he can afford it and has a Bentley, but he never ever showed a greedy side. And he was generous with his time every time I saw him.'

As calendars tipped into January 1990, Spurs were hoping to continue with their momentum up the table, but it wasn't to be. A winless month that saw them take two points from a possible nine in the league – including a 1–0 defeat to North London rivals Arsenal – was only exacerbated further by two cup exits, to Southampton in the FA Cup third round, and over two matches to Nottingham Forest in the fifth round of the League Cup.

Lineker had only scored once in those six matches, but that barren spell only looked worrying based on his usual prolific nature. It had got to such a stage that if he didn't score, it was seen as a disappointment – although his overall record was still pretty impressive.

A RETURN HOME

'Gary's got 15 goals in less than 30 games,' Venables said to press ahead of the replay of the League Cup match with Forest. 'That's what you hope for from him and you feel he has got plenty more where they came from.'

As would England manager Bobby Robson, with the World Cup on the horizon. And so it was a universally welcomed return to form when Lineker started February with a hat-trick against Norwich, his second treble of the season. The *Belfast Newsletter* dubbed it 'a near perfect exhibition of finishing', while Venables said Lineker's 'finishing was outstanding'. It showed all the hallmarks of Lineker at his clinical best, rounding Norwich goalkeeper Bryan Gunn with two similar goals, before completing his hat-trick from the penalty spot.

'It's always nice to score three goals,' Lineker said in the *Reading Post* afterwards. 'But it is especially nice because it is an important time for us. Things have not gone so well for us in the past couple of weeks and it's nice to bounce back.'

The victory propelled Tottenham to fifth place in the league, but they couldn't quite shake their inconsistency. Lineker scored an 88th-minute winner in the next game at Chelsea, but then four defeats in five stalled the side's progress again.

There had started to be rumblings of Spurs' financial issues off the pitch too, with the money raised by selling Waddle at the start of the season seemingly not covering a sufficient amount of the club's debts. There had been talk before Lineker joined in June that Tottenham were struggling to raise the cash to complete the transfer before the payments were restructured, but it wasn't known quite how precarious the situation was.

When news came that the club hadn't paid Tranmere their share of gate receipts from November's League Cup tie and that Southampton had started legal action for the same thing after their meeting in the FA Cup, the picture started to become clearer. To make matters worse, Venables claims in his autobiography that Spurs were fined £20,000 after arriving late to one match after the team bus was towed for causing an obstruction in the West End while the players ate lunch.

If the storm clouds appeared to be building off the pitch, performances on it were about to keep the narrative more positive. A run of seven wins in the last eight games of the season from 21 March saw Venables' men jump up to third in the table – a feat they didn't match again until 2015/16. While Tottenham came in 16 points behind champions Liverpool, the finish was a big achievement and showed the quality Spurs had in their ranks.

During the end-of-season run, Lineker scored six times, taking his record for the campaign to 26 in all competitions, 24 of which came in the league, helping him to yet another Golden Boot – adding to those he'd won in 1984/5 and 1985/6.

'He's one of those players at the top of his profession,' Venables told the *Daily Mirror* in May. 'His record speaks for itself. He's got a high profile and the pressure's on him to score goals. If he does finish the division's top league scorer, then he really couldn't have done any better than that. I never doubted he'd do well.'

With the 1990 World Cup only weeks away, England's top striker was in red-hot form. And four years on from his Mexico '86 heroics, there were even bigger hopes that Lineker would deliver for the Three Lions as they headed out to Italy for the tournament. If he ever got there.

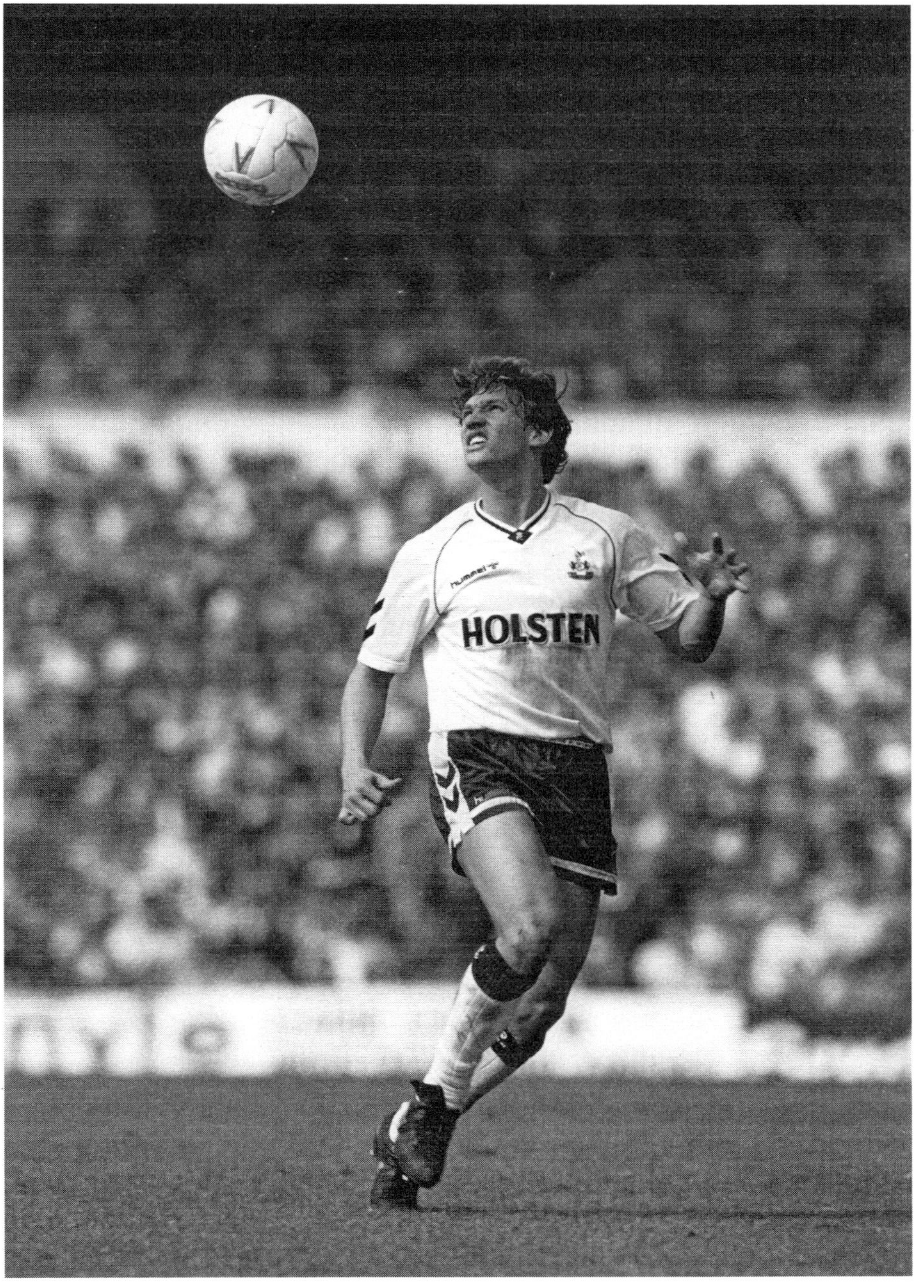
HOLSTEN

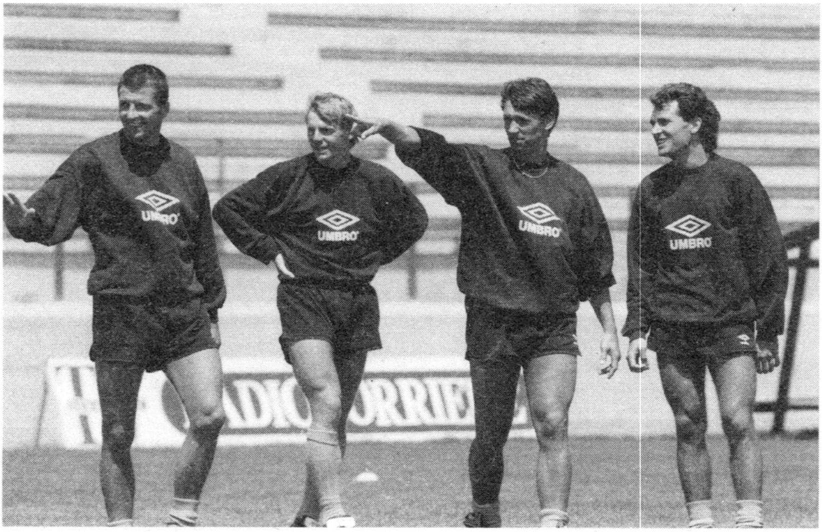
UMBRO
UMBRO
UMBRO
UMBRO

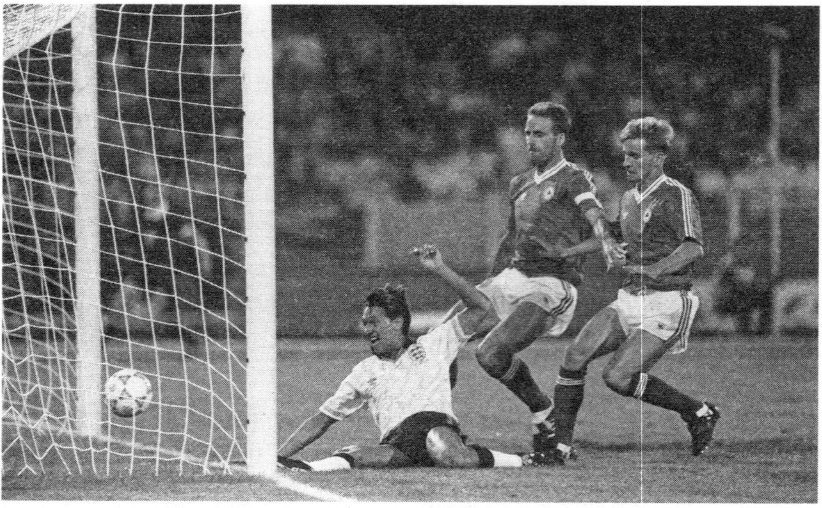

13

THE ITALIAN JOB

England, 1990

'To be honest, I did have a few things going through my mind – like if I miss this, I won't be allowed back in the country.'

It's inexplicable to think there was ever a question mark over Gary Lineker going to the 1990 World Cup. The Mexico '86 Golden Boot winner from four years earlier had shown he'd lost none of his finishing instincts after a goal-laden return to England with Tottenham and he was still the man his international teammates looked to for a goal.

Yet there was still uncertainty over whether Lineker would ever grace a pitch at Italia '90. In fact, when Prime Minister Margaret Thatcher encouraged the FA to 'consider very carefully' withdrawing from the finals, it triggered plenty of debate about whether the Three Lions should send a team at all.

Concern was growing that a World Cup in Italy could spell danger. England's now-notorious thug element had been kept away from the rest of the continent in club competition for five years since the Heysel Stadium disaster in 1985, but it hadn't done anything to improve the reputation of English fans abroad.

A match with Sweden in Stockholm in September 1989 had resulted in 100 England followers being arrested and deported, and with the possibility of a month-long stay in Italy on the cards if Bobby Robson's men were to make a sustained assault on the World Cup, there were genuine fears about what could happen. Thatcher's comments were unprecedented and raised the prospect that removing England – Lineker and all – from the finals could alleviate a potentially volatile situation.

Eventually, a plan was made to locate England on Sardinia, an island far enough away from the west coast of Italy to keep the English isolated from other fans. Housing everyone on Sardinia also meant it was easier to control who came on and off the island because the only viable routes to get there were by plane or boat. It was enough to assuage the English authorities' worries and convince them it was safe to take part.

The threat of England's hooligans wasn't the only storm setting the tone for the tournament back home. Negativity had never been too far away from the side, with a surge of criticism aimed at manager Robson in particular. Many felt he shouldn't have stayed on as boss on the back of the disastrous Euro '88 campaign in which England had returned embarrassed and pointless. But remain Robson did. His contract ran until after the World Cup and the FA bigwigs had no desire to replace him before then.

Just as England had done before the European Championships, they soon started building another long unbeaten run, although that stint was still pockmarked with displays that weren't always as impressive as most of an England persuasion would have liked.

There was a 1–1 friendly draw with Saudi Arabia, an uninspiring 0–0 stalemate with Chile in the Rous Cup, and then three consecutive 0–0 draws at the end of 1989 – England drawing blanks away at Sweden and Poland in World Cup qualification, before doing the same in a friendly against Italy.

The two doughnuts in qualifying at least secured safe passage to the finals in 1990, but only in second place behind the Swedes. England had impressively negotiated qualification without conceding a goal, but they'd only scored 10 times in six matches and could only win half of their games.

Even Lineker hadn't been immune to stick from the press during that time. He went through the worst dry period of his England career, going nearly an entire calendar year without finding the net for his country. It was a run that coincided with his odyssey out on the wing at Barcelona under Johan Cruyff, but nonetheless raised questions about his ability to lead England's attack in quite the way he had in Mexico in 1986.

'They [opposition coaches] have put their heads together and rumbled Lineker, even the Greeks shut him out,' scolded *Mirror* columnist Mike Langley, who penned a column predicting the beginning of the end for the striker. Langley claimed Lineker was starting to lose the burst of pace that made him so deadly and that he was starting to adapt his game in a way that required 'a fiercer partner than either Alan Smith or Peter Beardsley' or he should be dropped.

Robson, though, felt Lineker was simply a victim of his own success. 'It's not easy to play against,' the England manager complained in a February 1989 press conference after the 2–1 win over Greece, Lineker's sixth successive international outing without a goal.

'They put three defenders on him. Two of them mark and don't worry about cover or laying off because they know the third man is behind them all the time. It's so hard to get free from that.'

Despite Robson's defence of his man, those close to the set-up were aware that the prospect of replacing Lineker in England's frontline was something the manager was seriously considering. For a player who relied so heavily on his pace and goalscoring instincts, it was a natural conclusion that if the goals dried up, there would be questions over what else he brought to the team. Unthinkable only a short time ago, Lineker's place was now under threat.

Thankfully, the striker's barren spell eventually ended a month short of him hitting a year without netting for England. When it came, the goal against Albania was vintage Lineker, pouncing on a loose ball after Chris Waddle's long cross was only half dealt with by the Red and Blacks' defence to steer a header into the net from six yards. The relief at finally scoring was written all over Lineker's face as he peeled away with gritted teeth and clenched fists in celebration. Forget the murmurings of debate about his place in the team – a striker craves nothing more than that feeling of hitting the back of the net.

'His [Lineker's] first goal for seven matches justified the Barcelona striker's dance of delight – a sign that the smile was at last returning to the face of English soccer,' wrote respected journalist Harry Harris in the *Daily Mirror*.

Once Lineker had freed himself of strikers' block, goals followed in the next two matches, registering against Poland and Denmark, but it was only a temporary reprieve. Another run of four without scoring came next, as England and Lineker didn't seem as free-flowing as they once had.

There were still flashes of hope among the disjointed displays, not least a 1–0 win against World Cup favourites Brazil at Wembley when Lineker scored the only goal, while playing in an odd pair of boots. The curious situation occurred after the England hitman discovered one of his Quasar boots – which he wore as part of an endorsement – was split. When he was unable to find a replacement, he borrowed one of Bobby Robson's Adidas kicks instead. To avoid showing favouritism to either boot brand, Lineker's winner came courtesy of a header.

Despite England's bitty form, the side reached 17 matches unbeaten from the end of Euro '88, a run they only ceded less than a month before Italia '90 began when they were vanquished 2–1 by Uruguay in a pre-tournament warm-up. There were green shoots of hope even if England weren't firing on all cylinders – not that anybody would have known it looking at the national press.

The furore was focused on Robson once more after it was revealed that the England manager had agreed to take over Dutch side PSV Eindhoven after the World Cup. There was nothing too scandalous about Robson's move, especially as he'd been informed prior to any negotiations with PSV that his England contract wouldn't be renewed, but it was seen as an act of treachery by some sections of the press. Robson's patriotism was called into question, while open season was declared on the manager's character.

THE ITALIAN JOB

On the eve of the tournament, Robson was accused by some tabloids of taking part in an alleged 'three times a night romp with redheads' while his wife Elsie slept. If he could swallow criticism connected to football, this was a bridge too far and he took a stand. As did his players, who took a vow of silence with the media.

Relationships were strained and a lack of trust festered among the squad, yet Lineker still found a way to ingratiate himself with the press without uttering a single word.

'It was the time of the worst excesses of the *Sun* and the *Daily Star* and there was all sorts of scurrilous stuff that was being printed by what we call in our business, the "rotters" – the news reporters who make our lives as football reporters more difficult by printing stuff that's nothing to do with football and gets everyone angry,' recalls Patrick Barclay.

'There was one there with Bobby Robson, and the squad were furious and refused to speak to press out in Italy for a week. I remember the day they had a complete strike and wouldn't talk to the press at all. The players were being driven away and I remember seeing Lineker's face out of the back of the bus and he flashed a V sign at us, but he was grinning all over his face. He had a sense of humour even in a situation like that, when it was them and us, he still had a really big grin on his face while he was doing it.'

By now, Lineker was a senior member of the England squad. Four years earlier, he had still been relatively green in terms of international experience, despite going into Mexico '86 as the Three Lions' premier goalscoring threat. In the time since then, he'd become a permanent fixture in the side – bad run of form in 1989 notwithstanding – and was a calming influence on the dressing room.

Lineker was a key part of Robson's leadership team and would regularly be seen in conversation with the manager, discussing tactics and ways to get the most out of the side. Lineker may not have been a leader in the traditional sense, but he undoubtedly had clout, even if he didn't like to show it.

'My impression of him was that he was clearly a smart individual and clearly had an idea of what direction things could go for him when he stopped playing,' remembers Pete Davies, who wrote the seminal Italia '90 book, *All Played Out,* for which he had behind-the-scenes access to the England camp throughout the tournament.

'He was already pretty canny and pretty cautious about speaking to anyone, and in a good way because he was never impolite. He was boring, but not because he's a boring person – he isn't – but he played up to it... because clearly he was as smart as anybody in the squad.

'He was never going to be shouting at anyone in the dressing room, but if he was expressing an opinion in private, I think people would defer to that. The crucial thing was it was them and it was private. He knew how to play the game and how to tip the wink that he might have an opinion on things, but you weren't going to get him saying it on the record.'

Lineker also played a key role in providing entertainment for his teammates during the tournament, forming one half of double act 'Honest Shilts and Links' with room-mate Peter Shilton. The duo organised race nights during days off, sourcing video tapes of little-known meets and masquerading as bookmakers, making the most of Lineker's experience of running the books as a kid at Leicester races to adjust the odds based on where the money was being placed.

Playing bookie was a lucrative business, apart from on one occasion when Paul Gascoigne got hold of a copy of the races 'Shilts and Links' planned to show before the evening took place. Gazza, captain Bryan Robson and others in the side concocted a plan to back against the horse they knew would win to get Lineker to lengthen the odds, before putting on a series of last-minute bets to win big. By the time the two bookies knew they'd been duped, it was too late.

'This is a person who's trusted, you know this is an honest man,' Davies comments. 'It's really simple, you know it's an honest man and if you're going to gamble, you don't want your bookie to be a crook or a fool – I don't think there's anything more remarkable about it than that.

'This is a person who will get on with everyone around him, if necessary on a needs-must basis because you're trapped in a hotel surrounded by journalists you don't want to speak to, so it might be needs must. But this is a guy who has got a smooth surface and is going to take things quietly and calmly, and keep his opinions to himself.

'He's not going to cause trouble, he is someone you can talk to if something is troubling you. It comes back to, on the surface, what you see is what you get, which is a thoroughly likeable, decent person.'

The real business was out on the pitch, and with a group consisting of the Republic of Ireland and the Netherlands – two of the teams that had knocked England out of the European Championship in 1988 – there was a chance for revenge. The scars of two years earlier were still raw and expectations were low outside of England's camp, despite the squad entering the tournament with a much more settled look than they'd had in West Germany.

Defensively, in particular, England looked much more solid with Terry Butcher and Des Walker flanked by Gary Stevens and Stuart Pearce, while Gazza's emergence in midfield gave the Three Lions an extra attacking thrust. Not blighted by the hepatitis that sapped him of his energy at the Euros, Lineker was also back to his best after a prosperous season with Spurs.

The Tottenham striker had released a pre-tournament duet with Roy of the Rovers called 'Europe Together' in which Lineker attempted a questionable rap (it didn't chart), and seemingly buoyed by his partnership with the fictional superstar, Lineker fancied an even bigger role for himself. Before the tournament, he asked Bobby Robson if he could take penalties, even though Pearce was the usual taker – a request the two accepted without a problem.

'Gary had won the Golden Boot four years earlier and I assumed he wanted to win it again,' Robson wrote in his autobiography, *Farewell But Not Goodbye*. 'I admired him for asking. Not for a moment did I think him big headed. A manager is hardly likely to find negative connotations in his senior striker asking to be given penalty-taking duties at a World Cup. Stuart Pearce, who I thought was our best penalty taker, was not remotely offended.'

Just as in Euro '88, first up for England was Jack Charlton's Republic of Ireland. Robson had warned his charges of the aerial bombardment they were going to face, and wanted to ensure the mistakes of two years earlier didn't come back to haunt them once more. Lineker had his own score to settle, having been denied on several occasions by Ireland goalkeeper Packie Bonner on the way to defeat during their last meeting. But he was trying to look forward rather than backwards in his quest for victory this time.

'We want to beat them because we're playing in the World Cup. The fact we lost two years ago I don't think will make too much difference,' Lineker said to the press ahead of the game. 'It's difficult to say whether playing Ireland first is a good thing. It's a tough game, that's for sure. We know their players very well; they all play in the league.

'They play the long ball game and it's very physical. It will be very difficult for us. We have got to match them physically first to give us the right to play and I'm sure we'll do that.'

Lineker did just that as he gave England the lead after nine minutes, wriggling between Mick McCarthy and Chris Morris to get on the end of a diagonal pass before hurdling Bonner to slide the ball into the net. The breakthrough was exactly what England needed as the game quickly reverted to the blood-and-thunder contest many had expected, a battle of attrition as much as a football match.

Unfortunately for Lineker, his goal isn't the contribution people remember most from the Ireland match. That moment would come shortly after half time when an alarmed Lineker overexerted himself by challenging an opponent and relieved himself in the middle of the pitch.

Unbeknown to anyone else, he'd been struggling with a dodgy stomach the night before the match but hadn't said anything because he wanted to play. Everything had seemed manageable until midway through the first half when he started to get stomach cramps, but after making it to the toilet at the break, he'd assumed he'd overcome the worst of it until he landed heavily after stretching for the ball. Then his bowels emptied.

'This was kept secret for like 20-odd years – my family knew, the players knew, but it never came out,' Lineker said on the *Match of the Day Top 10* podcast. 'Then I was asked in an interview by someone [...] the last question was "By the way, there's always been this rumour that you had the accident on the football pitch at Italia '90" and I told the story.

'Then people found the footage and you can see me on the floor doing like a dog does when he wipes his arse on the ground and shovelling the sh*t out of my shorts and rubbing it into the pitch – thankfully it had rained. There is also a bit when you can see me look up and Gary Stevens comes and I remember him going, "Links, what's wrong?" and I went, "I've sh*t myself." I felt like crying.'

Things got even messier for England with less than 20 minutes to go. Steve McMahon failed to clear his lines properly, presenting the ball for Lineker's former Everton teammate Kevin Sheedy to hit a left-footed drive that arrowed past Shilton for 1–1.

Both teams toiled, but that's how the scores stayed. Once more, England had failed to beat the Irish in a major tournament and they'd feel the wrath of the press at home. Among the negative headlines was a particularly brutal headline in the *Sun*, which simply read: 'Send them home.'

The truth was that with European champions the Netherlands up next, England might not need any extra help achieving that aim themselves. Just like in Euro '88, the Dutch had also failed to win their group opener – drawing 1–1 with Egypt – and while the best third-place finishers in the six groups would also progress to the knockouts, a defeat for either side would leave their future in the tournament looking precarious.

Robson and his players were determined not to let history repeat itself and used the days before the Netherlands game to devise a new plan for the match. The manager and his assistant Don Howe didn't do this alone, though, and consulted with several senior players – including Lineker – about how to get the best possible result from their next outing.

'My main memory of Bobby Robson was that he was one of the most collegiate of coaches,' says Barclay. 'There was a lot of stuff getting into our domain about discussions about tactics that was reflected again in 1990. There were discussions and forums between the players and the manager about tactics, selection and everything else. Robson was obviously making the decisions, but he was very open-minded.

'In 1990, Robson really understood the strengths of his players, that was possibly it. His collegiate approach could be seen in his switch to a more flexible defensive system against Holland. They built from there.'

The result of the discussions was a 5–4–1 formation that saw Mark Wright deployed as a sweeper behind Butcher and Walker. Most notably for Lineker, that meant the sacrifice of his strike partner Peter Beardsley to make room for Wright – leaving the forward ploughing a lone furrow up top, with John Barnes in more of a free role behind him.

If the ploy was to make England harder to beat, it certainly worked. Robson's men were more solid and resolute, keeping the Netherlands at arm's length from Shilton's goal, even when they dominated possession. The extra man at the back provided the cover and assurance for England to press forward whenever they got the chance, with Lineker the main beneficiary. Another day he might have scored a hat-trick, but for some wayward finishing and a borderline refereeing call.

Each of the openings came in the second half. The first was a well-worked move that ended with Paul Parker teeing up Lineker with a low cross into the Dutch six-yard box, with goalkeeper Hans van Breukelen blocking the forward's first attempt with his feet, before England's number 10 fired in the rebound. The celebrations were short-lived as the referee ruled Lineker had handled the ricochet as it bounced back up on his body.

If that decision was a tight call, Lineker had ample opportunity to make up for it. Minutes after the disallowed goal, Barnes slipped him in but with Van Breukelen closing the angle, the normally reliable poacher skewed his effort wide instead. The final chance came from a deep cross on the right that Lineker got on the end of but then couldn't convert with his header.

England undoubtedly had the better of the chances and thought they'd finally got their breakthrough in stoppage time when Pearce rattled in an indirect free-kick that somehow managed to travel across the face of the box without taking a touch off anybody. A point would have to do.

'We didn't look good against the Irish and that was a bitter disappointment,' Lineker said post-match. 'Most of the lads have played in a sweeper system. We certainly felt more comfortable with it. It was just a shame I didn't score. The chances came but I couldn't put them away and I was very unlucky with the handball disallowed goal – the ball hit my hand and not the other way around.'

England were back to a 4–4–2 for the must-win final group match with Egypt, with Wolves striker Steve Bull getting the nod with Lineker up front. But it was a defender who got the decisive goal of the game when Mark Wright flicked a Gascoigne free-kick into the net with a deft header just before the hour mark.

It hadn't been pretty, but Wright's goal gave England the only win in any of the six matches in what had been a turgid group, therefore giving the Three Lions top spot. They'd been relatively unimpressive so far, but Robson's side could now see a pathway to the latter stages of the competition, facing Belgium in the last-16 before a possible quarter-final clash with either Colombia or Cameroon.

Lineker's form was not such good news. He seemed out of sorts against Egypt and with reports he was struggling after aggravating a toe injury against the Netherlands, there was talk in the newspapers of the painkilling injections he'd need to keep playing throughout the tournament.

There was little question of Lineker starting in the Belgium match, though. The discussion was more about England's formation and if Robson would stick with the 4–4–2 that had served them well against Egypt or revert to the new-look 5–4–1 they'd used in the draw with the Dutch. Ultimately, it was the latter that prevailed, with Lineker playing as a lone striker once more.

But while the approach had kept the Netherlands at bay in the group, England relied on more than a little bit of luck in Bologna. Belgium were the better side, carving out a series of chances – most notably a Jan Ceulemans effort that smacked back off the post with Shilton well beaten in the first half, and then a long-range sighter from Enzo Scifo that also hit the woodwork in the second.

Barnes did have a goal ruled out by a tight offside call before half time, but it was Lineker who had England's best chance again, though he couldn't force a bouncing ball into the net when put clean through by Waddle. The game appeared to be destined to be decided by a penalty shoot-out until a free-kick from the impressive Gascoigne sat up for substitute David Platt, turning like a spinning top, to hook in a volley in the 119th minute to settle the tie. England had narrowly done what was required of them again.

Despite their progress, the media were still critical of England – particularly in an attacking sense. They'd scored only three times in four games, two of those from set pieces, and had failed to hit the heights their talents suggested they were capable of. It appeared that Robson was getting frustrated too and used the press to call out Lineker before the quarter-final with Cameroon after it emerged the striker hadn't trained at all since picking up his toe problem against the Netherlands nearly two weeks earlier.

'I thought he would have trained this morning, but he has told me it's still a bit sore,' said Robson. 'But I'm going to make him train tomorrow. It has been too long since he has done a session he now risks [his] selection if he doesn't train. It seems he is fit to play, but not to train. I've got to work that one out.'

Thankfully for England supporters, the striker was named on the teamsheet because Cameroon was Lineker's night. Without him, the Indomitable Lions, who had shocked holders Argentina on the way to becoming the first African side to reach a World Cup quarter-final, may well have had another scalp.

THE ITALIAN JOB

Things had looked to be going swimmingly when Platt headed in Pearce's left-wing cross to give England a half-time lead, but when the Cameroonians hit back through an Emmanuel Kundé penalty and then a clipped Eugène Ekéké finish, things were looking bleak.

Platt missed a chance when clean through on goal as the clock ticked down. Then with less than 10 minutes to go, Lineker got to a loose ball in the box ahead of anyone else, before being scythed down for a penalty. With the weight of an entire nation on his shoulders, Lineker picked himself up to take a nerveless spot-kick that sent goalkeeper Thomas N'Kono the wrong way to force the game into extra time.

Lineker wasn't finished there, though. After being expertly played through on goal by Gascoigne, the forward tried to go round N'Kono, but was tripped on his way and won a second penalty of the night. Once more, he dusted himself down to fire a powerful strike past the goalkeeper to give England the win. After four goalless appearances, Lineker was the toast of the country, keeping his cool despite the pressure back home.

'To be honest, I did have a few things going through my mind – like if I miss this, I won't be allowed back in the country,' Lineker said of those crucial penalties in a press conference. 'But the most amazing thing was that I was thinking of my brother, sitting in a bar in Tenerife, because I know the agonies he suffers watching me.'

Thanks to Lineker's courage, Robson's men had become the first England side to ever reach a World Cup semi-final on foreign soil. It set up a showdown with old adversaries West Germany for a place in the final, with the English press inevitably stoking up the rivalry by comparing the match to the two World Wars the nations had fought against each other.

The players tried to ignore all the hysteria, but there was no avoiding the historical connotations. The night before the match, the team gathered for a meeting and were waiting for Robson to join them to start, when Lineker spotted a moment to relieve the tension. The squad's resident bookie turned over the clipboard and wrote 'Even money he mentions the war' and covered it up again before Robson arrived.

173

The squad waited patiently, stifling bursts of giggles as the England boss finally arrived, completely unaware of the stakes on his words. For some of the more impulsive members of the squad, it must have felt like an age as Robson, dressed casually but with grey hair still in its trademark side parting, put the last touches to his preparation. Any indication of the jape would mean the game was up before it had even begun.

When the manager finally started his team talk, his north-east lilt ready to deliver the motivational speech of his life, Lineker's odds suddenly looked almost too generous. 'We beat them in the war,' uttered Robson, prompting an eruption of huge cheers and celebrations from the players in front of him. Robson was confused until he turned over the sheet to discover what had been written. He knew who the culprit was, seeking out his striker, impish grin painted across his face, before jokingly retorting, 'You bastard, Lineker' to roars of laughter.

While Lineker had found the perfect way to relieve the pre-match tension among the England squad, his name was being mentioned in a different context in the West Germany camp. German boss Franz Beckenbauer was doing his own preparations and had pinpointed who his side should be most wary of.

'We were afraid of three players: Waddle, Gascoigne and Gary,' recalls West Germany winger Pierre Littbarski. 'In terms of Gary, he was very consistent and the other two were artists, but he was very consistent, so we said, "He can't get the ball in the penalty area, he is very sharp in the box" and we conceded a goal exactly like that.

'We were maybe most afraid of him [Lineker]. He looks kind and he's not really a dirty player, but very dangerous, good technique, good at protecting the ball, good at getting to the near post for crosses and was very dangerous. Not a nice player to play against.'

Many of the newspapers concurred with that assessment, pinpointing Lineker's ruthlessness as one of the key weapons in England's arsenal if they were to reach a first World Cup Final on foreign soil. If he was at his razor-sharp best, as he was against Cameroon, he'd take some stopping.

THE ITALIAN JOB

The match conjured up memories of one of Lineker's earliest football heartbreaks, too – the 1970 World Cup quarter-final defeat he watched as nine-year-old boy. 'I remember that match in Mexico so clearly,' he told the *Daily Mirror* in a pre-match interview. 'I sat with my mum and dad and watched our television in the back lounge. With the great Gerd Müller, what a team they had. As a kid, you have your dreams, but I never believed that one day I would play in a match of this importance against them.'

There was no doubting the sense of occasion as kick-off approached at the Stadio Delle Alpi on that fateful July evening. As the fans teemed into the ground, a special electricity hung in the air. This was a night that would go down in history, two great enemies set to duke it out for a place in football's ultimate match.

The two huge banks of fans, adorned in white replica shirts and giant flags, covered the ground. The noise the two sides created, barracking each other from across the stands, only added to the cocktail of tension and excitement around the ground.

It was a match brimming with quality and while Lineker was expertly marshalled, there was a sense that one mistake or a moment of quality from one of the match winners on the pitch would be enough to settle the contest.

Gascoigne saw a volley turned around the post by Bodo Illgner; opposite number Shilton tipped over a powerful Klaus Augenthaler effort; Olaf Thon got free of Parker in the box but fired straight at the goalkeeper. Then disaster struck for England. Andreas Brehmer's drive looped up off Parker, flopping up in the air like a golfer's sand wedge out of a bunker and dropping just beyond Shilton's reach. The Germans were ahead.

England needed their goal poacher to step up as half chances came and went. With 10 minutes left of normal time, Lineker finally got the sniff he was hoping for – the ball dropping for him to hit a first-time left-foot strike across Illgner and into the corner of the net. It was exactly as Beckenbauer had predicted: give Lineker a chance in the box and he'll punish you. Lineker was mobbed by Beardsley and Pearce. England were still alive.

'What's Lineker there for?' Davies poses rhetorically. 'Look at the goal in the semi-final, it's an absolutely rapacious goal. It's "I'm having this", it's at speed. Parker's put a fantastic cross over and he's taken the ball on his thigh at speed and buried it. It's blink of an eye, it's an opportunity, one time and that's what you're going to the match for.

'Understandably, everyone talks about Gascoigne throughout the tournament because he was miraculous in his moment, but actually who scored the goal against the Germans? Look at how utterly clinical that finish, just how quickly it's done, it's a great goal and it's a perfect goal for the moment – it's Lineker at his best. When you're watching a game as titanic as that one, that's what puts breath in your body.'

Extra time could have gone either way. German forward Jürgen Klinsmann went agonisingly close on two occasions, before Waddle hit a drive that had Illgner beaten but slammed back off the post. Guido Buchwald then repeated the trick, hitting the same upright as Waddle with an effort that had Shilton grasping for fresh air.

Lineker had been starved of openings in the additional half an hour, but it didn't stop him from being one of the protagonists in one of its most famous moments. With extra time ticking by, Gazza overreached for the ball and clattered into Thomas Berthold, picking up a yellow card that would have ruled him out of the final if England made it. As the realisation dawned on Gascoigne and the tears started to fall, Lineker rushed over to comfort his Spurs teammate before signalling to Robson on the sidelines to 'have a word with him' – his reaction almost as well-known as Gazza's.

'The guy [Lineker] knows what's going on, he understands people, he's sharp,' says Davies. 'They all knew Gascoigne, they'd been together for six weeks by that point, they all knew each other and didn't play that way in the semi-final without being a unit – and Gascoigne was very obviously somebody who could flip in an instant.

'The miracle is that he didn't have a meltdown in that moment, but Lineker knew that was an obvious possibility and he made sure he got that message across, just with a gesture and an expression in a quiet way. It shows his awareness of people around him. It's just an indicator of him not being self-obsessed, but a considerate, thoughtful person.'

And so the match went to penalties. Lineker was the first taker on England's list but felt so at ease in such a highly pressurised moment, he still found time to give Shilton some advice to be on guard for West Germany putting their spot-kicks down the middle, after seeing so many similar approaches during the tournament. He had no idea how prescient that prediction would be.

Lineker's tip may not have come to fruition, but he held up his end of the bargain, slamming in a low penalty to Illgner's right. The Three Lions had their noses ahead, but despite Beardsley and Platt following suit with the next two penalties, the Germans kept responding with faultless efforts of their own.

So when Pearce struck his penalty down the middle and saw it come back off the goalkeeper's legs, the writing was on the wall for England. Thon slotted home the next to make Waddle's a must-score shot, but he could only blaze over. The World Cup dream was over. As England's crestfallen fans rolled up their flags and made their way to the exits, the players traipsed off, tails between their legs, after coming so close to achieving their dreams.

England lost a low-key third-place play-off to Italy a few days later, but they returned home as heroes – particularly Gazza and Lineker for their decisive moments in the run. The *Sun* newspaper, which had only weeks earlier demanded the side to be sent home after drawing with the Republic of Ireland, turned full circle and sent the players medals to congratulate them on their performance.

A side that it felt like nobody wanted at the tournament had won over the nation's hearts by refusing to come home.

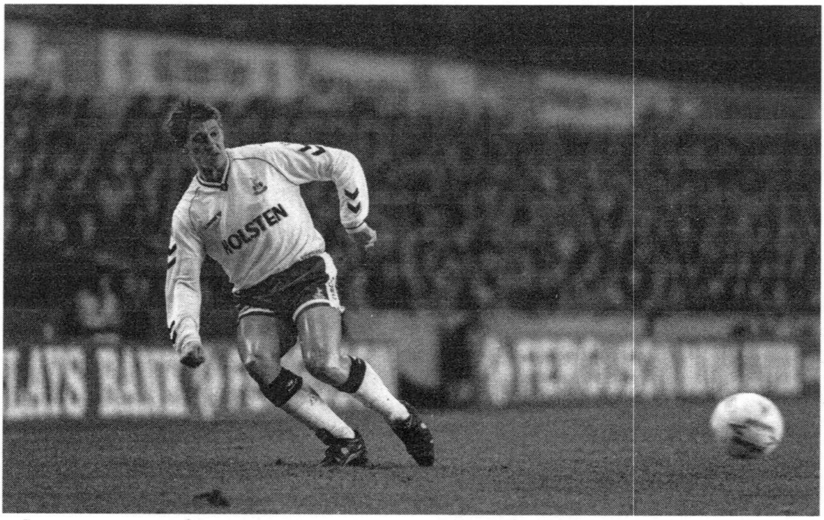
HOLSTEN

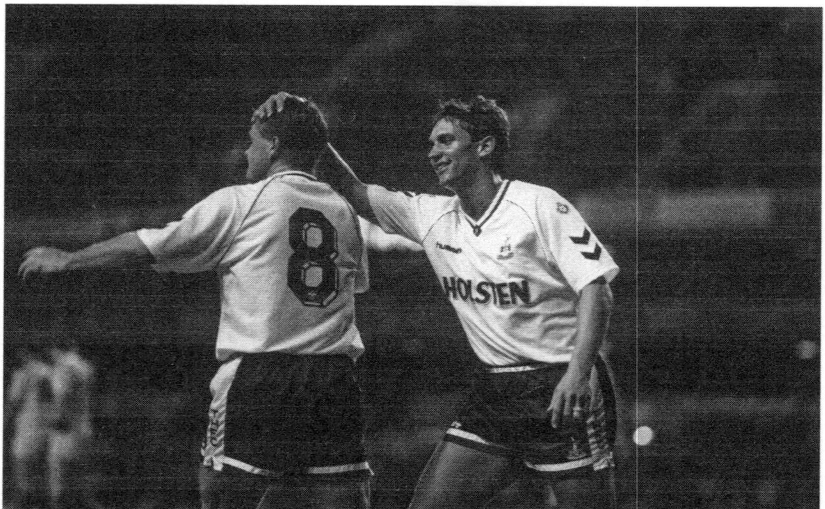
HOLSTEN
8

14

WHITE-HOT LANE

Tottenham, 1990–1991

'This was Gary before the game, going around the dressing room, charging the young guys up, getting us ready for the game, driving up that spirit and passion.'

A trip to White Hart Lane in August 1990 was like buying a ticket for the Gazza and Lineker show. The pair were two of England's biggest Italia '90 heroes and there was even more clamour than previously to see Tottenham's star turns in action.

The duo had been crucial in the Three Lions' run to the World Cup semi-finals, although despite his four goals during the tournament, Lineker had to accept he was Gascoigne's support act. Gazzamania was in full swing as the new season arrived, with the fervour surrounding the midfielder's all-action displays and semi-final tears still burning brightly.

A pre-season trip to League of Ireland side Derry City was championed as having 'phenomenal interest' by the local newspaper, with the 'flamboyant' Gazza and 'explosive pace' of Lineker drawing a crowd of more than 10,000 for the friendly. Wherever they went, they were box-office news.

It was the same at home, too, with Tottenham's office staff inundated with demands for tickets for the sold-out First Division opener with Manchester City.

'I've been here for eight years and I've never known anything like it. It's been like a whirlwind – we stopped selling tickets for the game three weeks ago,' Spurs' ticket office manager Chris Belt told the *Scarborough Evening News* before the league curtain-raiser.

'I think most of it is down to Paul [Gascoigne]. You pick up any paper and his name and picture are in it. He is the number-one attraction in football at the moment. Perhaps he is attracting people who wouldn't normally watch football.'

Gascoigne and Lineker's World Cup showings, paired with Spurs' surging run to third at the end of the previous season, had built expectations in North London that the side would kick on to even bigger and better things in the 1990/1 campaign. Despite continuing talk of the threat of administration hanging over the club thanks to a reported £20 million debt, the core of the side had stayed together.

Even widespread interest in Tottenham's England stars from other clubs had been dismissed, regardless of the club's financial plight. One report suggested Juventus had offered a £12 million deal to sign both Gazza and Lineker in a bumper purchase that would have seen them move to the Italian giants in 12 months' time, yet chairman Irving Scholar said there was no truth in the rumour.

The combination almost guaranteed goals, so the Spurs hierarchy would have known that keeping their two prized assets together to work in tandem was key. Gascoigne was arguably at the peak of his powers, constantly scheming to find openings for his teammates and carrying a goal threat himself, while having a poacher like Lineker was perfect to feed off the supply.

'They [Lineker and Gazza] had a really good relationship,' says forward Paul Stewart. 'When they were both playing on the field, Gary knew what Paul could do and knew Paul could do something that could give him a chance. He [Gary] knew the ability that Gazza had so they had an unbelievable football relationship because you had two world-class players and when you've got them singing from the same hymn sheet, it was only dangerous for the opposition. And those two playing at the World Cup only enhanced it.'

It couldn't be said that the pair didn't have a sense of show about them either. With the fans packed in to the rafters for the opening-day match with Man City, they dazzled with a performance dubbed the 'Gaz and Gary Show' by the *Sunday Mirror* – Lineker grabbing two goals to Gascoigne's one in a 3–1 win. It was exactly what the watching masses wanted.

Lineker had them off their seats within two minutes of kick-off, pouncing on a mistimed header by City's Paul Lake to slot home, and although the visitors levelled things up soon afterwards, the England striker showed his clinical finishing again to finish off a through ball from Nayim.

The England striker's two-goal haul may have been enough for him to take the man of the match award, but Gazza had the final say as he embarked on a mazy run before firing an excellent finish to round off the victory.

'I thought Gary Lineker looked very sharp,' said manager Terry Venables at the press conference afterwards. 'And Paul Gascoigne not only played good football but showed great determination.'

There was a positivity about Spurs and they carried on their great form from the previous season, not losing any of their first 10 league matches. Combined with the run at the end of 1989/90, the Lilywhites had only lost one of their past 18 league matches between the middle of March and October.

Surprisingly given the good form, Lineker wasn't scoring quite as freely as he had been previously, only netting three more times after his double against Man City to sit on a paltry five strikes in all competitions by the end of October. Gazza, on the other hand, had nine.

With the goals being shared around and Tottenham flying high in the league, there was a lot of excitement that this could be a special season for Venables' side. Even a 3–1 defeat at home to champions Liverpool in which Lineker scored couldn't put too much of a dampener on proceedings, with Spurs running off another seven points from the next three games to keep up the momentum.

The only thing that risked upsetting things were the storm clouds that were building off the pitch. In late October, it was reported that dealings in Tottenham's shares on the Stock Exchange had been suspended. The move had been taken after chairman Scholar revealed that media mogul Robert Maxwell had loaned him £1.1 million, therefore indirectly giving money to the club.

The figure had been used to pay the final instalment of Lineker's transfer from Barcelona, after the Blaugrana had demanded the return of the striker because of Spurs' failure to pay the money on time.

The move had raised questions about the financial situation at the club, with the Stock Exchange saying it required more details about the company and that there was 'insufficient information at present available' for deciding on the value of the club's shares.

Maxwell, who was Derby County chairman at the time, had also reportedly been involved in raising £13 million from shareholders, which could have given Maxwell a sizeable stake in Spurs. It was a distraction that was only just getting started.

Behind the scenes, a battle for the ownership of the club was beginning to emerge. It was clear Scholar's time as chairman was coming to an end, and with Maxwell and Amstrad owner Alan Sugar waiting in the wings, it was unclear where the future of the club lay. To make things more complicated, Venables was starting to get involved in off-the-field issues as he tried to secure the future of the club.

The challenge was to keep the boardroom noise away from the dressing room, with the senior players – including Lineker – trying to keep the focus on what they could control rather than matters that were out of their hands.

'He wasn't a typical leader like a Bryan Robson or Tony Adams who would grab someone by the scruff of the neck if they needed to,' says Stewart. 'Gary was cool, calm and collected. When the problems were going on at Spurs, when Terry was trying to acquire the club and they were skint, what they did well was that they kept it away from the players.

'The players didn't really feel the anxiety because of the way Lineker, [captain] Gary Mabbutt and Terry Venables were. We could only affect what we could do on the field, not what's off the field, and they did a good job of keeping all that away from the playing staff.'

Lineker's sense of calm was priceless. 'To be fair to Gary, when we had meetings, he was the one who was very level-headed, he'd keep everything low-key, wouldn't let anything spill over and was always good to go to,' says defender Terry Fenwick. 'And, of course, he was Gary Lineker, so everybody listened to him and he was great for the younger players.

'He calmed everybody down, he kept everything above board, he made sure he didn't do anything that would have been a contradiction to the situation. We of course backed Terry. Everybody loved Terry Venables, and we knew this was a very difficult time at the club when the board were at each other's throats. Gary was great with the young players; he wouldn't allow them to spill over, he wouldn't allow them to get out of hand with anything.

'Several of the younger players were quite aggressive, this was people like Neil Ruddock, but Gary calmed it all down. He was the one who sympathised with everybody, calmed everybody down and made sure they knew what position we were taking on.'

By now well established in the Spurs dressing room, Lineker and his impeccable temperament were having more of an impact than simply helping to deflect off-pitch distractions. Notorious for his serene character and ability to stay unruffled in the face of high-pressure situations, the striker had never been booked throughout his entire career and had become a prized target for unscrupulous defenders wanting to break that record.

'I remember playing in one particular game when we got battered by Wimbledon at the old Plough Lane and he got absolutely battered that day – they really kicked lumps out of him, it was brutal. But he never lost his head once,' recalls midfielder John Moncur, who was on the periphery of the first team at the time.

'I remember thinking to myself, "Wow, that's something to learn by," but I never learned by it because I was the total opposite. I never saw him lose his cool once. The one thing is, you'd find out people's characters in training because it's behind closed doors, but I never saw him once have a tear-up with anyone, which is very unusual.'

Instead, Lineker had his own way of getting revenge for the agricultural challenges he was subjected to. 'Nothing seemed to fluster Gary, whatever the occasion, whoever we were playing against, if he was getting kicked up hill and down dale, he'd just get on with it,' says Stewart.

'He had this belief in his ability that, at some point, he'd get one over on the individual who was trying to kick him. And his way of getting them back wasn't by getting involved in any sort of altercation, it was by banging the ball in the back of the net. That's a trait you're born with and when you see what the game was like back then, with centre-halves that wanted to kick you about, it was impressive.

'From a personal point of view, I'd start getting involved in the altercations, whereas Gary would be totally the opposite. Again, nothing would stop him from taking that opportunity to answer back by knocking the ball into the back of the net – that's the trait he was born with.'

That sense of sportsmanship was now world renowned and Lineker's record for never being sent off or booked during his career led to him being awarded the FIFA Fair Play Award for 1990, picking up a £19,500 prize. FIFA called Lineker 'a living example of how enacting the spirit of fair play in top-level football can be crowned with personal success' and his record was difficult to disagree with.

Lineker led by quietly and unassumingly showing the way for others to follow. It was a characteristic that would increasingly come into focus as Tottenham's promising early start gradually dissipated. They maintained some decent form before Christmas, but those levels dropped thereafter, with the side catapulting down the table with a run of only two wins in 20 games from Boxing Day to the end of the season.

The mood in the dressing room could have become toxic, but Lineker played his part alongside the other senior players to try to keep morale high throughout the run.

'He wasn't someone who would be revving everyone up for a game, he wasn't that type,' explains Fenwick. 'But he would sit down with you after the game and talk about how we'd done, what we could do better, and all of those things. He would be very measured with his thought process about how we'd move forward, which was great. The younger players needed that when they were being thrown into games.'

Lineker wasn't immune from being a victim of Spurs' bad form, though. While he was continually being linked to big-money moves away from North London, the England striker found himself on the sidelines for the Easter double-header against Coventry and Luton. Venables said the decision was due to Lineker being in need of a rest and that he'd given him a break from training to fully recuperate.

Some members of the press speculated that a series of transfer rumours about Lineker's future and the hands of Old Father Time were starting to impact his performance – a notion his manager rejected.

'Gary can go on playing at the top level for another three or four years, but he needs a rest,' Venables claimed. 'Unlike most other players, he has had five years with no real break from football through his commitments with Barcelona, Tottenham and England. I had a chat with Gary and we agreed the best thing was for him to have a rest.'

Despite Tottenham's disastrous post-Christmas form that saw them drop to 10th place, the season wasn't a complete write-off. Punctuating those winless league games was the FA Cup, which provided solace in among the doom and gloom as Spurs continued to march through the rounds.

There was almost an inevitability about their progress – after all, the season ended in a year ending with a number one, which usually spelled success for Tottenham, with four of their previous seven FA Cup wins coming in 1900/01, 1920/1, 1960/1 and 1980/1. They'd also won league championships in 1951 and 1961, and the League Cup in 1971.

The cup run was of particular significance to Lineker too. Although he'd won silverware in Spain during his three-year stint with Barcelona, he hadn't yet managed to get his hands on a trophy in England and at 31, there were unlikely to be too many opportunities left for him to set that record straight.

'Realistically, I've only had two seasons where winning something has been a possibility,' Lineker said in an article in the *Kent Evening Post* on 15 February in typically balanced fashion. 'I had eight years at Leicester and much as it would have been nice to think they were going to challenge for the league title, it was never that way.

'I did win the Second Division championship with Leicester, came very close to winning both the league and cup with Everton and then had a successful time in Barcelona, which I count just as highly.

'Naturally I would like to win something domestically and hopefully it could be the FA Cup this season. But I've been very fortunate in my career, I've enjoyed every minute of it. It's been far more than I could ever have expected.'

The run started with a hard-fought 1–0 win away at Blackpool in round three, with a single goal from former Seasiders striker Stewart in the 68th minute all there was to separate Spurs from the fourth-tier Tangerines.

Next up were Second Division Oxford United at White Hart Lane and while the home side triumphed, they didn't have it all their own way in a 4–2 win. It looked to be a comfortable afternoon for Tottenham when a powerful Lineker effort added to an early Mabbutt strike to establish a two-goal lead. But two goals from Martin Foyle kept the First Division side honest, leaving Spurs to rely on a Gascoigne brace to guarantee their progress.

There was more lower-league opposition in round five in the shape of Portsmouth, with Gazza the hero once more as Spurs won 2–1. A goal from Mark Chamberlain put Pompey one up at half time and when Lineker uncharacteristically missed a sitter, it didn't look like being Tottenham's day. But then Gascoigne took charge, heading in Paul Allen's cross to level things up before scoring a goal of real quality to win the tie with six minutes remaining – cutting inside to beat a defender before ramming a left-footed strike into the net.

The quarter-final was a similar story, with Notts County going ahead shortly before half time, only for a Craig Short own-goal to restoring parity after the break. And it was Gazza again who came up with another late winner. This time, though, Lineker was unfortunate not to get on the scoresheet himself, posing a constant threat to the Magpies' back-line and being denied on three occasions by goalkeeper Steve Cherry.

As Spurs progressed, there was increasingly more talk of Lineker's quest to win his first domestic medal in England and he appeared to be warming to the task.

'Going down that cup run as it built, he got better and better,' says Moncur. 'He gathered momentum and he wanted to win the trophy, him and Gazza. As the rounds got bigger, he got better – that's the sort of player he was.'

That was certainly true when it came to the semi-final. After a run of more favourable draws against teams from further down the pyramid, Tottenham were pitted against title-chasing Arsenal in the last four. The Gunners had lost only once in the league all season and had only conceded 14 goals in 33 matches up to that point, so the odds were stacked in their favour to get the better of their North London rivals in what was the first FA Cup semi-final to be played at Wembley.

If there was any glimmer of hope for Spurs, it was that the two league matches that season had ended in 0–0 draws, with the two sides cancelling each other out for long periods. And Venables had devised a plan to not only stop Arsenal, but also cause more problems for their watertight back-line.

The Tottenham boss had identified that creating space behind full-backs Lee Dixon and Nigel Winterburn was the key to getting more joy going forward and hoped to draw them out to create more space for Lineker, Gascoigne and co. to get at them. To do that, Spurs lined up more conservatively with David Howells on the left and Allen on the right, with instructions to sit deep in order to lure out Arsenal down the flanks.

'Before the game, I don't think anyone gave us a chance against Arsenal – they were top of the league and doing amazingly well, and we were doing so-so in the league,' says Vinny Samways. 'They didn't give us a chance, but on our given day, we could beat anybody.'

The match was an occasion fitting of its build-up. Nearly 78,000 fans armed with giant flags and banners made from bedsheets had squeezed into Wembley, a setting that made it feel like the final itself. For every Arsenal and Tottenham fan creating a rowdy atmosphere in the stadium's bowl-shaped stands that wrapped around the pitch, this *was* their cup final.

Any tension that was being felt in the stands wasn't evident on the faces of Tottenham's main protagonists as they walked out in line towards the pitch. Lineker, who would have expected a tough afternoon ploughing a lone furrow against the Gunners' stingy back-line, looked as nerveless and composed as ever, while Gazza shot two manic grins towards the camera as it panned into his face. If Spurs stood any chance of upsetting their North London counterparts, they'd need their two charmed players to step up.

And so it proved. From early on, Spurs were finding pockets of space to put pressure on their rivals, with their quick passing in the Arsenal half mimicking that of a pinball bouncing off the bumpers of its course in perfectly choreographed fashion. Ping, ping, ping to push and probe the country's best back-line.

There were glimpses of openings. Gascoigne flashed a shot wide of David Seaman's far post after a neat interchange between Lineker and Paul Allen to pierce the often-impenetrable red blockade; another move pulled the Arsenal sentries away from their stations only for the move to evade Howells on the left.

There was promise for the team in white. Although the opening goal was more to do with Gazza's genius than any tactical ploy, as Tottenham's number 8 rattled in a 30-yard free-kick that remains one of the most memorable strikes in FA Cup history. The second goal five minutes later was more of an example of Venables' nous, with Allen getting in behind Winterburn on the right to get a cross into the box that fell to Lineker, who stabbed home from a few yards out. After only 10 minutes, Tottenham were two up.

It was a start the champions elect would never recover from. Lineker's old Leicester teammate Alan Smith did halve the arrears with a header right on half time, but Arsenal couldn't find a way to restore parity. And with time running out, Spurs hit the Gunners on the break to make it 3–1 – Lineker taking hold of the ball 40 yards from goal before running into the space created by Samways' decoy run to gain entry into the box and firing beyond goalkeeper David Seaman.

Lineker's strike was one of his best in a Tottenham shirt in that he made it for himself rather than relying solely on his merciless goalscoring instinct, but it is often forgotten because of Gascoigne's mesmeric free-kick earlier in the game. In many ways, the forward's brace is a mere footnote in the semi-final due to his teammate's genius, with Lineker regularly joking since about his anonymity in the game's narrative as a result.

'Gazza scored that amazing free-kick and Gary scored two goals in that game, but it wasn't all "Gazza, Gazza, Gazza" [in the dressing room],' argues Samways. 'Everyone was delighted to have won an FA Cup semi-final, especially against Arsenal. It's understandable when people are talking about Gazza, look at the goal – if someone can score two goals, but someone else scores an amazing goal, then that's getting spoken about, and rightly so.'

With the poor post-Christmas league form leaving Spurs in mid-table, the focus was now solely on preparation for the FA Cup Final with Nottingham Forest. Venables rested Lineker again in order to keep him fresh, this time leaving him out of the defeat to Crystal Palace. However, his star striker was back in the team for a cup final dress rehearsal two weeks before the match when Forest arrived in town in the league.

Ever the wily competitor, Lineker's mind was already focused on how he could get the upper hand at Wembley and he spotted the perfect opportunity when defender Steve Chettle was given the job of marshalling him rather than England colleague Des Walker. Lineker freely admitted he didn't enjoy playing against Walker because of his pace and ability to read the game, so he deliberately let Chettle get the better of him in the league match, hoping Forest manager Brian Clough would stick to the plan for the final.

As the two teams lined up in the Wembley tunnel two weeks later, Lineker discovered his plan had been successful, with Walker creeping up behind him before kick-off and whispering, 'It worked' in his ear. Chettle had been given the job of marking him.

The news was a welcome boost to Lineker, who had shown signs in the dressing room of feeling the weight of the occasion for one of the only times in his career, according to teammate Fenwick.

'At the time, the FA Cup was the biggest competition in the world and was shown all over the world and I could see it in Gary's face,' the 20-cap England defender says. 'I'd broken my ankle in an earlier round of the cup so I wasn't fit, but I was watching from a distance and I was in and around the squad.

'It was nice seeing Gary was a little nervous before the game, that's not him at all because he's normally clear as day, knows his job and gets on with it. I could see it in the dressing room. Before the game, he was charged up and ready for the game, but Gary was never like that – he was so laid-back, it was unbelievable and everybody just let Gary get on with it.

'But this was Gary before the game, going around the dressing room, charging the young guys up, getting us ready for the game, driving up that spirit and passion. That wasn't what he was like at all, but [during] the FA Cup Final, I looked at him and thought, "That's a different Gary Lineker to what everybody is used to."'

Regardless of the preparation, the game couldn't have got off to a worse start for Tottenham. With little over 10 minutes on the clock, Gascoigne launched into an overzealous challenge with Forest's Gary Charles, chopping the full-back to the ground and leaving both players writhing around on the floor. Gazza had already got away with planting a foot in Garry Parker's chest a few minutes earlier, but he wasn't so lucky this time and would have to be withdrawn due to a knee injury.

To make matters worse, Stuart Pearce fired a piledriver of a free-kick into the top corner to give Forest the lead. Spurs were one down and with their talisman coming off minutes later, any pre-match exuberance was quickly dissipated.

'When we went 1–0 down, I remember Gazza going off, but I don't think Gary panicked – it wasn't in his nature,' recalls Stewart. 'When Gazza went off, I looked around the team and you could feel everybody's shoulders dropping and thinking, "Oh my god, that's the last thing we need." But if you looked at Links, I don't think his shoulders had dropped.'

All eyes were on Lineker to get Spurs back into the game and he appeared to have done just that, finding a pocket of space in the box to sweep home an Allen cross, only for the linesman to rule it out for offside. The replays showed Lineker was comfortably on and the rueful look on his face as he walked away, hands on hips, suggested he knew as well.

Tottenham's number 10 was running rings around his marker, Chettle, so more chances were sure to arrive. And when he was hauled down by goalkeeper Mark Crossley as he bore down on goal, Lineker appeared to have the perfect chance to make up for the incorrect offside. But it wasn't to be, as Lineker struck his penalty to Crossley's left, at a comfortable height for the 21-year-old goalkeeper to parry it to safety. It was starting to look as though it wasn't going to be the London side's day as they went into the break one down.

'In the cup final, Links was magnificent and kept us all on track,' says Fenwick. 'Gazza got injured, but that's where Gary did the same for us that he did for England when Gazza got out of control and was crying because he got a yellow card in the [World Cup] semi-final. These are times when his experience and knowledge and the Gary Lineker we know him for comes out. He was the one who calmed everybody down and got our thinking back on track.'

It wasn't just in Tottenham's dressing room that there was a reset, though. Emerging for the second half, Walker caught up with Lineker, ominously saying, 'I'm back' in reference to Clough rejigging his defence so Chettle would no longer be responsible for keeping the striker quiet. The change may have made Lineker more muted after the break, but it couldn't stop Spurs pulling level, thanks to Stewart's low, angled drive from the right side of the penalty area. Cue relief, not least from Lineker.

'When I scored, you can see my momentum takes me over the barriers behind the goal,' reminisces Stewart. 'The first person who caught up with me was Gary. All I heard him saying was, "Thank you, thank you, thank you" because he'd missed the penalty and [I'd] managed to get us back in the game. It's a memory that sticks out because he tried to grab hold of me to thank me.'

The game remained at 1–1 until extra time when Spurs seized the initiative. Substitute Paul Walsh saw his header crash off the bar after looping over Crossley, with Pearce putting the ball behind for a corner. From the resulting set piece, Nayim's cross narrowly avoided Lineker but a stretching Walker inadvertently headed it into his own net as he tried to get it away.

Lineker allowed himself a show of emotion, clenching his fist and bellowing out into the Wembley sky. It would be the first of a long night of celebrations, since the goal proved to be enough as Spurs held on to win – giving their England striker that coveted first piece of silverware on home soil.

'To win an FA Cup Final was a dream and having lost one before – and I was getting towards the end of my career now – I just had to win this final,' Lineker said in an interview for Goalhanger Films' YouTube channel in 2015. 'It had got financial implications for the club at the time, the club was in a real mess and it was vital that we'd go on to win it.'

With rumours suggesting Lineker would be sold that summer to help ease Spurs' financial issues, it appeared to be the perfect farewell. But, like anything at White Hart Lane at the time, nothing was set in stone.

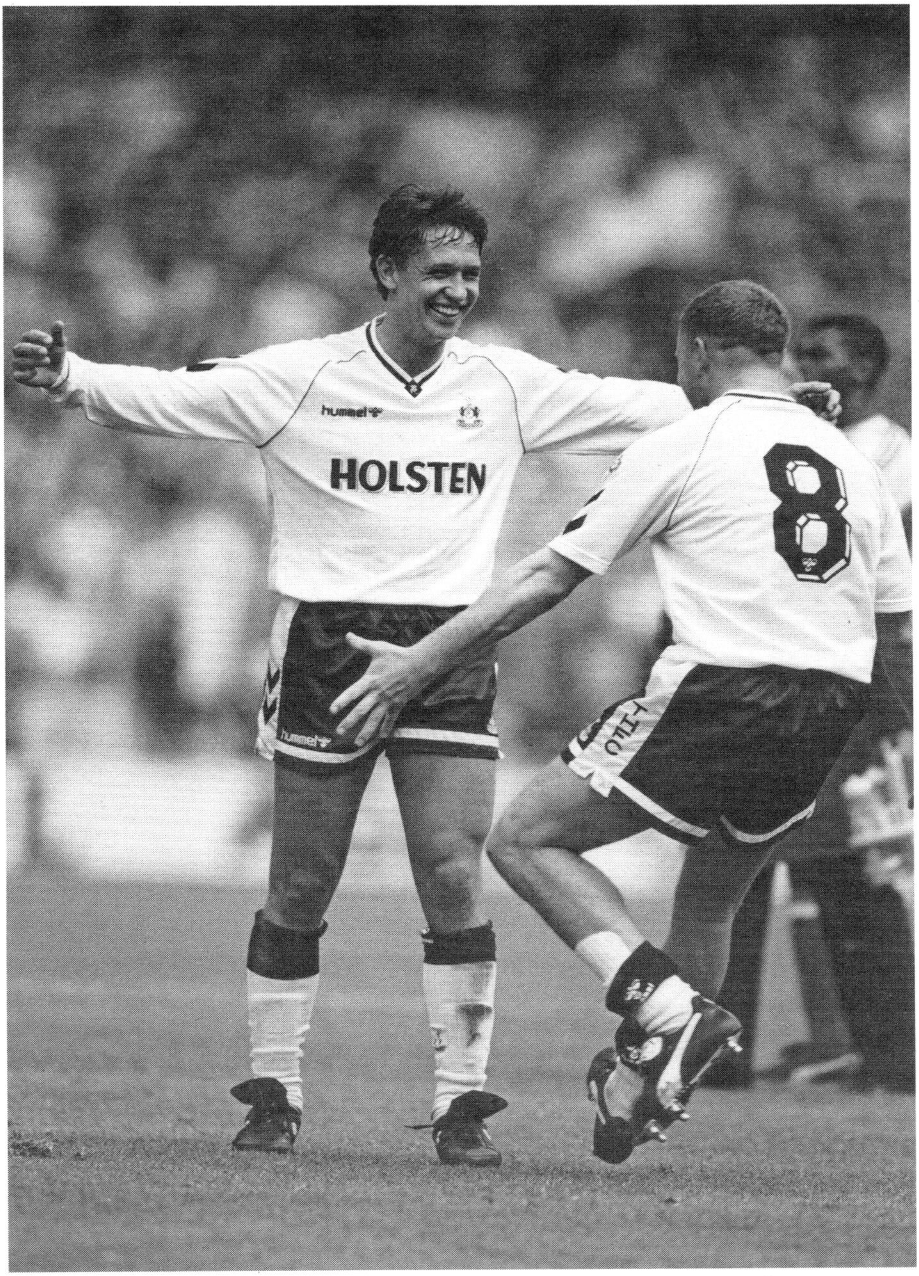
hummel
HOLSTEN
8
hummel

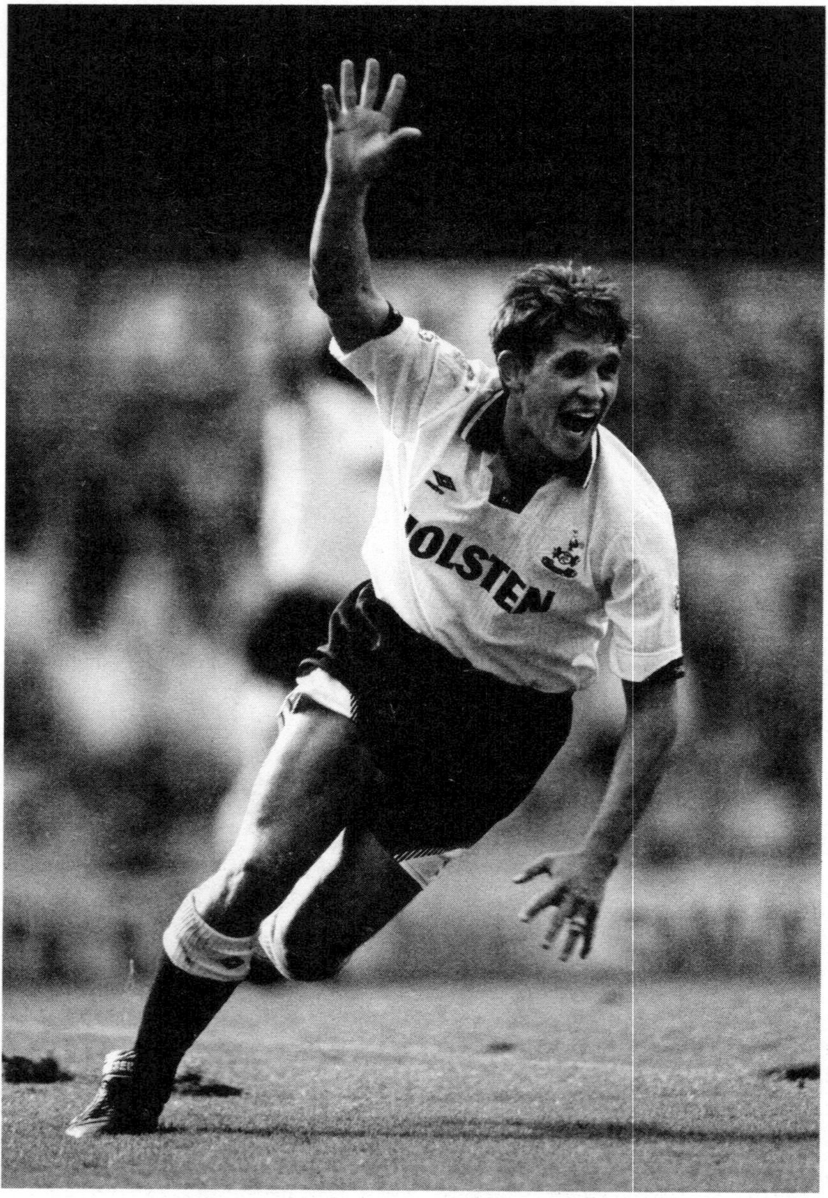

15

SO LONG, FAREWELL...

Tottenham, 1991–1992

*'My agent actually phoned me and said,
"I think this is some kind of publicity stunt."'*

Gary Lineker was said to be furious. Only days before Tottenham's FA Cup Final with Nottingham Forest, news broke that Spurs had been touting his name about in an attempt to sell him – without any consultation with him or his agent Jon Holmes.

Publicly, the England striker was keeping his counsel, with Holmes telling journalists they'd wait until after the Cup Final to comment. Privately, it was reported that Lineker was upset about the possible unsettling nature of the story before such a big game and that nobody at the club had spoken to him about a move.

His contract still had two years left to run and Lineker had expected to stay for the duration. A host of clubs from home and abroad – ranging from Aston Villa and Everton to past admirers such as Napoli, Torino and Monaco – had been linked with a move, and there had been talk that Spurs had 'engaged an agent' other than Holmes to broker a transfer.

The financial justification was obvious to everyone. The strain to balance the books at White Hart Lane had long been known and it was no surprise the club was looking to raise money by selling their assets. Prior to the end of the season, a deal had already been agreed to sell Paul Gascoigne to Lazio that summer, although the damaged cruciate ligament the midfielder injured in his rash tackle on Gary Charles in the FA Cup Final had raised questions over the move.

A proven goalscorer like Lineker was bound to garner interest too, despite now being the wrong side of 30. He'd only scored 19 goals in all competitions in 1990/91, the first time he'd failed to surpass 20 strikes in an English league season since his early Leicester days, but his ability to produce when it mattered still looked as strong as ever.

While the FA Cup win had papered over some of the chaos behind the scenes at Spurs, Lineker was said to be happy at the club. He was settled in London, his wife Michelle was pregnant with their first child George, and life was good. The striker had also been voted as Britain's sexiest footballer in a Radio 1 Breakfast Show poll, so why would he want to leave such an adoring public behind?

Lineker had also found somewhere he could balance his football career with his passion for cricket. He now had a playing membership with the Marylebone Cricket Club (MCC) at Lord's Cricket Ground and would regularly don the whites and take guard in front of the stumps for Cross Arrows – a team made up of MCC members – when time allowed.

The team would play at the Nursery Ground at Lord's, with Lineker still capable of showing his prowess with the bat by racking up big scores, and happy to keep wicket or pick up the ball to bowl as well. It wasn't always a popular pastime with Terry Venables though, with the Spurs boss once banning Lineker from playing cricket after his forward tore a muscle in his back when bowling, causing him to miss a match for Tottenham.

During pre-season for the 1990/91 season, Lineker was even persuaded to turn out in a charity match for Bunbury Cricket Club in Finchley, hours before a pre-season friendly with West Ham. Facing West Indies fast bowler Courtney Walsh, Lineker asked him to try him with a few 'real' balls, before settling in to score 112 not out by lunch. With the day job calling, Lineker had to declare so he could get to the match, where he duly scored a hat-trick that evening. There can have been few better sporting days.

It was the sort of lifestyle that suited Lineker. And with such a happy life around him, he hoped that once Tottenham's ownership wranglings were sorted, the off-field distractions would quieten down. While that calm ultimately didn't arrive, a new owner did – in the shape of Alan Sugar – and assuaged any immediate concerns of the club going into administration.

Sugar had been touted as a possible buyer for months and teamed up with manager Venables – who had himself been a potential buyer at one stage – to put together a deal to beat media tycoon Robert Maxwell to the purchase. The deal meant Venables stepped down from his managerial post to become chief executive, making way for Peter Shreeves to take over.

That wasn't the end to the Lineker transfer rumours, though, with ambitious Second Division Blackburn Rovers tabling a £2 million bid. Spurs agreed to take the offer seriously and put it to their striker's representatives, although as it turned out, it was Lineker's agent who didn't give it much credence.

'My agent actually phoned me and said, "I think this is some kind of publicity stunt,"' Lineker said in a 2015 interview with *FourFourTwo*. 'Obviously, it turned out that Jack Walker actually did have a few bob and was ready to spend it. But I was ready to do something different at that stage.'

Lineker may have had his sights set on what was going to come next, but there was no sign of it impacting his performances on the pitch as he started the 1991/92 season in inspired form. A brace at The Dell helped Spurs to a 3–2 win at Southampton on the opening day, following that up with at least a goal in all but one of Spurs' next six league games.

The crowning glory of Lineker's run was a four-goal blitz away at Wimbledon in a 5–3 win that saw him score a first-half hat-trick. By the end of September, he'd already totted up 11 goals and had matched last season's league total of 13 before October had finished. With more goals coming in the League Cup and the Cup Winners' Cup, Lineker's form appeared to put paid to any suggestions at the end of the previous season that age was beginning to catch up with him.

Worryingly for First Division defenders, Lineker suggested he wasn't fully fit after his haul against Wimbledon and told the press he was carrying toe and back injuries. Not that any of his teammates noticed.

'You'd go through 20-minute phases of the game and not see him, but people wouldn't realise that was his game,' says Terry Fenwick. 'People didn't realise that was his game, that's what he was doing: he was trying to manipulate the opposition so he could get in a position where he'd pop up and score. That was the measure of the man; that is what he did. Quite often as a captain or senior player in the team, you just let him get on with it and deal with everybody else, then wait for Gary to pop up when he did.'

When Lineker was in a run of form like he was, it almost became second nature to provide him with assists. Get the ball in the right areas and the hotshot striker would do the rest.

'He was an absolutely fantastic goalscorer,' remembers John Moncur. 'What struck me was the sharpness of his runs, he was nigh-on impossible to mark and he just knew where the ball was going to go. He never scored spectacular goals, but if you look at them, it was like he had a telepathic idea of where the ball would be and it always seemed to come to him.

'People would say, "That's lucky, how's that come to him there?" But if you watched him through his career, it's something you can't really coach. Midfield players loved to play behind him because he could sometimes make a bad ball into a great ball, that's how electric and intelligent he was. The thing is, it's all right running about, but there was a sixth sense with him.'

Lineker may have been on his best ever goalscoring run in a Tottenham shirt, but privately he was starting to spot signs of slowing down. It was a factor he had to take into account as he considered his next move beyond the end of the season – there may still have been interest in his signature from top clubs across Europe, but he was increasingly doubtful whether they were the right option for him.

As autumn wore on, the prospect of another alternative started to grow. The Japanese J-League was launching and its clubs were looking to recruit a handful of marquee signings to attract interest in the competition. Lineker fit the image perfectly and he'd been approached by Nagoya Grampus Eight about joining on a lucrative two-year deal starting in February 1993. It wasn't the most obvious move for a player still considered to be one of the world's best strikers, but the project appealed to Lineker and he called a press conference to announce the move in November.

'It was always my intention to go out at the top and hopefully with the European Championships next summer, I'll be doing that,' said Lineker in the media briefing announcing his move. 'My original plan was to finish my contract with Tottenham, which runs for the rest of the season and the one after, before retiring. But the Japanese interest came up and it gave me an interesting option.'

Spurs agreed a deal for £1 million to sell Lineker to the Toyota-backed club, with reports at the time suggesting that Lineker would trouser more than £2 million in salary alone, before considering the sponsorship opportunities the transfer would provide him with. Venables said in his autobiography that Alan Sugar wasn't happy that Tottenham hadn't made more from the agreement, believing a player of Lineker's quality should have commanded a higher transfer fee, despite his age.

By announcing the move with several months of the season to go, Lineker was almost giving himself a farewell tour. There were still five months before the end of the season and with an extended gap before his contract started in Japan, he could throw himself into the cut and thrust of the First Division for the final time – and after starting the season like a train, he was in contention to win yet another Golden Boot before his time was out.

Sadly, it wouldn't be a time of celebration for Lineker. Two months after his first son was born, baby George was diagnosed with a rare form of acute leukaemia and rushed to Great Ormond Street Hospital in London for treatment. The news of George's diagnosis sent shockwaves around the football fraternity, with

Lineker taking compassionate leave to allow him to stay at his son's bedside as he battled the disease.

'I'll never forget that first night,' Lineker told The Athletic's *The Moment* podcast in 2022. 'I was with [then-wife] Michelle and they did all these tests and stuff. At the end of the night, they gave us some sort of evaluation of prospects and they said it's not good. They came to us with a somewhere between 10 and 20 per cent survival rate with this thing at his age.

'It was such a difficult time because we were being told that it would be incredibly difficult for him to make it through the night. They said they've got to start chemotherapy immediately because the leukaemia was in such a state. So the first thing they told us was "We've got to try and get him over the next two or three days and then we'll evaluate." So it was pretty grim.'

Football understandably took a backseat as Lineker stayed at the hospital, praying for good news. He admitted to having recurring dreams of carrying a tiny white coffin as he went through the torture of watching helplessly as specialist doctors and nurses fought to save George's life.

After sitting out several games, Lineker asked to be integrated back into the Spurs camp to attempt to get a short respite from the turmoil of waiting in hospital for any news about George.

'Football was the only time I could almost get it out of my mind,' said Lineker on *The Moment*. 'I had three weeks without training and then I said, "Right, Terry [Venables], can I come in?" because I needed it for me, in a way. There's a little bit of an escape from a whole day in the hospital ward looking for the worst signs or sometimes looking for good signs or whatever it was.'

Lineker made his return in a 2–1 defeat to Liverpool at White Hart Lane and then played in the following three matches – each of which was in London, allowing him to dash straight back to Great Ormond Street Hospital after the match. The Spurs hierarchy was more than happy to provide him with the leeway to manage his time and put no pressure on him to join the squad for the away trip to Coventry on New Year's Day, which would include an overnight stay in the Midlands before the match.

'Gary will come up to Coventry with us on New Year's Eve and spend the night at a hotel with the rest of the team before we play at Highfield Road the next day,' said boss Shreeves. 'He has put himself up for the game. It is delightful news.

'We have put no pressure on him to play, but he is training every day with us and is back in his old routine. Gary always had a ritual of preparation before matches and he has gone back to it. When he first came back against Liverpool the other week, it was a traumatic experience for him, but ever since then he has been sharp and bright, and it is a very good sign.'

The trip coincided with the news that Lineker was being awarded an OBE in the New Year's Honours List for his services to the game. But every achievement now paled into insignificance alongside George's recovery in hospital.

Lineker and Spurs' form understandably faltered, with the striker failing to score in any of 10 winless league matches following the trip to Coventry. Their FA Cup defence ended meekly too, with a 1–0 replay defeat to Aston Villa – a side Lineker never enjoyed playing against, never scoring at Villa Park in his entire career.

The only piece of light relief was a fifth round League Cup win against Norwich, in which Lineker scored, but that run ended a few weeks later, going down 3–2 on aggregate in a two-legged semi-final with Nottingham Forest.

Tottenham's poor run had left them looking over their shoulders at the relegation battle behind them, so a return to form in spring was a welcome relief to the Spurs hierarchy, especially after news that the Sugar and Venables reign had managed to get the club's accounts back into the black.

Lineker scored in a topsy-turvy 4–3 win against Coventry for their first league win in nearly three months, before he struck a hat-trick – the 18th of his professional career – to beat West Ham 3–0 a few days later.

For all the disruptions he'd suffered, Lineker was still sitting at the top of the goalscoring charts and with Shreeves setting his striker a target of reaching 35 goals before the season was over, there was hope he'd finish his final season at Tottenham in a blaze of glory.

'I leave other people to set targets,' Lineker said to press after the West Ham match. 'I just hope to get fit and have the chance to score goals. It's nice to keep the habit going. Hopefully we can stave off relegation fears and I can finish the season with a bit of a spurt. I wanted to go out to Japan still at the top of my form and hopefully that will be the case. There's a few games to go yet.'

That's just what he did, scoring five in the next five games to help Spurs to three important wins to take them away from danger. And wherever he went, Lineker received a largely favourable reception from supporters, showing the appreciation his reputation had afforded him with English fans over the years.

'I remember that wherever we went and played, away fans could sometimes be ruthless, but I don't think Gary ever got the backlash from any of the teams,' says Stewart. 'I think he had the respect of a lot of football fans, whereby they wouldn't jump on his back.

'He earned that from what he'd done on the pitch, whereas sometimes I remember when I used to go to Forest, the fans used to absolutely despise me and from walking out on the pitch an hour before the game, they'd be on my back. But Gary didn't endure any of that sort of animosity from other fans because they respected what he'd done within the game.

'The goals he scored for England gained the respect of supporters and he never did anything controversial to get the back up of opposing fans – he scored goals that showed he was one of, if not the, best and he didn't really antagonise fans by going into tackles or anything. He was a clever man because I think he knew what he was doing.'

As Tottenham went to Old Trafford for the final match of the season against Manchester United, Lineker was in the box seat to win his fourth First Division Golden Boot. With 27 goals, he was one ahead of Arsenal's Ian Wright, with the Gunners at home to Southampton.

At half time, Lineker checked what was happening at Highbury and with neither having registered a goal, he was 45 minutes away from achieving his aim.

With half an hour to go, Spurs were 3–0 down and heading for a heavy defeat. So when Wright netted in London, it looked as though the best Lineker would get was a share of the boot – until he struck with four minutes to go. The goal came in classic Lineker fashion, the departing frontman peeling away from his marker at the back post to head home a Gordon Durie cross, taking him to 35 goals in all competitions.

More importantly, Lineker was sure the goal would be enough to keep him ahead of Wright for the Golden Boot. Alas, his England teammate had other ideas, scoring in the 89th and 90th minutes to not only draw level with Lineker, but take the trophy with almost the last kick of the season. Wright's hat-trick had come in the last 20 minutes of the game and much to Lineker's frustration; the gazumped striker called his friend to say, 'You bastard.'

From a playing perspective, it had still been an impressive way for Lineker to wave goodbye to the English game. He'd been crowned the Football Writers' Footballer of the Year a couple of weeks before and received his award at the Royal Lancaster hotel a few days after his Old Trafford farewell.

Lineker topped the poll with more than four times the total number of votes received by runner-up Stuart Pearce and became only the sixth player to win the award on more than one occasion, following in the footsteps of Stanley Matthews, Tom Finney, Danny Blanchflower, Kenny Dalglish and John Barnes.

'It's a great honour to win such a prestigious award for the second time and join such top company,' said Lineker. 'It's a magnificent finale to my career here.'

While the curtain had fallen on Lineker's club career on home soil, he wasn't ready to walk off into the shadows just yet. His final hurrah would come at the 1992 European Championships and the little matter of trying to break Bobby Charlton's England goalscoring record.

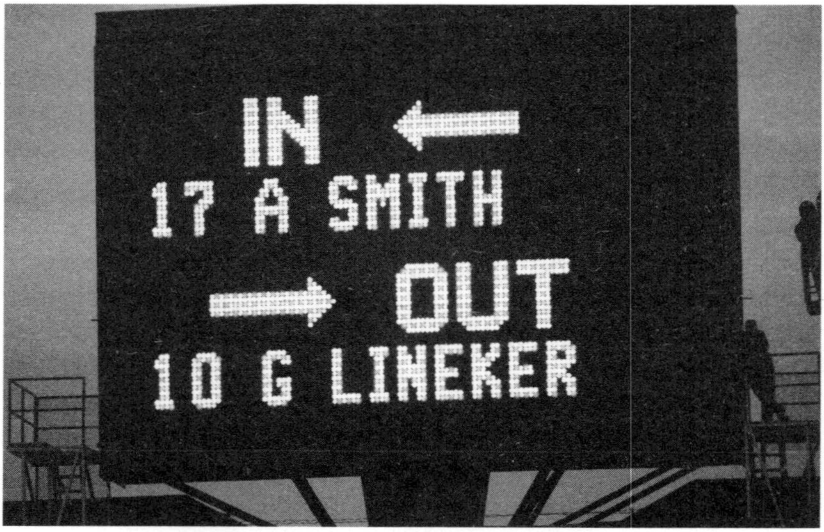
IN
17 A SMITH
OUT
10 G LINEKER

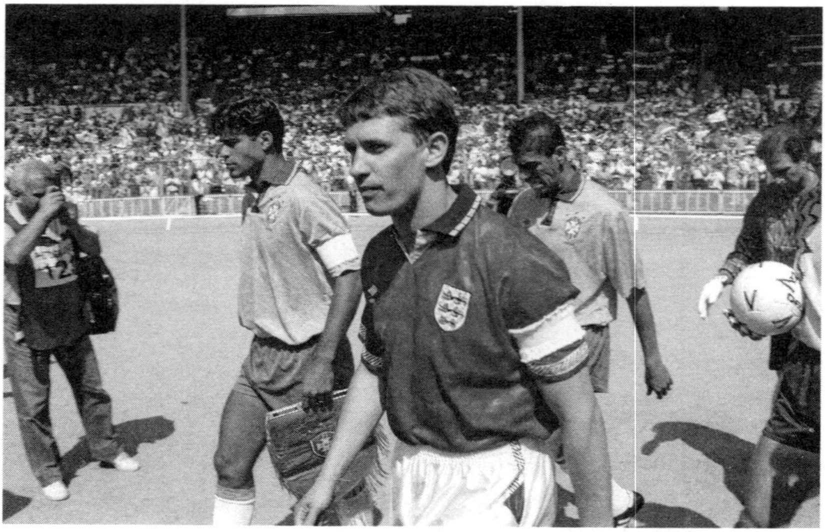

16

CAPTAINCY, RECORDS AND FALL-OUTS

England, 1990–1992

'Graham Taylor had been having a go at Gary for not holding the ball up. [...]

Even so, [...] when his number came up, I was surprised.'

The yellow placard emblazoned with number 10 was held aloft on the touchline. Gary Lineker glanced up at it, then looked again to double-check that what he was seeing was correct. There could be no doubt. His number was up.

There was little under half an hour remaining of England's crucial Euro '92 clash with Sweden and they desperately needed a goal to progress through to the knockout stages, but it was England's second-highest goalscorer of all time who was being withdrawn. The man who had so often been the Three Lions' saviour when they needed it most.

But this time he'd have to watch on from the bench as his teammates tried to rescue the situation without him. If they couldn't, the slow trudge to the sideline to be replaced by his former Leicester City strike partner Alan Smith would be Lineker's final action in an England shirt.

Ever the professional, Lineker kept his emotions in check – regardless of the frustration he must have felt bubbling inside. He shook Smith's hand and stoically walked towards the substitutes' bench, knowing his 80-cap international career might be ending in ignominy.

It was a narrative nobody had seen coming.

'[England manager] Graham Taylor had been having a go at Gary for not holding the ball up, which was never Gary's strength anyway,' explains Smith more than three decades on from being the unwitting replacement who brought down the curtain on Lineker's England story.

'Once or twice the ball bounced off him and [Taylor's assistants] Lawrie McMenemy and Phil Neal were having a bit of a go, and me and Alan Shearer were both asked to warm up. Even so, you still think you're going to play with him because we needed a goal, so when his number came up, I was surprised. But you don't have much time to think about it because you're going on for England at a major tournament and we needed a goal.'

Unfortunately for Smith, Lineker and England fans, that goal never arrived. In fact, not only did they fail to get themselves ahead, but with the minutes ticking away, Swedish playmaker Tomas Brolin danced through the England back-line, shimmying past defenders and playing a one-two with Martin Dahlin before prodding a superb finish into the top corner of the net.

England were out of Euro '92. Lineker's international career was over. And a full-scale post-mortem ensued.

'It wasn't the ideal way to finish,' a reserved Lineker said in a press conference the next day when facing questions about ending his England career only one goal short of equalling Bobby Charlton's scoring record. 'But those decisions are out of my hands. I was just disappointed because it meant I couldn't score the goal that got us through.'

Softly spoken and well-mannered as always, Lineker appeared to take the setback in his stride. But privately, the circumstances reportedly rankled him and it summed up a less-than-harmonious relationship with Taylor that had ebbed and flowed for the two years since the former Watford boss had taken over the England job from Bobby Robson.

Very few people would have predicted what the future held for Taylor and Lineker when the appointment was first made. The manager had been plucked from Aston Villa to take the reins of the international side shortly after Italia '90 and promptly named the experienced striker as his captain in the wake of Bryan Robson's continuing injury issues and a number of retirements after the World Cup.

Many in the press weren't overly enamoured by Taylor's appointment and while he was respected as a club coach, there was concern about how he'd step up to the international stage. Critics pointed out that he'd never won a major trophy and hadn't represented England as a player, so would struggle to get to grips with the demands of taking charge of the national team. Add to that that the side was in a state of transition after the departure of Robson and several senior players, and it was a big job to take on.

Giving Lineker the captain's armband seemed to be a canny pick, though. The forward had been part of the England set-up for several years, was one of few guaranteed starters and had a proven track record of handling high-pressure situations – even if he had limited experience in the role at club level.

'Not too many forwards have been given the job,' Lineker said after being named skipper for the friendly with Hungary in September 1990, Taylor's first match in charge. 'I don't know why because goalkeepers have been given it and it's even more difficult for them to communicate with players. I think I can do the job quite well.'

A winning goal in a 1–0 win over the Magyars suggested Lineker was right, the weight of the armband not causing him any issues as he swept home a close-range finish after a flowing move including David Platt and Paul Gascoigne bounced to him a few yards out.

'I enjoyed being captain and it was a wonderful feeling leading the side out as I walked up the tunnel,' Lineker said after the match. 'The crowd were great; it was nice to feel the expectancy among them, instead of the fear we have sometimes experienced. It was great to score and a nice way to repay the boss for giving me the captaincy.'

It was the perfect start, with the mutual love-in continuing as Taylor waxed lyrical about Lineker's prospects of breaking the England goalscoring record during his tenure. The strike against Hungary had taken Lineker's total to 36 goals, eight short of second-placed Jimmy Greaves on 44 and record-holder Charlton with 48. Given the rate at which he was scoring, it felt as though Lineker would be in with a shout of breaking that record.

'That is another goal of Gary's: to be the leading goalscorer,' Taylor told the press. 'I haven't spoken to him about it, but I would bet my last dollar that that is what he's after. He's got 14 to go and that is not beyond him. He's a naturally fit lad and he's only 29.'

England's new dawn had started well, with Lineker stating he didn't feel the need to change anything about his game now he was captain. He admitted, though, that it wasn't all plain sailing for him.

'I've always tried to talk a lot and encourage people. I found it very enjoyable,' Lineker said post-match. 'The biggest difference for me was the captain's armband – it kept slipping down, it was driving me crazy.'

Lineker repeated the trick in the next match too, scoring and retaining the captaincy for the 2–0 European Championship qualifier victory over Poland. He was so at ease with the armband now that he didn't relinquish it when a cut to the head caused him to be replaced early in the second half in order to get stitches.

After the match, Taylor revealed that Lineker would remain captain for the next qualifier against the Republic of Ireland in a month's time. There appeared to be no question of how highly the new England manager rated the striker's abilities as a player or a person.

CAPTAINCY, RECORDS AND FALL-OUTS

Bryan Robson's return for the matches with Cameroon and the return match with the Republic of Ireland at the start of 1991 did see Lineker temporarily hand back the captaincy to the Manchester United midfielder. But when it became clear Robson's international career was never going to rekindle, Lineker took over once more.

'I went for Gary for a number of reasons,' Taylor wrote in his autobiography, *Graham Taylor: In His Own Words*. 'He was well respected and when he spoke, people did listen to him. I can't say he was a leader of men like Bryan Robson or Stuart Pearce, who would roll up their sleeves and show the way for the rest, but he had a quiet authority about him. If I'm honest, I knew I needed Gary's influence on my side rather than against me, and giving him the captaincy was one way to do that.'

If Lineker was fit and starting, then he appeared to be Taylor's man – publicly at least. Behind the scenes, however, there had always been an inkling that Taylor was constantly testing Lineker to see if he was fit for the role. One such test, according to Lineker's agent Jon Holmes quoted in Colin Malam's 1993 biography *Gary Lineker: Strikingly Different*, was to tell him that Gazza would be dropped for the away match against the Republic of Ireland – a revelation Lineker refused to divulge to anybody else.

There had also been some discontent about how Taylor managed the two games when Robson returned as captain. While it was reported at the time that the captaincy was being judged on a game-by-game basis, there was some unrest about how that was handled, with Holmes stating again in *Strikingly Different* that the first he and Lineker knew about the change was after they received off-the-record tips from journalists in the know.

The Ireland game appeared to be a key moment in the relationship. After Lineker was substituted in the 76th minute, the striker told the media that he was feeling tired, while Taylor responded with his less-than-complimentary thoughts.

Lineker took up the comments with Taylor at the next England camp, explaining he felt any issue should have been dealt with behind closed doors. Relations were strained, but the issues weren't having too much of a material impact on performances.

England were hardly free-flowing but they were effective under Taylor and – despite some of the alleged games going on out of public view – Lineker continued to score regularly. The forward bagged a brace in the friendly with Cameroon, notched up another in an exhibition match with Argentina and scored five in three games in an end-of-season tour to the southern hemisphere.

It was while on that four-match summer trip that the differences between Lineker and Taylor began to grow larger. After playing in a 1–0 win against Australia less than 24 hours after landing Down Under, Lineker scored the winner two days later in a victory over New Zealand. But with England due to play the All Whites again less than a week later, Lineker ducked out of the camp for five days to join up with his Tottenham teammates as they toured Japan.

While the break was pre-arranged for Lineker to return for the final match of the tour against Malaysia, Taylor remained cynical about how selfless his captain's intentions were when he was accompanied by his agent Holmes for the trip. Arguably Taylor was proved right as the trip to Japan became the prelude to Lineker's move to Nagoya Grampus Eight a year later, but the scepticism further tainted what should have been a close bond between manager and player.

A jet-lagged Lineker played for Spurs in a 4–0 defeat in Tokyo, before getting back in time for the Malaysia game in a sweltering Kuala Lumpur. If there had been any question that Lineker wasn't fully committed to the tour, though, the four goals he scored to slay the Malaysians 4–2 surely put paid to any suggestions that commercial interests were his priority.

Each goal highlighted Lineker's sharpness in the box, snaffling up a first within a minute and a perfect hat-trick within half an hour. Each of the goals were clinical first-time finishes – the first lashing in with his left foot, the second a tap in with the right, and his third a flicked header from a few yards out. With 20 minutes remaining of the second half, he added a fourth, drifting into space in the six-yard box before heading home John Salako's centre. It was goal poaching at its finest.

'It wasn't the best preparation, but it's all been worthwhile,' conceded Lineker to a Press Association reporter. 'The last time I played in conditions like that was Monterrey in the 1986 World Cup in Mexico, but at least then we had three weeks to acclimatise.

'The whole team showed tremendous resilience to keep going. I'll get all the glory, I suppose, I was just there on the end of things while the rest of the team were carving out the chances.'

Lineker's four-goal spree took his England total to 45, going past Greaves into outright second place and only three goals behind Charlton. It now seemed a case of when rather than if Lineker would break the record, but he was typically blasé about the prospect.

'I seem to spend half my life talking about this record,' Lineker said modestly. 'It's my job to score goals and all the time I'm doing that I maintain my place in the side. If the record comes, it comes but I'm more concerned with helping England be successful, whoever scores the goals.

'It's just nice to be in the company of people like Jimmy Greaves and Bobby Charlton. Jimmy did it a little bit quicker than me [Greaves hit 44 goals in 57 caps, compared to Lineker's 68], but it's great because he's one of the all-time great goalscorers and everyone always talks about him. I only saw him at the very end of his career, but I've seen clips of lots of his goals on television. He's an all-time great and I'm happy to be up alongside him.'

Lineker's next England goal turned out to be of crucial importance for both his country and his hopes of topping Charlton's record. Needing a point to qualify for Euro '92, the Three Lions found themselves 1–0 down away at Poland with less than 15 minutes left to play. Missing out on the tournament would have been unthinkable for a side that were World Cup semi-finalists less than 18 months earlier, but would also significantly reduce the number of games Lineker would have to add to his goals tally.

Roman Szewczyk's heavily deflected long-range drive had given the Poles the lead just past the half-hour mark and as much as England huffed and puffed, they were struggling to make much headway.

A long punt forward to Lineker by Lee Dixon would provide the impetus for that to change, with the number 10 taking the ball down brilliantly before playing a one-two with David Rocastle to give him enough space on the right flank to win a corner. Then, from the resulting set piece, Gary Mabbutt leapt highest to head at goal, where Lineker was lurking – finding enough space to volley while falling backwards as the ball flew into the net.

That goal had rescued England and Taylor from humiliation and was enough to earn a 1–1 draw that saw them take the only qualification spot by finishing top of the group. And Lineker was in no doubt about the significance of his strike, both for his team and on a personal level.

'I was fully aware that if we hadn't qualified, this could well have been my last game [for England] because the manager would have had to look to 1994,' England's goalscoring hero said to the press. 'That would be the common sense thing to do and it's debatable if I would still be around then, especially with the calls for change.

'It's got to be one of the most important goals I've ever scored. If we hadn't qualified, it would have been disastrous for English football.'

Despite playing the role of England's saviour against Poland, Lineker found himself on the bench as the tournament preparation started with a friendly against France in February. Alan Shearer and David Hirst were the preferred partnership up front instead, although Lineker proved he didn't need the full 90 minutes to make an impact as he scored the second of a 2–0 win after being introduced at half time.

Lineker was benched again the next month for the friendly trip to face Czechoslovakia in Prague, only coming on for the last 12 minutes after Taylor opted to start Nigel Clough and Mark Hateley together. When Clough came off at half time, it was Lineker's Tottenham comrade Paul Stewart who got the nod.

There were conspiracy theories doing the rounds that Taylor wasn't keen on Lineker matching Charlton's record and so was reducing his playing time to cut down the chances of that happening. It was a premise Taylor vehemently denied, although it hadn't gone unnoticed within the England squad that there was friction between Lineker and the manager.

'I think people notice it, teammates notice, Gary would mention it,' recalls Smith. 'With Bobby Robson, it was certainly a lot different. It was just a different approach to football that Graham had and it's difficult. It just didn't click between them, which is odd really because Gary was an established international goalscorer and a star having done so well at Italia '90. He was the man most likely to get goals for Graham's side, but for whatever reason, there was just a little bit of something between them.'

Lineker was given the full 90 minutes when England came together again for another friendly against the Soviet Union in April, netting the opener to move within one goal of Charlton's record. With three tournament warm-up matches still to come against Hungary, Brazil and Finland, and a minimum of three matches at the Euros, Lineker would now expect to have six shots at the record.

The first opportunity came and went in a goalless 68-minute spell against Hungary, although Lineker did set up the only goal of the game by teeing up Neil Webb to score. Lineker's blank did cost Taylor, though, who had made a wager before the game that it'd be the night Lineker would go into the England history books.

'I bet one member of staff £5 that Gary would score twice and break the record tonight,' lamented Taylor to press after the match. 'And anyone who knows me will know how upset I am about that. But I can confirm that he'll be starting on Sunday [against Brazil] and I'll probably go for double or quits and hope he does it then.'

Despite Taylor's backing, there were some quarters of the press that questioned his decision to bring Lineker off for Ian Wright midway through the second half and suggested that keeping him on would have been the right thing to do in order to help him get the goals he needed.

'It was always my intention to give him [Wright] what is not necessarily a final chance, but an opportunity and it was just the way it worked out that it was Gary who had to come off,' insisted Taylor. 'Like the rest of the Great British public, I want Gary to break the record, but I don't base my decisions on emotion. We've got a lot of fish to fry as well as that goalscoring record. And I'm sure he'll get that.'

Perhaps it was fitting that Lineker's next bite at the cherry was also his final match at Wembley against Brazil. It was a narrative the media gobbled up, lauding the 'goal-den moment' that presented itself for the perfect ending that wouldn't look out of place alongside the striker's other career achievements.

'Gary Lineker's Wembley send-off could rival a Frank Sinatra farewell concert for emotion if England scores against Brazil,' one Press Association reporter wrote poetically. 'Lineker's soccer CV reads like a fairytale so few would bet against him penning a Wembley epitaph with the goal he needs.'

The story was almost too good not to buy into. To say the Wembley crowd expected to witness history being made may be a bit much, but they were certainly braced and ready for it to happen. Lineker had scored the previous two times the Seleção had visited Wembley, so as he lined up in the pristine red shirt and white shorts in the summer sunshine, he knew he had what it took to do the business.

Only 10 minutes in and the moment looked to have arrived when Lineker was upended by goalkeeper Carlos to win a penalty that the striker himself would take. As the Brazilians protested the decision, Lineker calmly took the ball, playing keepy-uppy on the spot before settling himself for the spot-kick. Renato ruffled his hair as he prepared for his date with destiny. It was a scenario Lineker had rehearsed, and now he attempted to follow through with his plan.

As the visitors' complaints were waved away, eventually only Lineker, Carlos and the referee were left in the box. Moving over to the spot, the striker bent down to position the ball and ran his hand through his hair, before turning to make his way to where his run-up would begin. Time may have felt like it was moving slowly for Lineker, but his eagerness to get the penalty taken was clear as he set off to strike the penalty like a 100-metre sprinter reacting to the starter's gun, reacting immediately.

The goalkeeper dived to his right, guessing where the would-be record breaker would aim. But Lineker had other ideas, nonchalantly chipping his spot-kick down the middle of goal. With Carlos vacating that space, all that was left was surely for the net to bulge. But it didn't.

As Lineker's dink slowly floated towards the goal, Carlos had enough time to alter his body shape, throwing out his big left arm to stop the ball and then dive on it before his opponent could reach it. Lineker's head dropped and he grimaced, eyes down, before trotting back into position. He'd missed what would prove to be his best chance of the afternoon in an otherwise subdued display. This wasn't written in the script.

In the years that followed, Lineker was asked with regularity why he elected to go for the dinked penalty in a situation of such significance.

'The same reason I chipped five or six others; you've got to vary them because people monitor how you take penalties – every other time I'd done it, I'd scored,' Lineker told *FourFourTwo* in 2015. 'I'd done a bit of research and noticed their keeper always went down early, so I thought it was perfect for a little dink.

'I used to practise penalties in the week before a match, so I'd been hitting 30 or 40 of them a day on a crappy surface at Bisham Abbey. Then when it came to taking one at Wembley, the surface was lush and I hit it a bit fat. It was very embarrassing. The annoying thing was that the keeper actually did go down early, but my penalty was so pathetic it still went straight to him.'

Taylor suggested after the match that pressure had played its part in Lineker's miss. Yet as Patrick Barclay points out, the anxiety surrounding the record must have been less than that he'd experienced in previous situations, in which he'd thrived.

'I can remember thinking it was amazing that he missed the chance because he'd taken penalties under far greater pressure,' says

Barclay. 'The most pressure he ever felt taking penalties was the Cameroon game [in the Italia '90 quarter-final] when he must have dragged his legs up to that spot because of the pressure.

'But for those penalties, Cameroon would have knocked England out of the World Cup and it would have been portrayed as one of England's most inglorious episodes. So to be quite honest, there was much less pressure in the Brazil game.'

The missed penalty would be Lineker's best chance against Brazil and despite seeing out the full match, he couldn't make many more inroads against the South Americans' defence. Taylor hadn't been thrilled by Lineker's performance, record attempt or not, and made an ill-advised comment about his striker that ended up plastered across some of the next day's newspapers.

'By then I was on the *Observer* and, at that time, the England manager would do a separate briefing with the Sunday papers so we had some different angles to come at,' recalls Barclay. 'In his [Taylor's] briefing with the Sunday papers – and it appeared to be on record – he talked about Lineker and no doubt alluded to his lack of tracking back on opponents. He said it was like playing Brazil with 10 men.

'It struck me as a fantastic quote, so I used it. One or two of the others tried to protect Graham from it, but he certainly didn't say it was off the record. He didn't think Lineker was unalloyed to the team, [but] he didn't think the goals he scored made up for his perceived lack of contribution to the team's defensive effort.'

Whether or not the comments were initially intended to motivate Lineker, they didn't come across well and there was little doubt what Taylor truly felt. Regardless of any fall-out, Lineker's hunt for that elusive goal went on – hitting the bar against Finland in the last pre-tournament match.

The longer the goalless run went on, the more interest grew around Lineker. Surely he wouldn't miss the chance to break the record?

He barely had a sniff in the group opener with Denmark as England played out a stalemate with the eventual winners. Next up were France and a similar tale. It wasn't as if Lineker was fluffing his lines, he simply wasn't getting the chances.

CAPTAINCY, RECORDS AND FALL-OUTS

A second consecutive stalemate left England needing something from the final group match against hosts Sweden to reach the last four. A high-scoring draw could have been enough, as long as France and Denmark shared the spoils in a low-scoring encounter in the other group match, but victory was the only way for them to guarantee progress.

David Platt's fourth-minute goal had England on their way early on, but when Janne Eriksson levelled things up after the break, the onus was on Taylor's side to find another goal. Then with 61 minutes on the clock came the infamous change that ended Lineker's England career, the board going up to call him prematurely off the pitch.

It was seen as the culmination of a challenging two years, with the subtle snipes and digs finally resulting in a move that shook the nation.

'They weren't the kind of people to be nasty, but it was a strained relationship. An extraordinary relationship between manager and captain, you'd have to say,' Barclay explains.

'Another thing Graham had said to us in a [press] briefing and we didn't use was that when Alan Smith came on in the qualifying match away to Poland, he told the players, "Don't lump it up to the big man because if you do, the media will slaughter me." Well, that's exactly what happened when he brought Lineker off against Sweden in the tournament. The public support was 100 per cent for Lineker because substituting him like that was seen as demeaning a national treasure.'

Not only did Taylor's substitution rob Lineker of half an hour more to get the goal he craved, but it also failed to deliver the returns for England in a tournament context, with Brolin's late goal consigning the English to bottom spot in the group.

'It was only afterwards that you had all the reaction, but I still think it was a strange decision to take off Gary,' Smith says now. 'Graham Taylor and him never quite clicked and there was a little bit of friction between them, but I think Graham made the wrong call then – not by bringing me on, but by bringing him off for me.'

The post-mortem appeared to concur, with many pundits in shock at just how things had ended. Even now, BBC commentator Barry Davies talks of his 'absolute amazement' at Taylor's decision. It would characterise the entire tournament.

The treatment of Lineker at such a crucial time became a major talking point in the ensuing weeks. Taylor was naturally in the crosshairs of many after presiding over the Euros failure, with several journalists suggesting his 'humiliation' of his captain was an indication of the issues England were currently facing. There was sympathy for Lineker at not just his treatment but also having to contend with the manager's long-ball tactics, with the *Liverpool Echo* branding them 'Taylor-made for disaster'.

The man whose record Lineker was aiming to beat, Bobby Charlton, also came out in support of the retiring goalscorer. 'Graham Taylor was wrong,' said Charlton in the wake of the game. 'I was surprised to see Gary come off; he was unlucky.'

But not everybody agreed. In fact, two England legends were vehement in their belief that it was the correct decision for Lineker to be brought off and had shown why the striker himself had decided the time was right to bow out of international football.

'Let me remind you that I said before the Championship that Gary Lineker was finished,' former Three Lions captain Emlyn Hughes wrote in his *Daily Mirror* column. 'I was treated as though I had a screw loose. But I was proved right again. Gary didn't do the business because he's lost that killer instinct and doesn't have anyone around him to help get it back.'

World Cup-winning boss Alf Ramsey shared Hughes' opinion and backed Taylor for not letting sentiment affect his judgement, saying he would have done the same. 'The cold, cruel facts are that Lineker was out of the game, hadn't had a chance and wasn't scaring the Swedes,' said Ramsey in the *Daily Mirror*. 'I know Taylor has been criticised for taking his skipper off, but he had to do it.'

Regardless of the debate that roared on, the fact remained that eight years after making his England debut, Lineker's international career hadn't ended in the blaze of glory many had envisaged. There was a feeling of incompletion, that the nation had been robbed of a narrative it had yearned for.

Some more dewy-eyed observers even called for Lineker to reconsider his decision to cease playing for England beyond the end of the tournament. The Japan-bound striker would have none of it, though, snapping back with 'no chance at all' when asked if he'd perform a U-turn. Instead, Lineker was left to rue what might have been in his eternally humble way.

'I felt good and I nearly got on the end of a couple,' Lineker told the written press. 'Of course I didn't want to come off, but managers make those decisions and managers have to live or die by them. But there was nothing I could do about it. I just wanted the team to go on and score, whether I was on or off the field. I would have been happy then. Bobby [Charlton] deserves his record. He was a far better player than I am.'

Any of the defenders or goalkeepers who'd felt the full force of Lineker's goalscoring prowess would probably disagree. He may not have hung up his boots for England celebrating a milestone he'd looked destined to pass, but he had undoubtedly been one of his country's very best.

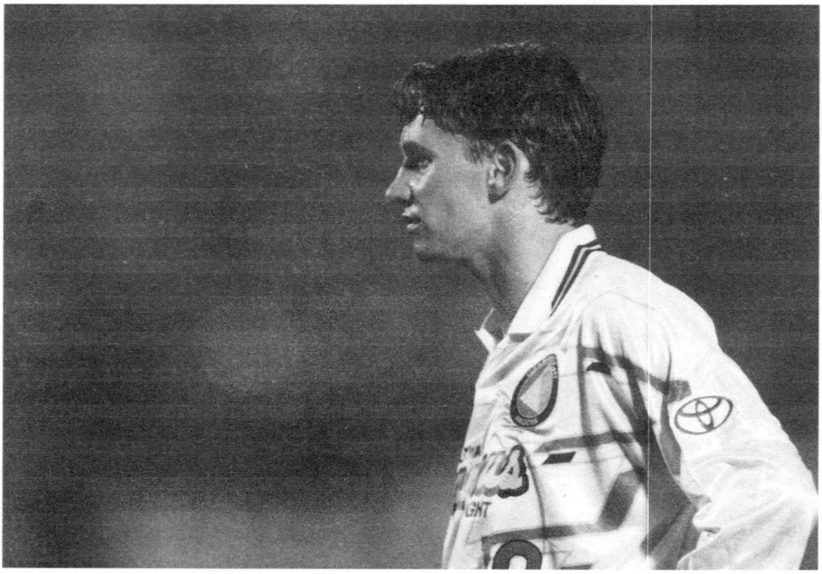

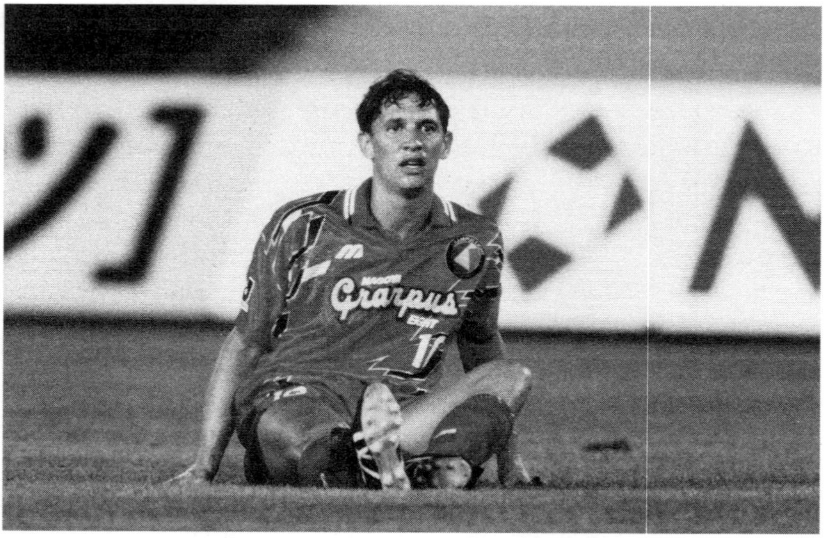
Grampus

17

A NEW ADVENTURE

Nagoya Grampus Eight, 1992–1994

'The fans were absolutely into the stars. For them it was a miracle that these players – Zico, Gary and me – were there. They couldn't understand that.'

A throng of Japanese fans gathered around the walkway, waiting for a glimpse of their hero. Lining the streets surrounding the gated-off passage, the supporters started to scream and shout like excitable groupies as they first caught sight of the star. It was the sort of reaction you'd expect to see for a world-famous boyband, with a predominantly female cohort waving autograph books, memorabilia and – bizarrely – holding out whiteboards to be signed.

Smiling to politely acknowledge the crowd, the man they wanted to see was Gary Lineker, Japan's new sports star. It had been more than a year since one of England's greatest ever goalscorers had announced he was joining Nagoya Grampus Eight from Tottenham and the excitement around his arrival hadn't lost any of its sheen.

Flanked by his teammates, including a couple of other foreign imports, Lineker was the undoubted attraction. He was one of three megastars to have joined the J-League for its launch, with former Brazil international Zico and West Germany's World Cup winner Pierre Littbarski posted elsewhere on the island nation to get the party started. And it was definitely working.

Lineker was in Japan's third-biggest city, Nagoya, based 260km (160 miles) south-west of capital Tokyo. Famed in the country for having the nation's biggest seaport, the city was also home to Grampus Eight, one of 10 professional football clubs that would form part of the new J-League.

The formerly amateur league had previously been made up of works sides, with Grampus Eight – a name derived from Grampus, a legendary dolphin that saved Nagoya, and Japanese lucky number eight – still run by the Toyoda family, who owned car firm Toyota. They'd used that financial clout to attract Lineker to the club, with the Englishman reported to be earning north of £2 million across his two-year deal with the side. But to them and the J-League as a whole, he was worth every penny.

'It's important for a new team to establish a good tradition and in order to fulfil our children's dreams, it has to play fair,' explained Grampus Eight managing director Narumi Nishigaki in an interview with the BBC in May 1993. 'For that reason, Gary Lineker is a very suitable person. We are glad to have him.'

It's true, Lineker's squeaky-clean image and commitment to fair play made him the perfect signing for a Japanese audience. The J-League was hoping to attract younger fans into the game and the England striker fed into that culture: respectful, polite and a bastion of doing things the right way.

The Japan Football Association (JFA) had devised a plan to drum up support for football in the country that would form an integral part of its joint bid to host the 2002 World Cup with South Korea. The strategy had been carefully formulated by taking into account where other leagues in emerging football nations – such as Major League Soccer (MLS) in America – had fallen flat previously, namely by stacking teams too highly with expensive imports, only for them to all leave at the end of their lucrative contracts with little legacy in their wake.

Instead, there was a strict limit of three overseas players per matchday team, meaning that sides were still predominantly made up of homegrown Japanese talent. The new signings would bring clout and attention, without blowing the bank and blocking the progression of the players who would be crucial to growing the national game after the foreigners had gone.

Lineker had certainly helped to raise the profile of his new club, with Nagoya Grampus Eight now a name familiar with British football fans in particular following the surprise announcement in November 1991 that he'd be leaving Spurs to move to Japan.

Although the transfer gathered pace in the run-up to Lineker's unveiling, the move had first been sounded out eight months earlier when Grampus Eight got in touch with Tottenham to enquire about the forward's availability. Some initial conversations took place between the clubs and Lineker's agent Jon Holmes, but there was no real movement until the following June when Spurs played a friendly in Tokyo.

Lineker had been on England duty on a tour of the southern hemisphere at the time but arranged a brief sojourn to line up for his club in the match. It provided an opportunity for him to get a flavour of the country and see first-hand what the JFA and Grampus Eight had planned. The intention had initially been for Lineker to see out his Spurs contract and retire in the summer of 1993, but the plan of being involved with the J-League appealed.

'The Japanese came in and we thought, "Well, this is something completely different,"' Lineker said in a BBC article published on 12 May 2023. 'Obviously it was a big payday, but I'd always been interested in travelling and experiencing other cultures after playing in Barcelona and this seemed like a really nice way to end my career, in a country that had always fascinated me and would also be safe for my family.

'I didn't want to just go gradually downhill in England, which I already felt like I was on the brink of doing because I knew my powers were waning, so it appealed for footballing reasons. I thought I could go out there and still score a few goals and it would all be really positive.'

Despite signing and announcing the deal in late 1991, there was still some doubt over the transfer until relatively close to the Linekers upping sticks and flying to Japan. The family had been rocked by baby George's illness and while his treatment continued, they were unwilling to promise that a move halfway around the world was feasible. Thankfully, with George in remission and showing no signs in his regular blood tests of relapsing, Lineker and wife Michelle felt it was possible to make final preparations.

There was still some level of disbelief when Lineker finally touched down to join up with his new side. It was as though the idea had seemed unlikely until he was actually there, wearing Grampus Eight colours.

'I was surprised Gary was there because I'd never have expected he would go,' says Littbarski, who joined JEF United Ichihara. 'From my point of view, this was something after my career had finished, but Gary still had a lot to give to the league, so it was different.'

The German winger, who is also known for his friendly demeanour, was blown away by the reaction he and his other big-name signings were greeted with. The level of interest was huge and the Japanese public had taken to the idea of the J-League in a big way.

'The fans were absolutely into the stars, for them it was a miracle that these players – Zico, Gary and me – were there. They couldn't understand that,' Littbarski continues. 'Every supporter I saw in the stadium was wearing the kit from the team and it was absolutely fantastic.

'There were thousands of people waiting for me on my first day and after every training session. There were so many supporters there every day and we'd do at least an hour of signing after each time we trained. Before the games, we stayed in a hotel and they'd have a long line, almost like a queue for a bus, that you could see from a long way away because there were so many people waiting for us to sign things. It was fantastic.'

The Linekers moved into a two-bedroom apartment in Nagoya and soon got stuck into Japanese life. The gap between the announcement and the completion of the transfer had given

Gary and Michelle the chance to start learning the language, and while Japanese isn't the easiest dialect to grasp, they had a basic understanding of how to ask the most important questions by the time they arrived.

Translators around the club made adapting to Japan's football culture easier, too. To his amusement, Lineker found some of the country's football lingo sounded almost familiar, with the locals shouting 'naisushotto' for good shot and 'ofusaido' for offside, among other quirks.

The training ground was pristinely kept and lined with rhododendron bushes to give it an attractive look, while everything was run with the utmost professionalism. The owner, Dr Toyoda, was based in a palatial office in Nagoya and as a neighbour of the Linekers, was never too far away from his star signing.

'For me, it's a great challenge. It's something totally different, very exciting and totally new,' Lineker said to the BBC upon his move. 'The start of a professional league, to help promote soccer and to live in a country like this is a fantastic experience and one we're going to try to enjoy, and I'm sure we will.'

Lineker threw himself into his assignment, with the BBC feature claiming the striker had taken to his responsibility by breaking the habit of a lifetime to train twice daily for three months. He was undoubtedly in good shape and was ranked top of a fitness challenge with his Grampus Eight teammates – an accolade Lineker admitted 'surprised' him – and was happy to offer advice to his fellow players to help develop their games.

The former England captain also threw himself into his promotional responsibilities, appearing at events and filming adverts to fulfil a series of commercial commitments, as well as promoting the J-League. In one particularly infamous gig, Lineker donned a Japanese police uniform and jumped aboard a motorcycle as part of a traffic safety campaign.

He scored his first goal in Grampus Eight colours with a diving header in a 2–1 friendly victory over Lazio, then added two more as the Japanese side got the better of Brazilians Grêmio. On the face of it, life in Japan had started well.

'I feel almost in 100 per cent condition,' said Lineker, who had been given the bizarre nickname 'Noble Barbarian' by his Japanese public. 'Taking goals when given space in the penalty area is my job.'

Only Lineker wasn't in the best possible shape. He'd been carrying a toe injury throughout the second half of his final season with Tottenham and played on by taking painkillers to reduce the agony. It was hoped an operation in October would relieve the issue before he arrived in Japan, but it did little to improve the situation.

On the morning of the new J-League season, an earthquake hit nearby, shaking the hotel Grampus Eight were staying in, yet it was far from the only shock they were about to face that day. Their new star striker was already aware he was unable to play to his full potential due to his injury, but he was about to discover his teammates weren't up to the job of carrying him.

Their opening match was against Zico's Kashima Antlers in front of a sell-out crowd. The JFA hadn't scrimped on any of the pomp and pageantry the launch of a new national football league deserved, with fireworks, flags and loud music creating a fantastic atmosphere. The excitement was huge, with a family-friendly feeling that Lineker later described as being like going to an England Schoolboys international.

Unfortunately for Grampus Eight, that's where the fun ended as Zico showed his enduring quality to inspire a 5–0 win. Lineker barely got a kick and didn't have a single sight of goal across the 90 minutes. For a player who relied heavily on good service and was in too much pain to take on the extra workload, it was a worrying sign – and a trend that continued thereafter, with only one goal in his first six matches.

The standard was always expected to be lower than Lineker and his fellow superstars were accustomed to. Yet it was still taking some time for them to make the adjustment.

'It was different. In terms of quality, it was generally OK, but the European style was different – faster and better,' Littbarski explains. 'It was quite difficult to play there [in Japan]. Firstly because of the surface, as the pitches were different, the grass was very high and I fell over the ball a few times, which had never happened before. I had to adapt to the climate and grass situation.

'There were also times when you were used to players moving into certain spaces, but they didn't go there – they hesitated and when I first arrived in Japan, I was thinking faster than the players could react. That took some time to adapt to and to change how the players did things. They were so polite and didn't want to do things that would upset you, but hesitation in football is very difficult.'

Lineker's issues were set to worsen. While he was managing his toe injury to play for his new side initially, he started to get shooting pains in the one next to it. He had his big toe checked and X-rayed by the club's doctors, who diagnosed a damaged tendon and gave him a painkilling injection in order for him to play. It appeared to have done the trick until Lineker's entire foot balled up into a claw, causing him to be brought off.

Upon arrival at the hospital, he underwent further X-rays, which revealed that the bone in his toe had completely snapped and he'd need a procedure to screw it back together. It ruled Lineker out for the next three months, but upon his return, the old injury flared up even more and required another round of intensive treatment.

'I'm not happy with the condition of the toe,' said Lineker. 'It's very frustrating, but luckily my club are being very supportive.'

In Lineker's absence, Grampus Eight limped to a ninth-place finish out of 10 teams. But there was a bigger concern for their striker, who for a short time contemplated retiring before deciding to go through with a full reconstruction of his foot, followed by eight months of recovery.

This was Lineker's first major injury in his entire career, but while he came to terms with having to spend a long time on the sidelines, he could at least spend more time with his young family, who had just welcomed its fourth member, with second son Harry – named after Gary's grandfather – born in July. After the travails following George's birth, it was a relief that this time everything went as smoothly as can be expected with a newborn.

In the meantime, the Grampus Eight top brass looked for an answer to their on-pitch issues. They'd identified Terry Venables as a possible managerial appointment and met with the former Spurs gaffer in September 1993, but couldn't agree a deal. They went instead for another Englishman and previous manager of Lineker's, Gordon Milne, who'd had a successful seven-year spell at Besiktas in Turkey after leaving Leicester in 1986.

'Gary was pretty influential in getting Gordon to go there, along with Gary's agent Jon Holmes,' says Lineker's former Leicester teammate Ian Wilson, who joined Milne as his assistant. 'Gordon got the job and he got in touch with me. I was working at Peterhead, a Second Division team in Scotland, at the time and he said, "Would you be interested in coming to help me with pre-season for a month?" and I said, "Yes." I was out there for a fortnight and got a contract to stay.'

Reuniting with Milne and Wilson was a welcome bonus for Lineker as he continued his recovery from injury. For his second season in Japan, he was still heavily involved in the promotional side of things, but the pressure to get back fit was relieved somewhat by the arrival of Yugoslavia international Dragan Stojković from Marseille.

Stojković was Lineker's heir apparent as a big-name player and while that left Milne's squad overloaded with foreign players – especially when the ex-England man was fit – it appeased the owners' demand for star quality out on the pitch. And with the former Leicester contingent on the bench, Lineker would still get in the team when fit, despite any injury issues.

'Although Gary had a sore toe that hindered the amount of games he played, he was a great ambassador for the club,' says Wilson. 'Anything promotional that was going on, Gary was the face of it and promoted the brand Nagoya was trying to produce. Gary was always going to play if he was fit because he could score a goal out of nothing.

'Even if you were say in the dugout and Gary wasn't in the game, you tended to leave him on because his first touch might be a goal, that was basically how good he was. Keep him on because if something drops to him or the defender doesn't deal with it very well, there's a chance Gary will stick it in the back of the net. That's the best compliment I can give him.'

Grampus Eight's struggles on the pitch continued, though, not aided by the J-League's rules to play golden goal extra time or penalties to decide drawn games – meaning several games that would ordinarily have ended a point apiece went down as another defeat. It made it difficult to build confidence and the Nagoya side found themselves near the wrong end of the table once more.

Lineker felt a sense of responsibility for those difficulties due to his injury and continued to throw himself into any off-field activities he could, to make up for intermittent absence from the first team. He was an ambassador in every sense of the word and would offer advice wherever appropriate. Lineker regularly referenced how patient the club had been with him and there was no sign of the Japanese public losing their infatuation with him even if he wasn't playing as much as anyone had hoped.

'They [the Japanese players] hung on his every word,' says Wilson. 'None of them had ever seen anything like him, they were signing one of the best players in the world, all of the players looked up to him and the fans did too. Wherever he went to play games – Nagoya, Tokyo, Kobi or Hiroshima – the local players were looked after, but the cameras would all follow Gary. He had a lot in his face, but he just dealt with it and I think he knew that was going to be the case, but it stood him in good stead further down the line when he moved into the media later on. They were everywhere with him.'

The striker had been given the all-clear to return to the side by doctors in June but held off until the second stage of the J-League began in late July. Two months later, he announced his intention to retire from playing at the end of the season, as he continued to struggle with running and had lost some of the pace that had made him so deadly down the years. He ended his career in Japan with only nine goals across his two seasons with Grampus Eight, a haul he wasn't proud of.

'People who knew him would have known why he wanted to go to Japan: out of curiosity,' says Patrick Barclay. 'He'd already been to Barcelona and that was a lot further away then than it is now. There was a curiosity about the way of life.

'But as it turned out, if fate had given him the toe injury, it's just that he let down the Japanese fans – and he did feel rotten about that and he felt he'd short-changed them because of the injury and wasn't able to give the chap value for money. It definitely wasn't one of the high points of his career. If fate had that injury in store, it was probably as well that it happened on the other side of the world from his point of view.

'Because Lineker's game relied so much on pace, he would never have gone on for as long as the likes of the late Ray Wilkins or Teddy Sheringham, who both played to a grand old age because they didn't have a lot of pace to lose. As a result, we do remember Lineker at his peak. Only a Japanese pundit would say his career fizzled out.

'He handled it well because all people remember are his great deeds at Spurs, the cup final triumph and long overdue medal, and the World Cups – those are what you remember of his career. Whether he micro-planned it or not, it worked out pretty well reputation-wise.'

Time on the sidelines had helped Lineker work out what he wanted to do next. While he'd always been drawn to journalism, the nature of his time in Japan had given the 33-year-old time to properly consider his priorities and a path to achieve it. Lineker's former England teammate Bryan Robson tried to convince him to keep playing by joining him at Middlesbrough, with Southampton reportedly sounding him out too. The idea of coaching had also been suggested, but Lineker's mind was made up.

'I want to stay involved in the game somehow, but certainly not as a coach or manager – that doesn't appeal,' Lineker told BBC Radio Five Live as he announced his retirement. 'I don't think I'm the type and I wouldn't be any good at it either. I think my ambitions are certainly, in the near future, towards the media side of the game – TV or possibly the radio or perhaps writing a little bit, something I've started to do recently.'

Lineker had started to feather his own nest in the closing months at Nagoya and had already started making plans for his post-playing career. He'd excelled in a promotional role for the J-League and was keen to explore those same avenues when he moved back to England. One relationship that was growing was with Walkers, a Leicester-based crisp manufacturer, for whom he'd first shot an advert in 1986.

At that stage, it hadn't turned into regular work, but by the time he was preparing to hang up his boots, it appeared Walkers and Lineker could see how a longer-term relationship could be beneficial. The trouble was, being in Japan meant shooting an ad back in the UK wasn't an easy one to swing.

'I always remember training one time and we're putting the boys through their paces and Gary comes up to me and says, "Ian, I need to go back to the UK,"' recalls Wilson. 'I said, "Gary, it's a Tuesday afternoon, it'll take you a day and a half to go back to get there and a day and a half to get back." He said, "You've got to speak to the boss, I need to go home." So I asked, "Alright, is everything OK at home or is somebody unwell?"

'He said, "No, I need to go back to do an advert." I said, "An advert?" and he said, "Yeah." I asked him if he minded me asking who it's with and he said, "Walkers crisps." He told me what he'd benefit from it financially and I asked if I could carry his bags. I spoke to Gordon and he let him go to get it done, and that was that. He's been doing it ever since.'

Japan had been the perfect breeding ground for Lineker's future career choice. He'd revelled in the role as Grampus Eight's star attraction and had handled the increased attention with the easy charm that had always accompanied his dealings with the media. He'd been a big name back at home for some time, but the level of attention he'd received in Japan was in an entirely different league. Lineker had sampled what it was like to be an A-list celebrity.

'He gained a lot of experience that people wouldn't have seen if they weren't in Nagoya, but me and Gordon saw him develop,' adds Wilson. 'He was standing in the right way, he was on interviews, on the microphone, taking pictures, he was dealing with press and TV cameras everywhere he went in Nagoya.

'He's got [a] character [that means] that he can promote himself, wherever he is – and he did it at Grampus Eight – and maybe he got better there and did presentations if something big was happening with Toyota. He began to adapt pretty well to TV cameras and there was a lot of them about at the time, wherever he went.

'There were TV crews following him wherever he went, whether it was on the Shinkansen [bullet trains] going from Nagoya to Tokyo, or coming out of the stadium, going out for a meal, they'd maybe follow and catch you there. He certainly did quite a lot there and I'm pretty sure that stood him in good stead for the future.'

Life in Nagoya had definitely prepared Lineker for life as a TV celebrity, although he must have hoped rather than expected he'd go on to achieve the level of success he has since experienced in the media.

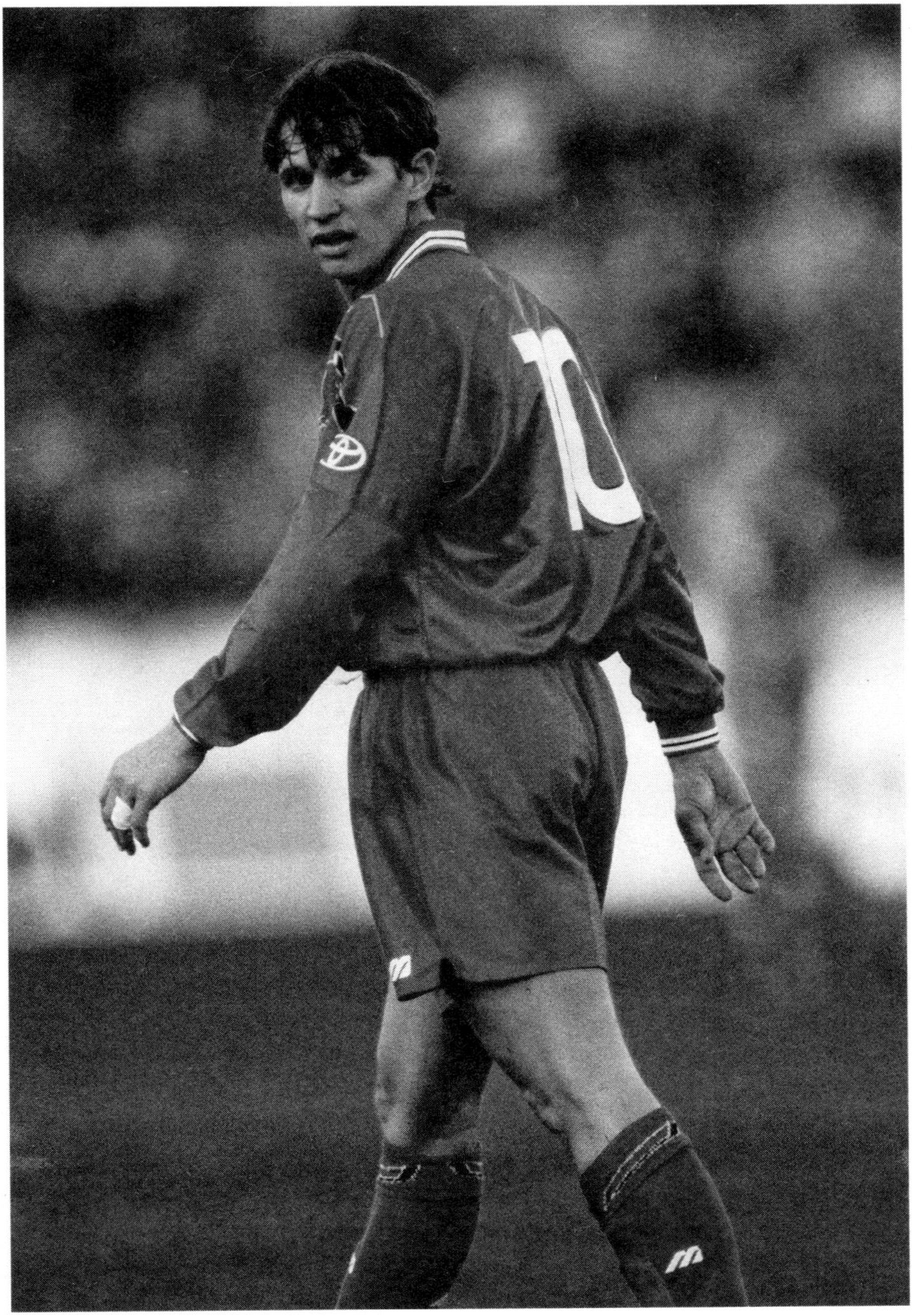

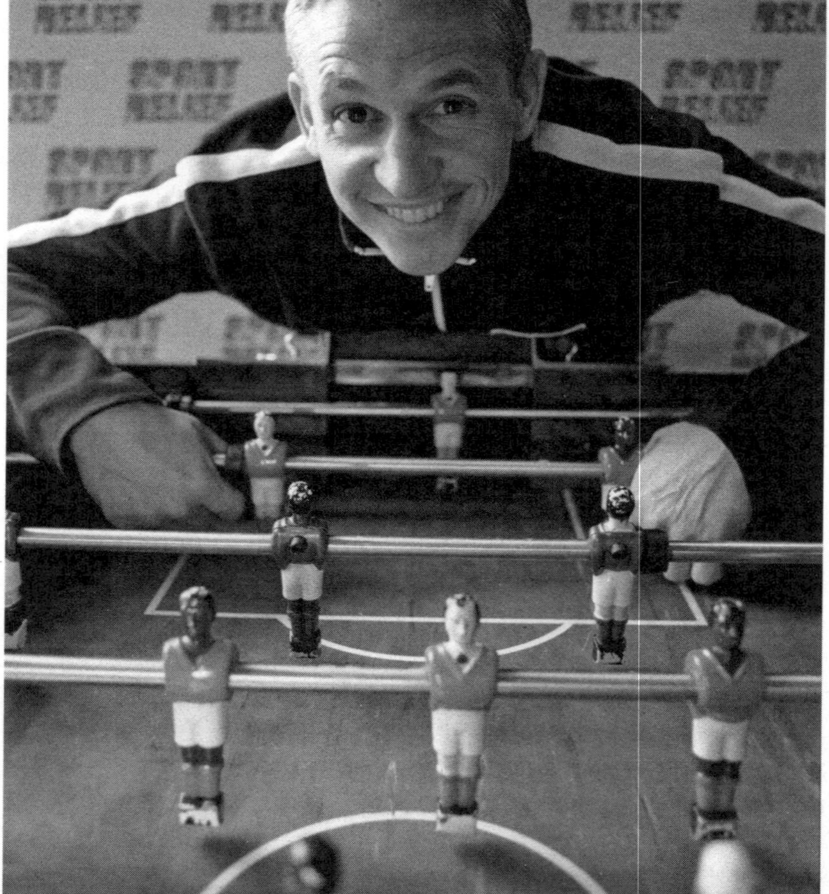
SPORT RELIEF

18

STAR TURN

1994–2000

'… maybe some people were waiting for him to fall on his backside. But he got to a really high standard very quickly. And he's a very nice guy. I hate him, really.'

Gary Lineker always had his eyes on the end game. He was from an era when being a professional footballer didn't pay anywhere near as well as it does today, so it could be argued that he didn't have much of a choice.

But, though he didn't realise it at the time, long before Lineker had even signed his first football apprenticeship contract, he had shown signs of where he wanted to go after his career on the pitch had come to an end. It traced all the way back to when he used to visit Filbert Street as a supporter.

In his formative days, a young Lineker would return home after watching Leicester City play and pick up a pen. As he wrote, all the match's events and his opinions would spill out on to the page as he pulled together a post-match report of what he'd just witnessed in the stands. Today, his words may be clung to by millions of social media followers, desperate to hear his thoughts about football and a whole manner of other topics, but back then, they were for his eyes only.

It was the earliest signs of Lineker's interest in becoming a sports journalist and was the career he's later said he'd probably have pursued had things not worked out as a player. And it's a fascination he never lost, even when he was the one being written and talked about.

Just as with the start of his playing career, though, it would have been impossible to foresee the unbridled success Lineker would have in the media as the highest-paid person at the BBC, and the most well-known face of football coverage in England for more than two decades.

Once Lineker had established himself as one of Leicester's star turns, it was no real surprise that he gravitated towards the idea of having a column in the city's newspaper, the *Leicester Mercury*. His first article was published on 26 November 1984, a few days before he turned 24 – a relatively young age to become a club mouthpiece and to have one eye on the future when he was still growing his reputation as a player.

That move alone provided a glimpse into Lineker's psyche, an almost entrepreneurial instinct that is always asking, 'What's next?' long before it's time to make the leap. He could never have envisaged where a close bond with the media would eventually take him, but hindsight shows the signs were all there.

'Throughout his life he was a quick learner, I remember at Leicester he was already interested in what was going to happen next,' recalls his former Foxes boss Gordon Milne. 'He was interested in the radio a bit and would do a bit of local stuff, but he had this Leicester accent and you'd think, "Christ almighty, who's going to listen to that?" He was looking ahead – his mind was not commercial, but he was thinking about his career and how he could use it to his benefit.'

Lineker's *Mercury* column would become synonymous with his later years at City and he used it to address many of the big matters that surrounded him at the time. He enjoyed sharing his thoughts on his gradual breakthrough into the England set-up and basking in Leicester's best moments in the top flight, but he also never shirked the tricky topics either.

Lineker regularly updated fans on his thoughts during downturns in form – both personally and as the team worried about First Division relegation – and spoke candidly about his contract situation as he neared his Leicester exit to Everton in the summer of 1985. He even announced in the *Mercury* his decision to leave the Foxes if a big club put an offer in front of him. At a time when players weren't as au fait with the inner workings of the media as they are today, Lineker understood how he could use his close relationship with the city's football journalists to communicate openly and honestly, not just with supporters but also potential suitors elsewhere.

When he moved to Everton, it was a brand-new world for Lineker. Where previously he'd been in a city he'd lived in for his entire life and where he was the undoubted star, Lineker was now just one of a host of big-name players in Merseyside. Liverpool and Everton were arguably the two best sides in the country when he first arrived, so the attention he received in the East Midlands wasn't likely to be replicated.

His move meant the end of his column with the *Leicester Mercury* and while his profile was higher as the chief goalscorer of an Everton side that went close to winning the double in 1985/6, the media exposure he received was of a different sort. When he first moved to Goodison Park, his name was initially more associated with the letters of complaint that Toffees fans were sending in to the *Liverpool Echo* about wasting money on him to replace Andy Gray.

What was starting to stand out about Lineker was how well he came across in interviews with journalists and how he was always willing to step in front of the camera – whether with Everton or as his career developed with England. There were no airs or graces about him, and he always showed an appreciation for the job journalists were doing.

'It was very late in the season, in April, and I interviewed Lineker for the first time leading up to the 1986 FA Cup Final,' says former

Liverpool Echo football journalist Ric George. 'I'd only just started at the *Echo* and I didn't know any footballers, so I'd never interviewed an Everton or Liverpool player before.

'I went out to Everton's old training ground, Bellefield, for the interview, and as an Everton fan, I was keen to do this. I wasn't sure what kind of a person he'd be, but he was absolutely brilliant and had no side to him. I liked him and it went OK. I must have made a good impression because while I'd never say I was a buddy of his, I became a journalist who over the next two or three years he could trust.'

Lineker was charming and intelligent in his interviews and as his stock continued to rise, there was an increasing clamour from the media to hear from him. But in fitting with his character, the Footballer of the Year never let that change how he dealt with people and he always remembered the journalists with whom he'd worked successfully in the past. That extended to George, who found that Lineker was still as amenable – if not even more so – to talking to the *Liverpool Echo* reporter when he moved to Barcelona in 1986.

'I interviewed him once or twice before he went to Barcelona and I got on with him,' George continues. 'You used to be able to ring the dressing room at the Nou Camp, so if I ever wanted an interview him, that's what I'd do and, fair play to him, he'd give me a few minutes before training.

'Once when I called him, I told him I wanted to come out and go to Barcelona. It wasn't at the *Echo*'s expense and I'd pay for trips like that myself and use my holiday because I was keen. When I went over to Barcelona to see Gary, it was for a Clásico against Real Madrid and he and his first wife, Michelle, invited me to their place. He was away with the team on the day of the game, but Michelle cooked me a pasta meal, drove me to the game and I sat next to her for the Clásico.

'After the game, we went to a very swanky, exclusive nightclub. I was sitting there with Gary and his wife, Julio Alberto, who was a big star for Spain, and Montserrat Caballé, an opera singer, walked in. It was only when she released "Barcelona" with Freddy Mercury a couple of years later that I knew how big she was. Gary was always good to me and made me feel welcome.'

George's relationship with Lineker continued when the forward returned to England with Spurs in 1989, with the journalist always getting an interview when he asked and even being invited to Lineker's home in North London on one occasion when he already had guests round.

That sort of relationship wasn't a rarity, either. Lineker enjoyed a strong bond with several different journalists and broadcasters, partly because he was interested in their craft. While on international duty, he even earned the nickname 'Junior Des' – after the BBC's totemic presenter Des Lynam – from England teammates Paul Gascoigne and Chris Waddle due to the time he spent with people in the press, watching how they did their intros.

'He wouldn't quite come across in the way he does now, but he had something to say – he wasn't just trying to make a point,' says legendary BBC commentator Barry Davies. 'He was interesting to talk to and interesting to listen to. He was a smiling guy, that's the way I saw him – he was an easy person to be with and he was very pleasant when he was talking to me.'

By the time his career hit its peak, Lineker had mapped out what he intended his post-playing career to look like. Despite speculative enquiries from Leicester – twice – and being 'sounded out' by Aston Villa, moving into management was never as appealing to him as sitting in a warm studio and talking about the action instead. 'I never saw myself becoming a manager,' Lineker said. 'I didn't enjoy training, let alone standing there watching other people do it.'

Besides, he'd spotted a gap in the broadcast market that very few others had filled previously and believed his natural ease in front of the camera made the perfect complement to his status as a widely recognised footballer. In the early 1990s, only the likes of Jimmy Hill and Bob Wilson had successfully straddled the two worlds and Lineker wanted in on the action.

'I was ahead of Gary in terms of not just being pushed to do *Football Focus* but working for the Beeb and not being a trained journalist,' says former Arsenal goalkeeper Wilson, who worked for the BBC from 1974 to 1994 after hanging up his gloves.

'Up until then, the likes of Des Lynam, David Coleman and Frank Bough had worked on the BBC and Radio 5, and all were absolute professional, trained journalists. Gary Lineker and Bob Wilson are not trained journalists, Jimmy Hill as well. To get into broadcasting then, you normally had to have gone through writing for a newspaper, working for a radio station or whatever first. None of us – Jimmy, me or Gary – had ever been trained in that way.'

Lineker's first TV appearance as a pundit was in 1986 for the now infamous post-World Cup Final debate with Lynam and Terry Venables that preluded his move to Barcelona. While the young striker lapped up the opportunity, his booking had initially been inspired by wanting him there in case he was crowned as the Mexico '86 Golden Boot winner, which he duly was.

Softly spoken, eloquent and with a cheeky glint in his eye, Lineker had performed well and pursued a plethora of other opportunities while still a player. He struck a deal with the *News of the World* to become a columnist for the high-circulation Sunday newspaper and started getting more exposure on TV and radio, not just in a football setting, but also on BBC Radio 4's popular *Desert Island Discs*, where he picked songs by the likes of U2 and comedy act Monty Python to take with him as a fictional castaway.

One of his most unusual gigs was in Barcelona, when he somehow managed to do co-commentary on a game he played in for Spanish TV. The quirk came about due to the coverage agreement at the time, which meant entire games were shown as if live on TV the day after they'd been played. Lineker hadn't realised quite what he'd let himself in for, initially assuming he'd been booked as a pundit.

Punditry wasn't Lineker's passion, though. Despite appearing on a variety of panels in his early years, the former England captain felt he only had so much to offer in the role because he was only really an authority on being a striker and didn't know enough about the other positions. Ironically, it was his playing experience that became such a strength as he established himself as a presenter.

'In the end, it's all about putting your own stamp on it,' says Wilson. 'If it's a massive disadvantage not being a trained journalist [as an ex-professional getting into broadcasting], there is also a massive advantage in the public sitting at home listening to you because they know you've been there and understand the game of football. A lot of the presenters haven't got a clue on the actual inside of the game and [about] things like what is a sending-off offence. If it came out of the mouth of Frank Bough, David Coleman or even Des Lynam, it wouldn't be the same as if it came out of the mouth of Gary Lineker or those of us who played the game.

'Ultimately when it comes to doing analysis with the guys [the pundits], you have a massive advantage. The journalists were guided into "You've got to ask them about that sending off, ask them about that amazing goal" and they would earmark the particular points they were going to pick out on *Match of the Day*. But when you've got Gary Lineker as a presenter, he knows the match and football, he knows the laws of the game, he knows refereeing, he knows everything.'

Lineker's prowess as a presenter saw him take on more than just football jobs for the BBC, even in the early days. During the gap between leaving Tottenham and joining Grampus Eight in 1992, the recently retired England international found time to be part of the BBC's commentary team for the Barcelona Olympics. With his playing career gradually winding down during an injury-hit two years in Japan, Lineker got his legs further under the table at the BBC, becoming a more regular fixture as a pundit on *Match of the Day* and hosting a weekly show on Radio 5 Live called *Gary Lineker's Football Night*.

By the time Lineker was anointed the new presenter of Saturday lunchtime programme *Football Focus* in 1996, he'd already been earmarked as the long-term successor for Lynam as the BBC's top sports presenter. He was on a collision course with the *Match of the Day* host's position, with Lynam beginning to offer advice to his protégé.

'He was taking over from Des Lynam and he watched him very closely and, of course, Bob Wilson, who was also a very good presenter. Gary looked and watched what he [Lynam] did, but he was intent on doing it his way,' Davies explains.

'I think Gary wanted to be himself because he knew Desmond wasn't going to say, "You've got to do something this way or that way." Desmond would definitely not have said that. Gary I'm sure would give the same advice now.'

Lineker was certainly listening, watching and learning whenever he could – even taking vocal coaching to help pep up his naturally flat voice. As in his playing days, that thirst to constantly develop saw him gobble up ground on his more experienced colleagues. The pressure to succeed wasn't insignificant, either.

'It was difficult for him coming in because he was already a superstar and maybe some people were waiting for him to fall on his backside,' Lynam told the *Guardian*. 'But he got to a very high standard very quickly. And he's a very nice guy. I hate him, really.'

Despite Lynam's typically amusing response to Lineker's career switch, he played more of a role in his would-be replacement's progression than he makes out.

'In the early days I used to fluff a lot of lines and get quite tense about that,' Lineker said in a 2001 interview with the *Observer*. 'He [Lynam] said, "Well, we all do it – I do it. The important thing is, rather like when you're playing golf, when you're struggling it's better to slow down rather than quicken up." So that helped significantly.

'And one of the things about Des is he'll never say, "Joining me", he'll say, "Joining us," basically including the people at home. Things like that he's advised me. And then – prepare your ad libs! It appears sometimes that you say things off the cuff but you've been thinking about them for some time.'

Lineker's broadcasting career might have been going swimmingly, but it wasn't without its bumps in the road. He became embroiled in a public spat with Premier League side Wimbledon after criticising Vinnie Jones in an opinionated *Radio Times* article that called the Dons' Welsh international midfielder 'a self-hyped personality – fine for him, but he isn't a good player and no benefit to the game', while also appearing to criticise Manchester United manager Alex

Ferguson and former England teammate Gascoigne. It's fair to say that didn't draw the best response from Wimbledon, which Lineker had also previously claimed were best watched on Ceefax due to their direct style of play.

A fax addressed from 'everyone at Wimbledon FC' was sent to the press in retort. 'As a BBC sports presenter, he [Lineker] should aspire to the high standards that organisation has always stood for, not resort to smearing three fellow professionals... In his typical selfish way, Lineker is trying to promote himself as a strong man with strong opinions. But it can never happen... Lineker has the charisma of a jellyfish. He is a jellyfish without a sting...

'The BBC has spent tens of thousands of pounds trying to make him the new face of television sport, but he simply has no charisma or presence about him... Lineker sends so many people to sleep, they'd be better off marketing him as a cure for insomnia... The BBC are lowering their usually high standards by trying to promote Lineker as a frontman. It is an insult to Des Lynam and all sports lovers.'

Lineker and the BBC tried to pass it off in good humour, putting an animated jellyfish alongside the *Football Focus* presenter in the next programme, but it showed the pitfalls awaiting their new star. This was a time when the public would take to writing letters of abuse rather than posting it online and while that weeded out some of the criticism any presenter expects to receive, the more incensed would still go to the effort of letting them know how they felt. Although as a former footballer, he was already used to the stick.

'He always liked to have an opinion and you've got to have a particular thing about you that you know not everybody watching that screen is going to like you anyway,' says Wilson. 'I still keep in my desk a couple of letters of some of the most filthy things you can imagine pictures of or words sent about me when I was presenting *Grandstand*, *Football Focus* or the World Cup.

'It doesn't matter who you are, it doesn't matter if you're the greatest presenter, you're still going to get stick if you have a little side angle to something or we say something, and that will have applied to Gary too.'

No matter the naysayers, nobody was going to stop Lineker now. His first live TV show was during Euro '96, and the second was the highlights between England and Scotland, which drew several million viewers.

He was getting closer to being entrusted with the BBC's crown jewels, although his debut fronting of the flagship Saturday afternoon sports show *Grandstand* came much sooner than anyone intended. On 5 April 1997, a bomb scare at the Grand National meant all 60,000 people – including Lynam, who was presenting the show live from Aintree – were evacuated from the racecourse, leaving Lineker being thrown into the anchor position.

Unaware of the drama unfolding at the National, Lineker had been spending a serene afternoon watching the day's Premier League action with Alan Hansen ahead of that evening's *Match of the Day*. The friends had been relatively relaxed, idly chatting over the games' talking points, drinking coffee and eating sandwiches, when news of what was happening in Merseyside filtered through to them. This was no cursory update of a breaking story for Lineker, though: he was urgently needed to fill in for Lynam.

The former England striker was quickly ushered into make-up, where he was neatened up, equipped with a mic, and put in front of the cameras in the studio. Not that the viewers would have known how hastily the presenter's *Grandstand* debut had come to pass, as the screen cut from Lynam back to Television Centre, where a smartly dressed Lineker greeted them. He cut an image as unruffled as his hairstyle, appearing as though he'd been waiting all day for the call.

Lineker later admitted that he wasn't quite as calm on the inside as he looked, ad-libbing as the story developed to keep the viewers informed. His only tell as he told the nation, 'Well, clearly the situation at Aintree is a very sad one indeed,' was the white pen he held with both hands as he stared into camera. Sometimes you don't know when you'll be called off the subs' bench.

Getting the call sooner than was expected became a habit for Lineker. When Lynam defected to accept ITV's lucrative offer and left the BBC in 1999, Lineker was given the keys to *Match of the*

Day. He refused to relinquish them for another 25 years, apart from a three-season hiatus when the Premier League highlights went to ITV instead. By the time it was announced Lineker would step down in 2025, he was *Match of the Day*'s longest-serving host.

Lineker's first show went live on 7 August 1999, with nine games to introduce, including Liverpool's win at Sheffield Wednesday and his beloved Leicester's loss to Arsenal. Starting as he meant to go on, the newbie presenter signed off the show with a now-trademark quip – another titbit he picked up from Lynam – saying, 'Hey, tell you what, football's back.' He then looked off camera and asked the production team, 'Any good? Have I got the job?'

Of course, he had. It was the culmination of a carefully curated plan set about by Lineker's agent Jon Holmes upon the striker's retirement. Lineker had been everywhere in the ensuing years between his retirement from the field and his first show, even enjoying a long stint playing up to his goody two shoes reputation as a team captain on sports panel show *They Think It's All Over*. The move was genius, as Lineker looked to shed the 'boring' tag he'd been given as a player, but still maintained his image as football's golden boy.

They Think It's All Over revealed a more laid-back Lineker than BBC audiences were used to seeing. He traded the smart presenting garb for a casual shirt and cut a more relaxed figure as he easily manoeuvred his way through the witty jibes and competitive jousting that bounced around the studio. The personality that made Lineker popular in dressing rooms throughout his career began to shine through to a national audience alongside the edgier humour of regular panellists Rory McGrath and Jonathan Ross. He was clean-cut with his words but conveyed his cheeky side with a wry smile and a twinkle in his eye. The former England captain wasn't given an easy ride, regularly handling comments about the end of his international career and some of the key personalities he'd faced along the way.

In one episode during a round of name-game impressions, in which McGrath did a series of impersonations for Lineker and comedian Frank Skinner to guess, Graham Taylor's name came up as one of the answers. 'Do I not like you, Gary Lineker?' McGrath posed, mimicking Taylor's distinctive lilt, with Lineker interrupting quickly with Taylor's name and a knowing laugh. It could have been an awkward moment, but Lineker's grin enabled the moment to slip away without a hint of animosity.

He was fast becoming more of a TV personality, but that wasn't going to be at the detriment of his sporting ambitions – it was designed to enhance it. Lineker became the BBC's golf presenter, took on the hosting role of *Sports Personality of the Year* and was a regular anchor for the corporation's multi-sports programming, such as the Olympics. He was now a media juggernaut and had come a long way since those early days in broadcast.

'He was quite shy and accepting [at first],' recalls Wilson. 'He obviously had a lot to contribute to the programme because of his experiences at World Cups, his England days, his Tottenham days and everything else. But he could do it in a way that he could find the right words.

At the very end of it, what it boils down to as a presenter on television is that you find the words, and that is something he has built up and built up from the shy lad I first knew and those early thoughts that when he finished playing, he might want to move into television.'

Lineker is so successful that he's arguably helped to shape the role of the sportsman-turned-presenter. Where Wilson and Hill had started the movement decades ago, Lineker has taken that on to such a point that it's easy to watch or listen to several ex-pros on TV, radio or podcasts without much conscious effort.

'Where things have changed in regards to the presenters is that they [producers] don't just go for a professional presenter now,' Wilson concurs. 'If you can find an individual [who] can be both fluent in finding the right words and able to challenge the two pundits alongside, that's good. That's what Gary has done and grown into.'

Over the years, Lineker has become more than simply someone known by sports fans. He branched out to appear on *Who Wants to be a Millionaire* with former England rugby international Austin Healey in 2008, winning £50,000 for charity in the process. He has also sat in the host's chair on *Have I Got News For You* on three occasions. Put that alongside his regular work for the BBC – a short stint hosting BT Sport's Champions League coverage – and his array of different newspaper columns, as well as an extensive number of podcast appearances, and it's hard to avoid Lineker.

It's difficult to pick out Lineker's presenting highlights when he's now so slick and accomplished at everything he does, although presenting the BBC's 'Super Saturday' coverage during the London 2012 Olympics and winning a BAFTA for the presentation of England's World Cup quarter-final victory over Sweden in 2018 are definite standouts.

His status means he's been the BBC's highest-paid star for several years, reportedly pocketing between £1,350,000 and £1,354,999 across the 2022/3 season. While this is a rate that's matched and bettered elsewhere in the TV industry, it's a figure that does draw some criticism from certain parties from time to time, although he tries to bat that off with his stereotypical good humour whenever it's brought up.

'I remember when I was at a Football Writers' Association fundraising event for victims of the Grenfell tragedy [in 2017] and Lineker agreed to go on a panel without hesitation,' Patrick Barclay says.

'He was asked about his BBC salary and he said something along the lines of "Yep, I get lots of money, but the joke's on you lot because you're paying it," while pointing at the audience. It could have gone terribly wrong that joke, but it brought the house down. There were hundreds of people laughing at themselves because Lineker had delivered the line so well. He's got great discrimination, a great discernment about what to do and say.'

That's the key to Lineker's presenting style: it's so effortless. And commentator Davies believes that's the case because the nation is simply presented with a true, authentic version of Gary Lineker, whether the camera is on or not.

'It's easy and it's just like when he's chatting and introducing himself to his other presenters on *Match of the Day*, that's him, he doesn't put on an act,' Davies says. 'His personality has helped him have the success he's had. As he's got more experience, he can almost do it with his eyes closed – he's knowledgeable, he smiles easily, he's aware of other people's problems in the game from time to time, and he's happy to disagree strongly with people in the game.

'He's not only a footballer, he's a television personality, he's an interesting guy, he's a man in the street you can talk to.'

But once you've established a reputation and stature as big as Lineker's, it's only a matter of time before people start shooting at you.

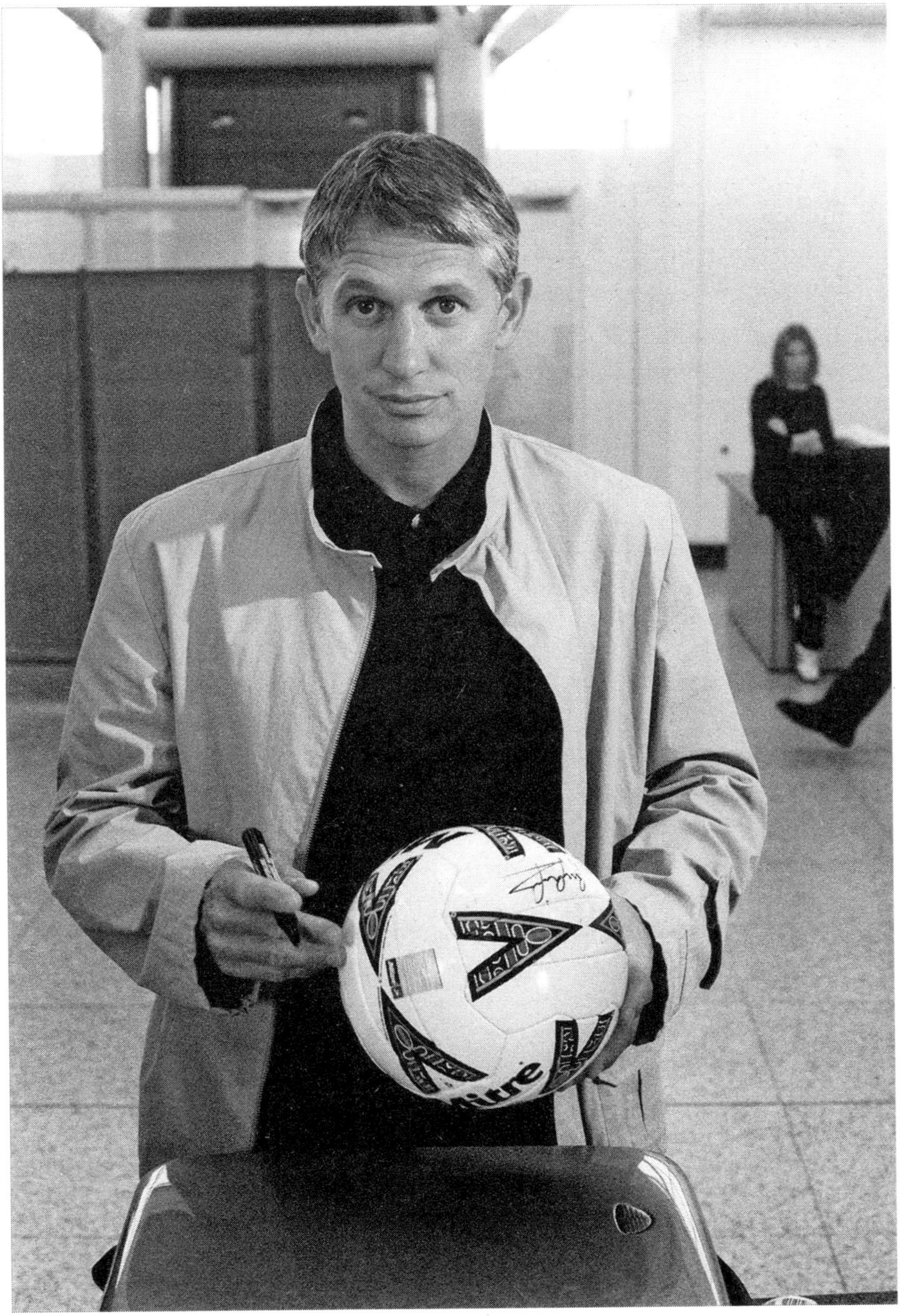

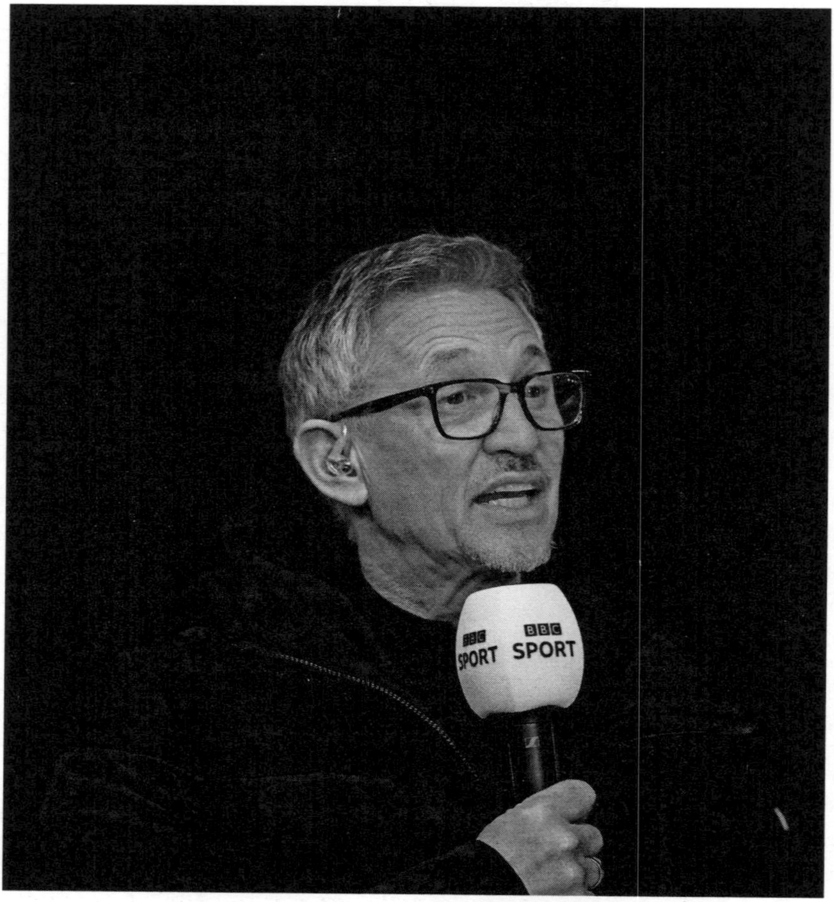
BBC SPORT
BBC SPORT

19

STANDING UP

2000–ongoing

'Gary has gone from being what I thought was quite a shy guy [...] to being the icon he has now become.'

'The BBC will only be able to bring limited sport programming this weekend and our schedules will be updated to reflect that,' read a BBC statement in March 2023. 'We are working hard to resolve the situation and hope to do so soon.'

The BBC's sport coverage had been paralysed. One after another after another, the corporation's extensive list of sports shows usually scheduled across the weekend had fallen by the wayside, as presenters and pundits refused to appear on them. First it was *Match of the Day*, which would now be a truncated 20-minute programme without commentary or analysis; then it was Saturday staples *Football Focus* and *Final Score*, followed by *Match of the Day 2* on Sunday. BBC Radio 5 Live was left with a skeleton staff of contracted workers to man the airwaves.

This was a full-scale public revolt, leaving the BBC in turmoil. And it had all been because of one man: Gary Lineker.

The highest-paid man on the BBC's payroll had been asked to step back from presenting *Match of the Day* until an agreement was reached on his social media use, following a tweet about the UK government's policy of banning illegal immigrants who tried to cross the English Channel from ever claiming asylum. Accompanied by the slogan 'Stop the Boats', the rhetoric was deeply controversial, with many opponents branding the approach insensitive to the plight of the people making the dangerous trip from France to Britain in tiny dinghies.

Lineker had reacted to news about the plans by posting from his personal Twitter feed that the stance was an 'immeasurably cruel policy directed at the most vulnerable people in language that is not dissimilar to that used by Germany in the 30s'.

While voicing such strong opposition to a government policy was likely to cause a stir from a public figure associated so heavily with the BBC, which aims to stay impartial at all times, the comparison to Nazi Germany was like pulling a pin on a hand grenade. Sure enough, it exploded, sending the right-wing press into a tailspin and demanding Lineker be taken off air immediately.

Anyone who's anyone had an opinion of the situation, including then Prime Minister Rishi Sunak, who reaffirmed his belief in the proposals in an attempt to make stopping the illegal Channel crossings a 'priority'. Home Secretary Suella Braverman, who initially outlined the plans, hit back at Lineker on the BBC's *Political Thinking* podcast, saying the Nazi comparison was 'lazy and unhelpful' and argued that her family 'felt very keenly the impact of the Holocaust' because her husband is Jewish.

Soon it was time for the BBC to handle the political hot potato it had been handed. If the contentious nature of the topic wasn't difficult enough to negotiate, the added nuance of Lineker being a freelancer contracted to the BBC further sullied the waters. The devil was in the detail and it all came down to the interpretation of the BBC's social media rules versus a freelancer's rights to have freedom of expression.

The decision was to ask Lineker to step back from presenting while they reviewed the rules, a move that led to criticism of BBC Director General Tim Davie as the action placated no one and triggered the mass strike of other BBC Sport freelancers in support of Lineker.

Not only had Lineker drawn up battle lines with the government, but the fall-out had now been positioned as Lineker versus the BBC. Regardless of personal opinions on the matter, it highlighted just how influential the former England striker had become – from being a scrawny teenager trying to break into Leicester City's first team, he was now single-handedly leading the nation's news agenda. If he had an opinion, he was going to use his status to air it.

'You think about the row with the BBC about language used around small boats and I'm sure he didn't land in that controversy by accident,' says Patrick Barclay. 'I don't think he would have said something he wasn't willing to defend, but he did defend it and came out with more credit than those who sought to limit him.

'I know what he was getting at. I personally wouldn't have said what he said, I don't think it was wholly accurate and I think he went too far, but who cares? It wasn't hate speech, it was thought-provoking, and it made me think and study whether the language was used in 1930s Germany. Well, it fucking well wasn't, but the point is, Lineker had that opinion and is perfectly entitled to express that. It made me think and study the subject, and that's surely what public discourse is about.'

Lineker knew his words would have clout and as a staunch supporter of immigrant rights – he's temporarily taken refugees into his own home to help them – it was a position he wanted to share with his nine million followers. He's previously said that he tries not to post anything without considering how it might be perceived and although his critics will claim he should 'stick to football', he's become synonymous with his strong views on a variety of topics, including climate change.

The grey area in the debate was how far was too far for the BBC. If they wanted to remain truly neutral on the day's most controversial topics, then could they accept its biggest star freely sharing his opinions in this way? And how much of a risk was Lineker taking with his own position by speaking out in the way he did?

'Where he should have understood something was that he was risking his job,' says former BBC presenter Bob Wilson. 'It doesn't matter what politics you've got; you can't do that when you're in a position like we were in to present those programmes, you can't publicly come out and say what he said about all those poor people who were trying to come into the country. Sorry, but that was daft.

'His politics will always be a talking point. I bet you can't tell me the political party of six of the best presenters in the country, you don't do that. Gary took a big risk and we saw it go to the top man and he's making a position about if they're going to keep him or not. He obviously got his loyal support from the guys who were sitting alongside him because they were very quick in coming forward in saying, "If you get rid of him, I'm off." Alex Scott joined that as well, so that says a lot.

'The bottom line is that Gary has gone from being what I thought was quite a shy guy when I was first involved with him to being the icon he has now become, whatever icon might stand for.'

Lineker's transformation into the impenetrable force he is today hasn't been an overnight thing. After establishing himself as one to watch in sports broadcasting, he has grown into not only the roles he had, but also the elevated status they provide him with.

His public image of being the clean-cut, nice guy provided a springboard for Lineker to naturally ease into the more socially conscious person he is now. He has become more comfortable with speaking his mind about topics broader than sport as he has gradually become more aware of the world at large in his older years.

Footballers – particularly at the time Lineker played – are often in their own little bubble and it's only after they retire that other things have a chance to flourish. Lineker moves in very different circles than he did as a young player and has naturally become more aware of various issues as he meets people with broad-ranging experiences and views. What he says and believes isn't universally popular and may not always be correct, but it's hard to disagree with his clear morals of justness and empathy.

Lineker has always been principled and single-minded – this is nothing new. He tried to play the game in a fair way, as highlighted by his famously clean disciplinary record, and always appeared to act in a respectful manner towards referees and opposition. He became an interviewer's dream due to his well-mannered eloquence, but never shied away from being honest when the occasion called for it – although the way it was delivered covered up the ruthless winning mentality that undoubtedly bubbled underneath his calm exterior.

And when it was time to make a stand, Lineker had never shirked away. In May 2010, the *Match of the Day* presenter quit his column for the *Mail on Sunday* following a sting operation by the newspaper that exposed FA Chairman Lord Triesman in a secretly recorded conversation. The Labour peer stood down from his position with the FA in part due to comments claiming that Spain and Russia were planning to bribe referees at that summer's World Cup.

The revelations, which Triesman complained had been as a result of *Mail on Sunday* 'entrapment', seriously harmed England's bid to host the 2018 World Cup – something Lineker wasn't prepared to condone.

'The story itself, the circumstances surrounding it and the actions of the *Mail on Sunday* in publishing it have undermined the bid to bring the World Cup to England in 2018,' Lineker said in a statement announcing the resignation of his column. 'I wholeheartedly support the bid because I believe that hosting the tournament would be brilliant for the country and I'm an official ambassador for it.'

Where Lineker's comments had been firm and forthright, his agent Jon Holmes failed to mince his words about the incident at all.

'The story showed crass judgement,' Holmes told the *Guardian*. 'It had dubious journalistic merit, was clearly obtained by entrapment and was timed to do the maximum damage to the World Cup bid, which Gary and all football fans in this country passionately support. We wanted to make our position clear and to do all we can now to help persuade FIFA that England is the best country to host a great World Cup in 2018.'

Those efforts ultimately proved fruitless, with Russia somewhat ironically winning the right to host the tournament in 2018. Yet Lineker's stance spoke volumes that he was acutely aware of the associations he made, which naturally puts a few noses out of joint along the way.

Lineker himself has been the target of attempts to uncover stories about his life, too. He's always attempted to keep his personal life out of the newspapers, although his two divorces naturally received coverage he'd probably have preferred to avoid. Yet he and his two ex-wives always managed to keep anything other than the legally accessible details out of the public eye.

The first marriage, to long-term wife Michelle, the mother of his four sons (the couple had two more after Harry), ended in 2006, with his wife of 20 years citing her husband's alleged 'unreasonable behaviour' causing her 'stress and anxiety' as the reason for the split. Lineker married again three years later to model Danielle Bux, although they announced their break-up six years after they tied the knot because Gary didn't want to have more children. Lineker has spoken since about his two 'wonderful marriages' and how he remains friends with both of his exes.

That hasn't stopped Lineker being the target of various attempts to dig up dirt on him, as people try to besmirch his whiter-than-white image. The most sinister attempt in the early noughties came when he was one of a long line of celebrities to be illegally tracked by undercover journalists trying to get their latest big scoop. Lineker says he was completely oblivious until he saw his picture come up on *Newsnight* as part of a piece with a former private investigator, who said he'd been hired by tabloids to track the presenter for two years.

The impression the story gave was that Lineker had been covertly followed as he went about his daily life, trailed with such regularity that it'd be impossible for him not to lead the investigator to a location or activity that would soon become salacious gossip in the papers. It was the most intense man-marking job anybody had ever done on him.

The investigator went on to claim that Lineker was 'one of the clever ones' because he never put a foot out of line to provide even a whiff of a story. The angle was that Lineker 'knew they were on to him', but the former England striker says completely the opposite was true.

'I was going, "Was I fuck?" I never had a clue,' said Lineker in an interview with the *Guardian* in January 2024. 'They showed video footage of me on the golf course taken through a hedge. I swear I never knew. The investigator thought I was clever because I never led them anywhere, but I wasn't messing about – all I did was play golf and go home.'

If his actions keep him out of the newspapers, his opinions don't. Much of that has coincided with the explosion of social media, specifically X/Twitter, which provides a platform for everybody – not just Lineker – to air their views in a way that wasn't previously possible. While his opinions are predominantly more left-leaning, he does stir up dissatisfaction from that side of the political spectrum too, particularly when he appeared to be in opposition to former Labour leader Jeremy Corbyn. In fact, Lineker has said previously that he's voted all ways in past elections.

One of Lineker's favourite pastimes in more recent years has been to criticise Conservative government policies, with a particular focus on environmental and asylum issues. These are topics close to his heart and he explained in a 2024 *Guardian* interview that these were subjects he'd okayed with the BBC to remain vocal on long before the incident that blew up in 2023.

'I had an agreement that I could carry on with that and climate change because for me those are humanitarian issues and they're going to get bigger,' Lineker said in the article.

People might not like that Lineker has stepped beyond the traditional sporting barriers by being more vocal on wider issues, but having proved he can reach the top of two highly competitive careers – albeit the second one significantly aided by the first – he's already shown he's capable of coming out of his wheelhouse.

'I don't think anyone has got any right to say, "Why doesn't he stick to what he knows?" although I don't always agree with how he does it sometimes,' says Barry Davies, who still sees Lineker in the Barnes district of London in which they both live.

'There are some footballers you can say that to, but I don't think Gary is one of them. He has an opinion on things and it's up to him if he wants to express points. But I don't see why people should say, "He's only a footballer" because he's not only a footballer – he's a television personality, he's an interesting guy, he's a man in the street you can talk to, so why turn on him as it were? There's a suggestion he's lost some popularity because he's given some opinions that other people don't agree with.'

As the incident with the BBC shows, Lineker isn't going to stop airing his views any time soon, so more controversies – perhaps not to quite the same extent – are likely to follow. After seeing how his peers rallied round him when asked to step back from presenting during the furore, Lineker has arguably been empowered and shown quite how much influence he wields now.

If nothing else, it was a victory for free speech and the ability to not censor public disagreement of policies or actions, wherever they come from. For it to have come from an ex-footballer whom no one who saw him play in his formative years initially pegged as a future international is a sign of what can be achieved when the stars align.

'He told the truth, what's the matter with doing that?' asked Lineker's former Everton teammate Neville Southall, who is well known for his left-wing political views. 'There's a horrible society where if you tell the truth and give your honest opinion, you get absolutely hammered for it. But I think he was just telling the truth.

'Gary stood up and said what he thought, and I don't see any problem with that... For me, I think he's allowed to have an opinion. And doesn't that prove that he's human? Don't the BBC rely on the relationship between the presenter and the viewer to stay in and watch? I think his views were honest and I think it proves he's human.'

And that's what Gary Lineker is: human. As his story shows, it's possible to accomplish seemingly impossible things while staying grounded and true to your roots. He's still a football-mad Leicester boy at heart.

A throng of reporters gathered at the bottom of Gary Lineker's drive, gazing up at the brickwork of his house. Some of them had grown accustomed to the spot, perched near the tall brickwork pillars that welcomed visitors to his home, they'd been stationed there so regularly in recent years.

But this time, it was different. Where previously the journalists had been there hoping for titbits of information on the latest rumour or scandal to surround the former England captain, now they already had the story. All they wanted was a first sight or cursory comment from their prey.

The news had broken on the evening on Monday 11 November that Lineker's contract as *Match of the Day* (MOTD) host would not be renewed beyond the end of the 2024/25 season, with confirmation from the BBC expected any time now.

The break-up had felt inevitable for a while. A long-standing couple that had gradually grown further apart across a 25-year union that had looked so perfect for so long. But things change and it was time for a separation of ways.

Some of the right-leaning newspapers who had sent paparazzi out to Lineker's home in the south-west London district of Barnes had been baying for the presenter's blood for a while, hoping to knock from his head the crown that had made him one of Britain's most recognisable TV personalities. That wish had now come true.

All of a sudden, there was movement as one of the windows sprung open, momentarily revealing Lineker like an actor waiting for his curtain call. The protagonist had stirred before disappearing again. Even when he did make a more sustained appearance, Lineker gave short shrift to the waiting reporters, preferring instead to refer them to the official BBC statement. 'After 25 seasons, Gary is stepping down from MOTD,' Alex Kay-Jelski, Director of BBC Sport, was quoted as saying. 'We want to thank him for everything he has done for the show, which continues to attract millions of viewers each week.'

The break wouldn't be immediate. The announcement in November would trigger a long goodbye for Lineker, one final lap of honour to see out the rest of the season. Even beyond that, he'd stay with the BBC for another year thanks to a contract extension that would see him present the corporation's FA Cup coverage for the following season before bowing out after the 2026 World Cup.

Choosing to focus on the contract extension in the BBC statement, Lineker simply said, 'I'm delighted to continue my long association with BBC Sport and would like to thank all those that made it happen.'

A day later, it was announced that Lineker had also stepped down as host of the BBC's annual *Sports Personality of the Year* awards show and the previous year's ceremony in 2023 was his last. This was a seismic shift in the Beeb's sports broadcasting strategy.

Lineker finally broke his silence on his *The Rest is Football* podcast a few days later, saying this was 'right time' to call time on his association with *Match of the Day* as he approached his mid-60s. Although several news outlets – including the BBC News – reported that Lineker was open to staying in post, a contract wasn't forthcoming.

The different narratives created a vacuum for speculation to build about what had happened behind the scenes. A natural conclusion was that Lineker's time on *Match of the Day* had come to an end because his polarising opinions on political and social issues had become too uncomfortable for the BBC, which prides itself on its impartiality.

The news triggered a host of views to be shared across the media. Lineker's former Leicester and England teammate Alan Smith appearing on Sky Sports News to declare his friend's tenure 'a mark in the sand' and congratulate him 'for the length of time he served in job because all eyes are on him every Saturday night.'

Regular *Match of the Day* pundit Danny Murphy paid homage to a 'warm, charismatic, intelligent man who knows his football' on TalkSport. Murphy's fellow radio show colleague Simon Jordan said he 'didn't really care' about the news, saying, 'it isn't a big deal to me because Gary Lineker can read an autocue and injects a bit of personality, there'll be plenty of other people [who can do that].'

If opinions on the man differed, there was a general consensus about why Lineker's departure wasn't as acrimonious as the official statements suggested. Talk host Mike Graham suggested Lineker had 'tweeted his way out of a job', while the *Mirror's* Darren Lewis bluntly said the presenter had been 'surrendered by the BBC for having an opinion'.

Whatever the truth was, one thing was for sure: it was the end of an era, both for Lineker and the BBC.

HOMES
journal
HOUSEKEEPING
Morning Advertiser
CABINET HOURS BOOST
PRIVATE EYE

EPILOGUE

It seems absurd to be debating whether one of England's greatest goalscorers would still make the grade today but that's the discussion I found myself having with several of the interviewees in this book.

Football has undoubtedly changed a lot since the 80-cap England striker made his Leicester City debut on 1 January 1979, so it's natural that the demands on a player have too. Lineker was an extraordinary goalscorer, a striker who combined lightning pace with an innate ability to find space and understand where a ball would drop that meant he was almost impossible to defend. Keep an eye on him for 89 minutes and he'd score in the 90th.

Lineker's figures were impressive wherever he went. He had a special talent – one he honed and made the most out of with determination and intelligence. Goals win games and the former England striker certainly had the ability to do that for whoever he played for.

Yet, he was always trailed by doubters – particularly in his early career. It was regularly levelled at Lineker that *all* he did was score goals, that he didn't contribute enough elsewhere on the pitch and that he wasn't as technically proficient as his peers. And when you compare the expectations on a striker in Lineker's heyday to those in the modern game, it's easy to wonder if it'd be possible for him to have the same career nowadays.

But his former Tottenham and England teammate Terry Fenwick says that those who claimed Lineker was one-dimensional revealed an inability to fully understand the striker's craft.

'When you're playing against Gary Lineker, you're always on your toes, you know where you're going and it's fantastic, never take him for granted,' says Fenwick, who came up against Lineker while at QPR.

'But again, if he's gone 10 or 15 minutes into the game and he's very quiet, it just lures you into that sense of "Oh, we're OK" and then bang, it hits you, and before you know it, he's scored a goal. He's done that to me before, when QPR played at Leicester – that's exactly what he did, and he was only a young man then.'

When I put the idea to Patrick Barclay, he pointed out that while the game has changed, players still exist at the top of today's game who possess similar characteristics to Lineker. The difference is that there are fewer of them now, but if they're truly exceptional at what they do, there's no better currency to offer a team than an ability to put the ball in the back of the net.

Lineker's record at Everton is proof of that. Provide him with better service and he'll find the net with frightening regularity. Given that today's elite teams are designed to play in a way that creates a higher number of quality chances, it follows that a master finisher would be hitting new, never-before-seen heights. Just look at Erling Haaland.

'[Manchester City boss, Pep] Guardiola has said to Haaland, "Look, I'm not too bothered about your defensive contribution as long as you score a goal a game or more,"' Barclay reasons.

'I think Lineker would have thrived on that. You watch a lot of Haaland's movement and he's bigger than Lineker, but not necessarily better. You can imagine Lineker drooling at Haaland's movement because it's just mesmeric to watch, the way Haaland thinks and plays chess with the defenders and moves them about. For Lineker, that's what he was about and what he was so very good at. If the manager had decided to do it – and Guardiola certainly seems to have been successful doing it with Haaland – they can use that sort of player.'

EPILOGUE

One of the things that stands out about Lineker's story is that desire to constantly improve. None of the people I spoke to for this book who played or worked with Lineker in his early years said they could ever have predicted he would go on to have the career he did. He was raw and clearly had the talent to make it as a professional footballer, but nobody predicted he'd make it at the elite level – certainly not with the success he had.

That's not a slight on Lineker, though. If anything, it's a compliment.

He may be renowned for his laid-back character, but beneath that unruffled veneer is a highly motivated, ambitious individual. Just because it's not streaming out of Lineker's every pore doesn't mean it isn't there – after all, after retiring as a player, he conquered broadcasting in just the same way.

So it's a fair assumption to make that if the game that a young Lineker was emerging into was more akin to today's sport, he'd have worked out where he needed to improve in order to succeed in that environment.

'Gary would be the first to tell you that he wasn't a genius, he was just a person who got the very best out of himself,' says ex-Leicester teammate Winston White. 'There's something commendable about somebody who goes out there every day to be the best he could possibly be. One thing you can say about good people is that they influence you almost remotely because of their professionalism and dedication, and even though I was older than him, I always looked at him and thought, "Wow, that's the level I want to get to."'

It's that sort of dedication that helped to create the Gary Lineker who is now one of the most famous – and influential – people in Britain and would probably mean he'd still make it in today's game. It's unquestionably one of the main reasons he achieved what he did in his era.

If he hadn't, it might just have robbed us of one of the most significant British footballers there has ever been.

LIST OF IMAGES

vi Lineker celebrates after scoring during England's final group stage match against Poland at the 1986 World Cup on 11 June in Monterrey, Mexico. Lineker scored a hat-trick as England won 3–0 to progress to the last-16. Credit: STAFF/AFP via Getty Images

xii Lineker on his father's fruit and vegetable stall in Leicester. Credit: Paul Popper/Popperfoto via Getty Images

8 An 18-year-old Lineker at Leicester City's pre-season photocall held at Filbert Street, August 1979. Credit: Bob Thomas Sports Photography via Getty Images

18 Lineker clashes with Jeff Clarke of Sunderland during their Division Two match held at Filbert Street in Leicester on 27 October 1979. Leicester City won 2–1. Credit: Bob Thomas Sports Photography via Getty Images.

33 Lineker during a friendly match between Leicester City and Australia at Filbert Street in Leicester, circa November 1980. Australia won 2–1. Credit: Bob Thomas Sports Photography via Getty Images

34 Lineker is challenged by QPR defender Bob Hazell during a Division Two match against QPR at Loftus Road on 9 April 1983 in London. Lineker scored both of Leicester's goals in a 2–2 draw to help the Foxes maintain an unbeaten run that would eventually stretch to 15 matches as they won promotion. Credit: Getty Images/Hulton Archive

49 Tottenham's Ossie Ardiles denies Lineker's attempt on goal during Leicester's 3–2 defeat to Tottenham Hotspur at White Hart Lane on 11 February 1984. Credit: Alan Olley/Mirrorpix via Getty Images

50 Lineker lines up before the British Home Championships match between Wales and England at Wrexham's Racecourse Ground on 2 May 1984. Despite getting his first international call-up, Lineker didn't make his debut and watched

LIST OF IMAGES

on from the bench as England lost 1–0. Credit: Paul Popper/Popperfoto via Getty Images/Getty Images

62 (left) Lineker sporting the short shorts that were all the rage during the '80s as Leicester draw 2–2 with Southampton on 7 April 1984 – Lineker scoring a brace. Credit: Mark Leech/Getty Images

62 (right) Lineker in action during Leicester's 4–1 league defeat to Arsenal at Filbert Street on 13 October 1984. Credit: David Cannon/Allsport/Getty Images

62 (bottom) Sniffing out a chance as Leicester lost 3–0 to Chelsea at Stamford Bridge on 29 September 1984. Credit: Robert Stiggins/Daily Express/Hulton Archive/Getty Images

72 (top) Lineker celebrates scoring his first Everton goal during a 1–0 win in the First Division against Tottenham at White Hart Lane on 26 August 1985. He'd go on to score 40 goals for the Toffees that season. Credit: Frank Coppi/Popperfoto via Getty Images

72 (bottom) Putting Everton 1–0 up in the 1986 FA Cup final against city rivals Liverpool at Wembley. Ultimately, it wasn't to be the Toffees' day as the Reds came back to win 3–1. Credit: Liverpool Echo/Mirrorpix/Getty Images

89 Lineker during Everton's 2–0 Charity Shield victory over Manchester United at Wembley in August 1985. Credit: Allsport UK /Allsport

90 (left) Gary Lineker at the team base in Monterrey, Mexico prior to the 1986 World Cup tournament. Credit: Monte Fresco/Mirrorpix/Getty Images

90 (right) A brace in the World Cup last-16 clash with Paraguay helped England to a 3–0 win at the Azteca Stadium and set up a quarter-final showdown with Diego Maradona's Argentina. Credit: David Cannon/Allsport

90 (bottom) Lineker basks in the glory of scoring a World Cup hat-trick as his treble helped England to a 3–0 win against Poland at the Universitario Stadium in Monterrey. Credit: Mike King/Allsport/Hulton Archive/Getty Images

106 Sporting Barcelona's famous red and blue stripes in 1986. Lineker played for the Catalan side for three seasons between 1986 and 1989. Credit: Allsport/Getty Images

121 Lineker scored 51 goals in 138 appearances in all appearances across his three seasons playing for Barcelona. Credit: David Cannon/Allsport/Getty Images

122 (top) Lining up alongside his England team-mates ahead of a 0–0 draw with Hungary in a friendly at the Nepstadion in Budapest on 27 April 1988. From right to left: Gary Lineker, Peter Beardsley, Steve McMahon, Trevor

Steven, Chris Waddle, Viv Anderson, Stuart Pearce, Tony Adams, Gary Pallister, Chris Woods and captain Bryan Robson. Credit: Simon Bruty/Allsport/Getty Images

122 (bottom) Lineker and England number eight Trevor Steven are left with their heads in their hands as a chance goes begging in the 3–1 defeat to Soviet Union at the 1988 European Championships in West Germany on 18 June. Credit: Monte Fresco/Mirrorpix/Getty Images

132 In the thick of the action as Barcelona beat Sampdoria 2–0 at the Wankdorf Stadium in Berne to win the 1989 UEFA Cup Winners' Cup. Credit: Allsport/Getty Images/Hulton Archive

146 (left) Turning out for Tottenham in a 2–1 victory over former club Everton in a First Division clash on 9 December 1989. Lineker cancelled out Tony Cottee's opener, before strike partner Paul Stewart grabbed the winner. Credit: Ben Radford/Allsport

146 (right) Donning his cricket whites for a Rainforest cricket match. Credit: Larry Ellis Collection/Getty Images

146 (bottom) Trying to break the deadlock as Spurs go down 1–0 at home to Wimbledon in a First Division match on 11 November 1989. Credit: Mike Maloney/Sunday People/Mirrorpix via Getty Images

159 Lineker keeps his eyes on the ball during a 2–1 win against Manchester United on 21 April 1990. Lineker scored Spurs' second of the day to clinch victory at White Hart Lane. Credit: Simon Bruty/Allsport/Getty Images

160 (top) England training during the 1990 World Cup. Left to right, Steve Bull, Stuart Pearce, Lineker, Tony Dorigo. Credit: Albert Cooper/Mirrorpix via Getty Images

160 (bottom) Lineker slides home the opener to put England 1–0 up against Republic of Ireland in their first match of the 1990 World Cup, only for Kevin Sheedy to equalise later on as the game ended 1-1. Credit: Independent News and Media/Getty Images.

178 (top) Attempting to make inroads against Chelsea in a League Cup quarter-final replay on 23 January 1991. Spurs would go on to lose 3–0. Credit: Mark Leech/Offside via Getty Images

178 (bottom) Lineker ruffles Paul Gascoigne's hair to celebrate one of the midfielder's four goals against Hartlepool United in 1990 League Cup tie. Lineker scored the other goal in a 5–0 rout. Credit: Mark Leech/Offside via Getty Images

193 Spurs goalscorers Lineker and Gascoigne celebrate Spurs' victory over North London rivals Arsenal in the FA Cup semi-final at Wembley on 14 April 1991. Credit: Photo by Dan Smith/Allsport/Getty Images

LIST OF IMAGES

194 Wheeling off in celebration after scoring the first goal in a 2–0 win over QPR on 14 September 1991. Lineker went on to score 33 goals in all competitions in what would be his final season in England. Credit: Photo by Bob Martin/Allsport/Getty Images

204 (top) The substitution that brought down Gary Lineker's England career, as he's replaced by former Leicester team-mate Alan Smith. England's 2–1 defeat to hosts Sweden in the group stage match in Solna saw the Three Lions crash out of Euro 92. Credit: Photo by Albert Cooper/Mirrorpix/Getty Images

204 (bottom) England captain Gary Lineker has history in his sights ahead of his last Wembley appearance for England against Brazil on 17 May 1992. Credit: Mark Leech/Offside via Getty Images

220 (top) A pensive look crosses Lineker's face as Nagoya Grampus Eight struggle in a J League match with Urawa Red Diamonds on 26 October 1994. Credit: J. LEAGUE/J.LEAGUE via Getty Images

220 (bottom) Lineker cuts a frustrated figured in a match for Grampus Eight against Sanfrecce Hiroshima on 19 November 1994. Credit: J.LEAGUE/J.LEAGUE via Getty Images

233 Lineker netted only eight times in two seasons playing for Nagoya Grampus Eight in Japan. Credit: J.LEAGUE/J.LEAGUE via Getty Images

234 Getting ready for some friendly competition during the Sport Relief Launch at London's Sport Cafe in March 2002. Credit: Warren Little/Getty Images

249 Lineker takes a break from filming at Stansted Airport as he starred in an advert for HMRC to warn England fans about drug smuggling during Euro 2000 in Belgium and Netherlands. Credit: Photo by John Rogers/Getty Images

250 Lineker presents Match of the Day at Leicester's King Power Stadium in March 2021 while the nation continued to adhere to Covid-19 restrictions. Credit: Laurence Griffiths. The FA via Getty Images

262 Lineker has never been too far away from the headlines, no less than when he took to a newsstand in 1985. Credit: Photo by SSPL/Getty Images

REFERENCES AND SOURCES

Quotations from contemporary press articles are from The British Newspaper archive and are available at http://www.britishnewspaperarchive.co.uk/. Outlets and dates are included in the text or in the reference list below when available. Other sources, including books, national newspapers and broadcast media, are cited below. Interviews I conducted and quotes from press conferences are not referenced here.

2	**to sample 'the fresh air of the market'**: Rob Hughes and Bob Thomas, *Lineker: Golden Boot* (HarperCollins, 1987)
3	**'It's a bit too much like hard work and at this time of year it's much too cold'**: *Football Focus* [TV programme], BBC One January 1985
5	**'I wasn't a great lover of school, but City of Leicester Boys was a good school'**: 'Passed/Failed: An education in the life of Gary Lineker, Match of the Day presenter and former footballer', *The Independent*, 4 March 2010
65	**'In the end, I'm standing there thinking, "What have I done here? I'm signing and I'm not going to get a game"'**: *Eddie Hearn: No Passion, No Point* [Podcast], BBC Radio 5 Live, 30 October 2020
78	**'unlike anyone I had at Everton at the time'**: Howard Kendall, *Love Affairs and Marriage: My Life in Football* (De Coubertin Books, 2013)
78	**'Players determine style'**: Rob Hughes and Bob Thomas *Lineker: Golden Boot* (HarperCollins, 1987)
98	**'Robson resign' and 'We want our money back'**: *The People*, 7 June 1986.
99	**'Mark Hateley and Gary Lineker haven't exactly the set the World Cup on fire up front'**: *Manchester Evening News*, 7 June 1986
99	**Sir Alf Ramsey, who specifically named Lineker in a *Daily Mirror* interview as one of a quartet of players he'd leave on the bench**: *Daily Mirror*, 6 June 1986
112	**'He took the move to Barcelona in his stride'**: Terry Venables, *Born to Manage: The Autobiography* (Simon & Schuster, 2014)

REFERENCES AND SOURCES

113 **'We've been good friends and there is no question of us trying to outdo each other'**: *Sunday Mirror*, 10 August 1986

115 **'There was one particularly poor match that ended with the team desperate and upset'**: Terry Venables, *Born to Manage: The Autobiography* (Simon & Schuster, 2014)

107, 116 **'His finishing is clinical'**: Terry Venables quoted in the *Daily Mirror*, 2 February 1987

118 **'We call our place the Hotel Barcelona'**: Lineker quoted in the *Daily Mirror*, 20 June 1987

124 **'I think there were some players that just didn't want to play'**: Bobby Robson in the *Daily Mail*, 19 June 1988

124 **'We're close to being a real force'**: Rob Hughes and Bob Thomas, *Lineker: Golden Boot* (HarperCollins, 1987)

127 **'Zubi was on the receiving end of one of Gary's more memorable goalscoring nights'**: Terry Venables, *Born to Manage: The Autobiography* (Simon & Schuster, 2014)

130 **'In the second game against the Netherlands…' Lineker told *FourFourTwo* several years later**: Maw, J., 'Gary Lineker: I almost joined Manchester United – but then Spurs pulled it off', *FourFourTwo*, 20 November 2015

138 **'Lineker is a good player and I have total confidence in him'**: Maw, J., 'Gary Lineker: I almost joined Manchester United – but then Spurs pulled it off', *FourFourTwo*, 20 November 2015

141 **'I won't score as many goals in this system I'm asked to play with Barcelona'**: Lineker quoted in the *Daily Mirror*, 3 March 1989

144 **'If I were a club chairman, I wouldn't pay that much for Gary Lineker'**: Lineker quoted in *Leicester Mercury*, 19 May 1989

148 **'neutered one of the world's top strikers'**: Terry Venables, *Born to Manage: The Autobiography* (Simon & Schuster, 2014)

148 **'Even before Gary had kicked a ball for us, I knew we had signed the bargain of the season'**: *Ibid*

155 **'It's always been one of my ambitions to'**: Gary Lineker quoted in the *Irish Independent*, 17 December 1989

158 **'He's one of those players at the top of his profession'**: Terry Venables quoted in the *Daily Mirror*, 5 May 1990

164 **'His [Lineker's] first goal for seven matches justified the Barcelona striker's dance'**: Harry Harris in the *Daily Mirror*, 27 April 1989

167 **'Gary had won the Golden Boot four years earlier and I assumed he wanted to win it again'**: Bobby Robson and Paul Hayward *Bobby Robson: Farewell But Not Goodbye – My Autobiography* (Hodder Paperbacks, 2006)

168	**'This was kept secret for like 20-odd years – my family knew, the players knew, but it never came out'**: *Match of the Day: Top 10* [Podcast], 'Greatest Premier League Hat-tricks', BBC Sounds 3 April 2023
169	**brutal headline in the *Sun*, which simply read: 'Send them home'**: *The Sun*, 12 June 1990.
175	**'I remember that match in Mexico so clearly'**: Gary Lineker quoted in the *Daily Mirror*, 3 July 1990
181	**'dubbed the Gaz and Gary Show'**: *Sunday Mirror*, 26 August 1990 **FIFA called Lineker 'a living example of how enacting the spirit of fair play in top-level football can be crowned with personal success'**: *Scarborough Evening News*, 18 December 1990
192	**'To win an FA Cup Final was a dream and having lost one before […] I just had to win this final'**: 'Gary Lineker's FA Cup Memories', Goalhanger, 29 May 2015.
197	**'My agent actually phoned me…' Lineker said in a 2015 interview with *FourFourTwo***: Maw. J, 'Gary Lineker: I almost joined Manchester United – but then Spurs pulled it off', *FourFourTwo*, 20 November 2015.
200	**'I'll never forget that first night'**: *The Athletic FC: The Moment* [Podcast], 'Gary Lineker on his son's battle with leukaemia', The Athletic Media Company 7 June 2022
209	**'I went for Gary for a number of reasons,' Taylor wrote in his autobiography**: Graham Taylor, *Graham Taylor: In His Own Words* (Peloton Publishing, 2017)
209	**according to Lineker's agent Jon Holmes quoted in Colin Malam's 1993 biography**: Colin Malam, *Gary Lineker: Strikingly Different* (Stanley Paul, 1993)
215	**'The same reason I chipped five or six others; you've got to vary them because people monitor how you take penalties…'**: Maw. J, 'Gary Lineker: I almost joined Manchester United – but then Spurs pulled it off', *FourFourTwo*, 20 November 2015.
218	**'Let me remind you that I said before the Championship that Gary Lineker was finished'**: Emyln Hughes, *Daily Mirror*, 18 June 1992
218	**'The cold, cruel facts are that Lineker was out of the game'**: Alf Ramsey, *Daily Mirror*, 18 June 1992
222	**'It's important for a new team to establish a good tradition'**: Narumi Nishigaki quoted on *Football Focus* [TV Programme], BBC One, 15 May 1993
223	**'The Japanese came in and we thought, "Well, this is something completely different,"'**: Lineker, G, 'Gary Lineker on the J-League: "It began with an earthquake and a 5-0 loss. And then things got worse", BBC Sport, 12 May 2023

REFERENCES AND SOURCES

225   'For me, it's a great challenge. It's something totally different, very exciting and totally new' and 'I feel almost in 100 per cent condition': Gary Lineker quoted on *Football Focus* [TV Programme], BBC One, 15 May 1993

230   'I want to stay involved in the game somehow, but certainly not as a coach or manager – that doesn't appeal': 'Football: Lineker retires to strike out in media', *The Independent*, 21 September 1994.

242   'It was difficult for him coming in because he was already a superstar': Des Lynam quoted in Ferguson, E., 'He's still the golden shot', *Guardian*, 8 April 2007.

242   'In the early days I used to fluff a lot of lines and get quite tense about that,': Barber, L., 'What's a boy to do?', *Observer*, 8 April 2001.

242   'a self-hyped personality – fine for him, but he isn't a good player and no benefit to the game': Quoted in Szreter, A, 'Football: Jones grabs Lineker by the tentacles', *The Independent*, 17 September.

251   'The BBC will only be able to bring limited sport programming this weekend': BBC Spokesperson, 11 March 2023. Available at: https://www.bbc.co.uk/mediacentre/statements/sport-programming

252   'immeasurably cruel policy directed at the most vulnerable people in language that is not dissimilar to that used by Germany in the 30s': Lineker, G. X.com, 7 March 2023. https://x.com/GaryLineker/status/1633111662352891908

252   **Home Secretary Suella Braverman ... hit back at Lineker**: *Political Thinking* [Podcast], BBC Radio 4, 9 March 2023

255   'The story itself, the circumstances surrounding it…': Gary Lineker quoted in Conn, D. 'Gary Lineker quits Mail on Sunday column over Lord Triesman Sting', the *Guardian*, 18 May 2010

255   'The story showed crass judgement…': John Holmes quoted in *Ibid*.

257   'I was going, "Was I fuck?" I never had a clue…': Gary Lineker quoted in Edwardes, C., '"The levels of attack are extraordinary": Gary Lineker on punditry, podcasts – and why he won't stop speaking his mind', *Guardian*, 20 January 2024

257   **these were subjects he'd okayed with the BBC**: Ibid.

259   'Gary is stepping down from MOTD' and **Lineker simply said, 'I'm delighted to continue my long association with BBC Sport'**, Helen Busby, 'Lineker to stop hosting Match of the Day, BBC confirms', BBC Sport, 12 November 2024

260   'surrendered by the BBC for having an opinion', Darren Lewis, 'Gary Lineker is being surrendered by the BBC for having an opinion …how sad is that?', *Daily Mirror*, 12 November 2024

ACKNOWLEDGEMENTS

Everyone has something to say about Gary Lineker. Whatever their age or background, there's always a memory, opinion or story they're willing to share about one of the most recognisable men in the United Kingdom. Of course, it helps that he's never too far away from a TV screen, the airwaves or a news headline.

Living in Leicestershire, this is especially true. People claim to have known one of the Lineker family, regularly shopped at the family fruit and veg stall in Leicester Market, or simply watched the future England captain's early years at Leicester City. There aren't many people to have hailed from the area who have enjoyed a bigger profile.

But what was most revealing was an interview England's latest world star, Jude Bellingham, gave to the BBC during the 2022 World Cup. The midfield prodigy was quizzed about how much he knew about Lineker, and replied, 'I think most people my age would say, "the guy off *Match of the Day*."' It was an answer that perfectly summed up how Lineker's public persona changes depending on the demographic you speak to.

Lineker has been part of the BBC's national sport coverage for more than 30 years now, so that's naturally where a lot of the younger generation know him from. But before he started to dominate our TV screens, he'd built a football career that put him among England's greatest ever players. It's just that those memories aren't remembered as readily any more because of everything else Lineker has done since.

ACKNOWLEDGEMENTS

A big part of writing this book was to bring those playing years back to life, reminding those who were around at the time – and those who are too young to have been – about the formative years that made Gary Lineker. To do that, speaking to the people who knew him was a crucial part of the project.

This book would never have worked without the generosity of the people who were involved at different points of Lineker's life sharing their time and memories with me. It's a testament to the impression that he left on so many people that they were willing to speak with so much warmth and passion about their memories of him.

Throughout these pages, there are a host of voices. Each one provided me with some valuable insights and information that have formed a key part of piecing together Lineker's story. From his former manager, Gordon Milne, who invited me into his home after I tentatively knocked on his front door asking for an interview, to the likes of Alan Smith, who squeezed in time among a busy broadcast schedule to speak to me about the strike partner who helped to kickstart his career, I'm very grateful.

As ever with books like this, it's not just the people you interview who make all this possible. There are also people who you talk to along the way who help to point you in the right direction, make an introduction or suggestion that sends you down a rabbit hole that adds a new dimension to the book. When you're working on a tale from decades before, those contributions that help you to track people down are so valuable.

A big thank you, as always, goes to my commissioning editor at Bloomsbury, Matt Lowing. Matt is a great sounding board for any different thoughts I have and suggestions – good and bad – to add to the book. This is the second book I've worked on with Matt and I've enjoyed it as much as the first. Having someone like that in your corner is crucial when embarking on a book like this.

I'd also like to thank Matt's Bloomsbury colleagues for their support in bringing the book to market, most notably editor Megan Jones and copy editor Lucy Doncaster for helping to polish everything up for publication.

On a personal level, I'm always grateful to those people around me who always show support. From my friends, who have endlessly listened to various Lineker-related anecdotes and ask for the umpteenth time how things are coming on with the book, to my family, who are always there to help, it means a lot.

To my dad, who is a Leicester fan, and used to make regular trips down to Filbert Street around the time Lineker was emerging on the scene, and was a great source of relevant knowledge. My mum, who never showed any interest in going to Filbert Street but is a saint for listening to us talk away about it all.

At the other end of the age spectrum, my daughter Isabelle was happy to share her thoughts on what the cover artwork should look like. Unfortunately for her, it wasn't that relevant to include a unicorn alongside the picture of Lineker on the cover.

Hopefully the fruits of my labours have created a book that does Lineker's story justice and captures the essence of a man who is revered by so many across the world.